On the Church of Christ

Jacques Maritain

ON THE CHURCH
OF CHRIST

The Person of the Church
and Her Personnel

Translated by
Joseph W. Evans

UNIVERSITY OF NOTRE DAME PRESS

NOTRE DAME   LONDON

Copyright © 1973 by
University of Notre Dame Press
Notre Dame, Indiana 46556

Library of Congress Cataloging in Publication Data

Maritain, Jacques, 1882-1973.
   On the church of Christ.

   Translation of De l'Église du Christ.
   Includes bibliographical references.
   1. Church.   2. Church history.   I. Title.
BX1746.M3513   282'.09   73-11559
ISBN 0-268-00519-2
ISBN 0-268-00525-7 (pbk.)

Manufactured in the United States of America

Preface

By what right has a layman lacking in authority to treat of such matters (he is not a theologian) ventured to write these pages on the Church of Christ, which is a mystery of faith? I reply that the sole authority one may avail oneself of in speaking to others is that of truth; and that in a profoundly troubled historical moment it is doubtless permissible to an old Christian philosopher who has thought about the mystery of the Church for sixty years to bear on it the testimony of his faith and of his meditation.

There is however a better reply and one of greater bearing: it is that philosophy, which even as *ancilla* of theology is never in a servile condition (it is rather an "auxiliary"—on the side of mere natural reason—than a "servant" of theology), has not only to furnish to the latter a metaphysics (I mean a metaphysics founded in truth); it has also for function,—at least if in the head of the philosopher it is itself strengthened by faith,—to enter, yes, onto the proper terrain of the *sacra doctrina* in order to make there itself an effort of reason and to propose there eventually to the competent doctors new views, I say by title of *research worker,* and of *research worker* freer than the theologian himself: for it suffices then for the philosopher to be suitably acquainted with theological questions and theological controversies, without however being charged himself, as is the theologian, with the concern

for the elucidations which the historical exegesis of the texts of
Scripture can furnish, and with the weight of a whole long patristic and conciliar tradition to be known in detail, to be scrutinized
and discussed, so as to order organically and to cause to progress
the treasure of truth which it transmits to us (I do not speak of
the appreciable number of pseudotheologians who employ themselves today to destroy it).

The philosopher leaves to the proper knowledge of the theologian the great interpretative and constructive work in question. He
profits by the fruits of this knowledge. But in his own manner of
thinking, the mind with its exigencies and being with its secrets
alone face each other; the reason of the Christian philosopher is
alone, in order to reflect on them, in the presence of the lofty
realities which are presented to him by the theologian. That is why
I have said that in the labor of research he is more free than the
latter, to whom he proposes views which it belongs to theology to
judge in the final analysis.

Let us add, with respect to the present work, that a philosophical approach demands that one regard the mystery of the Church
as an object placed before the mind and which one tries to
describe. In order to undertake to make thus the portrait of a
mystery, it was necessary to be an old philosopher resisting badly
the attraction of risks (of the beautiful risks). At least he is
without too many illusions about himself. To tell the truth, this
book has been written by an ignorant one for ignorant ones like
himself, but who like him have a great desire to understand as
much as possible, to understand a little.

The book in question has nothing to do with apologetics. It
presupposes the Catholic faith and addresses itself above all to
Catholics, to our nonseparated brothers who recite the Credo each
Sunday and who say: *I believe in the one, holy, catholic and
apostolic Church.* It addresses itself to others,—to our separated
brothers, to our friends of non-Christian religious affiliation, to
our agnostic or atheistic friends,—only to the extent that they
dialogue with Catholics and desire to know what Catholics believe,
even if the latter seem sometimes to have forgotten it.

This book has nothing to do either with a treatise of ecclesiol-
ogy. It is a kind of meditation which develops freely of itself as
the questions arise in the mind, so that in order to have an exact
idea of that which the author thinks it is necessary to have
followed to the end the curve which it describes.

After this, is it necessary to state (good authors do not advise that one insist on that which is obvious) that in the subtitle of the work and in the distinction between the person of the Church and her personnel, the word "personnel" has, neither in itself, nor in my thought, absolutely nothing pejorative? I have said "personnel of the Church" as one says "teaching personnel" or "diplomatic personnel." If it pleased someone to take this word in the supposedly humiliating sense of "service people" (a term which on any occasion whatsoever I would be ashamed to employ with disdain), well I would point out to him that there is nothing in the world more honorable than to be *engaged* by God in his service and in the service of his Church,—equerry of the king of kings or arms valet of his bride,—and that to belong to the "personnel" of the Church taken in this sense (which moreover restricts unduly my own) is a thing so incomparably great that, very far from being humiliating, it requires to go hand in hand with an incomparable humility.

I note finally that (and for this I apologize in what concerns the presentation of the volume) there are there some very short chapters and others very long. This is in no way due to the importance of the subject treated each time, but solely to the more or less great complexity of the discussion required.

11 June 1970 J. M.

Contents

The Revealed Data Concerning the Church

It is fitting first of all, clearly, to recall some of the texts which deliver to the Christian, concerning the Church, that which has been revealed in human words by the Word of God.

Matt. 28, 18-20: "Jesus [risen] came forward and addressed them [the eleven] in these words:
'Full authority has been given to me
both in heaven and on earth;
go, therefore, and make disciples of
all the nations.
Baptize them in the name
of the Father,
and of the Son,
and of the Holy Spirit.
Teach them to carry out everything I
have commanded you.
And know that I am with you always,
until the end of the world!' "

The apostles are sent
into the entire world, and
Christ will be with the Church
at each instant
until the end of time.

1

Matt. 16, 15-18: " 'And you,' he said to them, 'who do you say that I am?' 'You are the Messiah,' Simon Peter answered, 'the Son of the living God!' Jesus replied, 'Blest are you, Simon son of John! No mere man has revealed this to you, but my heavenly Father. I for my part declare to you, *you are 'Rock'* (Kepha) *and on this rock* (kepha) *I will build my church, and the jaws of death shall not prevail against it.*' "

> Primacy of Peter,
> and assurance
> that the Church of Christ
> is invincible to evil.

John 21, 15-17: "When they had eaten their meal, Jesus [risen] said to Simon Peter, 'Simon, son of John, do you love me more than these?' 'Yes, Lord,' he said, 'you know that I love you.' At which Jesus said, 'Feed my lambs.'

"A second time he put his question, 'Simon, son of John, do you love me?' 'Yes, Lord,' Peter said, 'you know that I love you.' Jesus replied, 'Tend my sheep.'

"A third time Jesus asked him, 'Simon, son of John, do you love me?' Peter was hurt because he had asked a third time, 'Do you love me?' So he said to him: 'Lord, you know everything. You know well that I love you.' Jesus said to him, 'Feed my sheep.' "

> Primacy of Peter.
> It is by reason
> of the love of
> charity that
> this primacy,
> like all authority
> in the Church,
> is conferred.

Matt. 12, 28: "If it is by the Spirit of God that I expel demons, then the reign of God has overtaken you."

> The kingdom of God
> has already begun
> here on earth,
> *in Christ and in
> the Church.*[1] We
> say: "Thy kingdom
> come," in order that

it come in the
world transfigured.

Ephes. 1, 17 and *1, 22-23:* "May the God of our Lord Jesus Christ, the Father of glory, grant you a spirit of wisdom and insight to know him clearly. . . . He has put all things under Christ's feet and *has made him, thus exalted, head of the church,*[2] *which is his body: the fullness of him who fills the universe in all its parts.*"[3]

Ephes. 4, 15-16: "*Let us profess the truth in love* and grow to the full maturity of Christ the head. *Through him the whole body grows, and with the proper functioning of the members joined firmly together by each supporting ligament, builds itself up in love.*"

Col. I, 17-18: "He is before all else that is. In him everything continues in being. *It is he who is head of the body,* the church."

Col. I, 24: "In my own flesh I fill up what is lacking in the sufferings of Christ *for the sake of his body, the church.*"

> The Church is *the mystical Body of Christ.*[4]

Ephes. 5, 29-30: "No one ever hates his own flesh; no, he nourishes it and takes care of it *as Christ cares for the church—for we are members of his body.*

'For this reason a man shall leave his
     father and mother,
and shall cling to his wife,
and the two shall be made into
     one.'[5]

This is a great foreshadowing; I mean that it refers to Christ and the church."

> The Church
> is *the Bride* of Christ.[6]

Ephes. 5, 25-27: "Husbands, love your wives, *as Christ loved the church.* He gave himself up for her *to make her holy, purifying her in the bath of water by the power of the word, to present to himself a glorious church, holy and immaculate, without stain or wrinkle or anything of that sort.*"

> The Church is
> *the Bride* of Christ. And

she is *without stain or wrinkle
or anything of that sort,
but holy and immaculate*
("indefectibly holy,"
the second Council
of the Vatican will say).[7]

I Tim. 3, 14-15: "I am writing you about these matters so that if I should be delayed you will know what kind of conduct befits a member of God's household, *the church of the living God, the pillar and bulwark*[8] *of truth.*"

Inerrancy of the Church.
She is *the pillar
and bulwark
of truth.*

I Pet. 2, 9-10: "You, however, are 'a chosen race, a royal priesthood, a holy nation, a people he claims for his own to proclaim the glorious works' of the One who called you from darkness into his marvellous light. Once you were no people, but *now you are God's people.*"

The Church is *the People of
God,* a name
which has been brought
to full light by the
second Council
of the Vatican.[9]

*   *   *

These texts show us in the clearest manner that the Church of Christ, *holy and immaculate,* is herself one of the mysteries which God has revealed to men and to the angels. She is a mystery of faith, and a supernatural mystery in the integral sense of the word (*quoad substantiam*), since she is the mystical Body of Christ and the Bride of Christ and the Plenitude of Christ, and since she lives by Him and by His grace ("by the truth in love," as St. Paul says).

He who loses from view that the Church is herself a mystery of faith has not in his thought the idea of the Church. He can certainly speak of her, and speak of her abundantly; he does not know of what he is speaking.

There are three who are holy and immaculate, although each in a different manner and by different title: Christ because He is

God; the Blessed Virgin because she was born without stain; the Church because, "purified in the bath of water by the power of the word," she shines, *sine macula, sine ruga,* with the purity in which she was born of the water and of the Spirit.

The Members of the Church Here on Earth
Are All Sinners and the
Church Herself Is without Sin

1. I do not speak here of the Church of heaven, but of the Church in pilgrimage on the earth. Except for the Virgin Mary, who up until her Assumption was a part of the Church of the earth, it is a fact that the members of the Church here on earth are all sinners. A few words first of all on this point.

Sons of Adam, they are all born deprived of grace, and it is in a human nature inclined to evil that at Baptism they have received the latter; they all bear in them the wounds of the first sin. They sin very frequently in a more or less slight manner, in many cases in a manner more or less grave, often without being aware of it themselves because they have neglected to purify their heart.

The sins of which each day the priest and the faithful accuse themselves at the beginning of Mass,—"I have sinned through my own fault, in my thoughts and in my words, in what I have done, and in what I have failed to do,"—do not prevent them from receiving the Body of Christ less than a half-hour after this avowal. They are sinners, yes: they sin each day through human weakness; and if it happens that they have sinned gravely they have had recourse to the Sacrament of Penance and have received absolution. They have habitually grace and charity.

And there are other members of the Church (they have received Baptism, which has imprinted in them,—as has Confirmation,—an indelible "character," and they have kept the faith) who live in evil and who have lost grace and charity, I say before the gaze of God, Who alone knows the bottom of hearts. One calls them because of this "dead" members. I don't care much for this word: for in fact, as I will indicate further on, they remain worked by ferments of life.[1]

Let us call them nevertheless, because the word is convenient, "dead" members. And let us say that in the reality of existence all the members of the Church here on earth, "living" members or "dead" members, are sinners,—more or less sinners; and that it is always to be feared that the best Christian will yield one day to temptation, and will slip away from grace, and even perhaps will install himself in a life of grave sin; just as it is always to be hoped that the worst rogue will turn indeed some day and will return to God, and will die perhaps as a saint.

2. On an entirely different plane, it is necessary to say also that in the consciousness that man has of himself, the more exalted a soul is in grace the more it feels itself a sinner, because then it knows a little, as its Master knew to perfection, "that which is in man." If the saints accuse themselves thus, it is less by moral scruple than by a crushing ontological view of human fragility in the face of the inscrutable grandeur and beauty of God,[2] and of the abyss of sufferings into which Mercy caused His Son to enter in order to save us.

And when they think of all the gifts which they have received without having merited them and which they have caused to bear so little fruit, and of the misery which remains in them, they are perhaps not wrong to put themselves below the great sinners for whom they pray, poor assassin gangsters and poor sordid prostitutes, or even poor rich men who feed their fortune and their mistresses with the blood of the starving, or even poor ones suffering from delusions of empire or of revolution who establish their power on mountains of corpses. The saints do not doubt that all these habitués of evil are indeed their brothers.

For the consciousness that the sinner has of himself it is quite otherwise. He seeks to justify himself in his own eyes, or at least to find some means of accepting himself without repenting. He does this in many ways. As the Russian writers have admirably seen, and Dostoevsky above all, there are some who say to themselves: "I am a scoundrel, I wallow in the mud," with tears of pity for themselves, of indulgence and of resignation, and not without

counting also on divine mercy. There are others who, while keeping the faith, say "I am right to live as I do, and I am proud of
myself, it is the morality of the priests which spoils everything by
imposing the impossible. . . ."

As for the non-Christians of our occidental civilization, they
doubtless do not have the sense of sin, but they know what
remorse is, and this is enough in order to destroy a man. How to
find an alibi? The whole question is to save my pride by accusing
things, for it is in them, is it not, not in me that vice is. In order to
disclose the latter, philosophy is fortunately there, with its discoveries and the new pictures of the world and of the human
condition that it reveals to us. Room then for the thinkers who
tell us that the sole hope is in the creative power of man, and who
deny God because there is evil on the earth. These people think
still that if the God of heaven existed, it would be good; and they
attach themselves still in some measure, Marx for example, to the
Judeo-Christian cultural heritage. And room finally for other
thinkers who have completely broken with this cultural heritage,
and who tell us to despair of man as of God. These people
announce the death of God,—and the death of man,—while dream-
ing of the superman with Nietzsche, the greatest among them, or
while offering like Freud a therapeutics to the depraved animal
that we are.

3. What is a modern Catholic going to do after this who is
filled with good will and the desire to show himself fully *of his
time,* as if it had not been said: *nolite conformari huic saeculo?* He
will think that the moment has come to change everything radically. It belongs to us therefore, and to him for his part, to work
to renew the faith. The old Church is dead or dying by dint of
having been soiled by history: it belongs to us to make another.
We understand now that if the transcendent God existed,—the
God of Abraham, of Isaac and of Jacob, the one Whom Jesus
called the heavenly Father (unfortunate expression, due to the
ignorance of the antipaternal complex),—this God of heaven
would alienate us from ourselves and would be for us worse than
evil: it belongs to us to cause to be the God required by the man
not alienated from himself and by the religion of pure exaltation
which is his, God of the earth only, inviscerated in the visible and
living force in us of the world in evolution.

These thinkers are Christians (neo-Christians), who think that
they have received for today the mission of prophets. There are

perhaps saints among them (man is such a bizarre animal), saints whose hearts would have caused them to lose their heads. The fact remains that to tell the truth the integral transformation of all the values preached by them is a dream of an adolescent sick with desires, and that they themselves are passing through a serious crisis of intellectual puberty which runs the risk of tiring them for a long time, although these crises are transitory by nature.

Be that as it may, one can ask oneself what becomes, in the consciousness that they have of themselves, of that profound feeling of being sinner, ashes and dust, which for centuries has inhabited the soul of the Christian. Be careful, they say to themselves, beware of the guilt complex! They know well, assuredly, that they are fallible like every human being. But there where there is no longer the sense of the infinite transcendence and of the infinite goodness of the All Holy One, it is inevitable that the authentic sense of sin will become blunted,—which has nothing to do with the guilt complex, for it allies itself with the joy (sacred) of deliverance and of salvation, with peace of the heart and confidence in limitless Mercy,—and which causes man to see his own truth, and the menace, inherent in all the fibers of his being, of the nothingness from which he has been drawn, and into which he can at each instant, through the liberty which is his admirable privilege, proceed morally to lose himself, but from which there suffices, in order to be drawn from it again, an act of this same liberty turning itself toward God.

How would the authentic sense of sin of which I have just spoken not be greatly blunted in our new prophets? It is doubtless because in the new teaching distributed by the clergy one speaks less and less of sin, instead of showing better that which it is truly, that many Christians who in a world more and more inhuman believe themselves made only in order to be more and more proud of being men regard recourse to the Sacrament of Penance as an irksome and superfluous drudgery.[3]

* * *

4. Composed of members who are all sinners, and who all bear in themselves the wounds of original sin, the Church herself, *holy and immaculate, without stain,* "indefectibly holy,"[4] is pure of all trace of sin. To state such a paradox is to say that the Church is essentially different from all the great human families or communities, temporal or spiritual, which we know, and that she pos-

sesses in comparison with them a privilege absolutely unique. If she is completely human, she is also completely elevated to a divine life which she is commissioned to communicate to us.

In the Apostles' Creed it is said that we believe "*in* Deum Patrem omnipotentem," and "*in* Jesum Christum," and "*in* Spiritum Sanctum," whereas for the Church (as also for the remission of sins, the resurrection of the dead, and eternal life) the preposition *in* is omitted. We believe "sanctam Ecclesiam catholicam,"— or, in the French translation (I refer here to the Profession of Faith of Paul VI): we believe "*à* l'Eglise une, sainte, catholique et apostolique." God, we "croyons *en*" Him, because He is the author of being and the author of salvation, and because into the uncreated abyss of his Truth and of his Goodness we cast our whole being, our intelligence and our love, in other words because we adore Him. The Church, we do not adore here, and therefore do not believe "*en*" her, but "*à*" her, because she is created, and a divine gift made to the universe of the created. (And likewise are gifts made to the creature: the remission of sins, the resurrection of the dead, and eternal life). But the difference of the prepositions *en* and *à*[5] does not signify in any way that the Church would be a thing purely and simply human, not implying in its being participation in the very life of God. (Would the remission of sins, the resurrection of the dead, and eternal life be likewise things purely human and natural?) The Church, who proposes to us by her teaching all that which God has revealed, and who perpetuates here on earth by the Mass the sacrifice of Christ, and who sanctifies us by her Sacraments, belongs essentially to the supernatural order, and she is herself a *mystery of faith,* as I have already noted.

In order to aid us to acquire some understanding of this mystery, I do not know a better guide than Cardinal Journet.[6] For more than fifty years it has been he who has been my master in the matter. And if in such a long protracted meditation it happens to me to depart from him on some point,—as this happens to me also for the Angelic Doctor,—it is in feeling myself his disciple more profoundly and more truly (a true disciple is a free disciple, is he not?).

5. Every living being, here on earth, has a soul which is the principle of its life, and a body in which and by the activities of which this life manifests itself visibly. Of the life of every living being, especially of the human being, we have thus external signs:

in itself,—or insofar precisely as immanent activity operating in the depths of the body, and, in man, of the spirit also,—this life is invisible, like the soul from which it proceeds.

It is the same for the Church. Her uncreated soul is the Holy Spirit, who, as the second Council of the Vatican says, dwells in the Church and in the hearts of the faithful as in a Temple,[7] and "by the power of the Gospel, rejuvenates the Church and renews her perpetually,"[8] so that "the holy Fathers were able to compare her role to that which the principle of life, that is to say the soul, exercises in the human body."[9]

But the Church has also, she, this great and mysterious human Figure, peregrinating under our eyes from century to century, a created soul[10] —and a created life—which she receives super-naturally from God and which are sanctifying grace ("entitative habitus") and charity ("operative habitus," as the jargon of the philosophers and of the theologians says). The soul and the life of the Church are grace and charity, which are realities invisible in themselves. There where grace and charity are, there there is the life of the Church, and there there passes the Blood of Christ. There where grace and charity are not, there there is not either the life of the Church, and there there does not pass either the Blood of Christ. To the extent that a man who has been baptized in the Church sins, to that extent he slips away from the life of the Church; if he installs himself in the state of sin (while keeping the faith, which without charity is itself "dead faith") he remains still a member of the Church, but then the life of the latter no longer passes in him. To the extent that he lives by grace and by charity, he lives also by the life of the Whole of which he is a member, and which is the mystical Body of Christ and the Bride of Christ.

All contradiction is therefore lifted from the moment one understands that, on the one hand, the Church herself is *without sin* because her own life is grace and charity,—in their plenitude, I shall return to this point further on,—and that, on the other hand, each of her members is *sinner* in the measure in which, in slipping away from grace, he slips away at the same stroke from the life of the Whole of which he is a member.

6. This is true, although in a manner essentially different, of the "living" members of the Church and of her "dead" members.

With regard to the "living" members, the part of evil in them remains greater than it could seem at first sight.

In man, indeed, there is not to be considered only moral evil properly so-called,—moral evil of free will,—but also that which one can call moral evil of nature, I mean by this the bad dispositions or inclinations for which we are not responsible—they come to us from Adam and from our personal heredity—and of which we are generally not conscious, they are as hidden to our own eyes as they are apparent to the eyes of the neighbor. Now in the "living" members of the Church these defects or failings of nature are there, coexisting with grace and charity,—below them if I may say, as the dregs at the bottom of a vase of some precious liquor which has not been decanted: self-respect, inferiority-complex or superiority-complex, obscure need to be recognized by another, and to please him, or obscure need to dominate him, and aggressiveness which impels one to blacken him in our judgments, morbid sensitiveness, etc. All of this can doubtless cause at some moment a "living" member of the Church to fall into sin, but much more often preys upon, while warping it, the good which is in him and which gives its fruits along the whole course of his existence. From the subterranean empire exercised by all of this many will deliver themselves little by little by dint of progressing in charity, and also by the effect of frequent Holy Communion; only the saints are *almost* liberated from it. Meanwhile, and as long as all of this has not been burned by charity, all that which in the "living" members of the Church proceeds from such failings of nature and spoils more or less the good which they do, is something which withdraws itself to this extent from the grace and from the charity which are in them, and at the same stroke slips away from the life of the Whole of which they are members, from the proper life of the Body of Christ passing in its members in the state of grace.[11]

As concerns after this the "dead" members, it is the part of the good that we risk not recognizing in them. It remains much greater than the word "dead" suggests.

First because if human nature is wounded since the Fall, in itself however it has been created good and keeps a fundamental goodness. What reserves of goodness and of generosity remain in those who have abandoned God and despair of themselves, and can at certain moments surprise us by profound movements of the soul and acts singularly beautiful! These interior movements and these acts are of the merely natural order, without doubt. And the life of the Church, which is supernatural grace and supernatural charity, does not at all pass by them, although however, if the souls in question belong to the Church by the baptismal character and by faith, the purely natural good at work in them belongs like them to the Church and is a part of her treasure.

But there is much more still: I am thinking of all the holy things, and depending on divine charity in our regard, which remain still in them: faith first, if these sinners have kept it and are still by this members of the Church. And theological hope, if they have kept it also. And, as long as the heart is not hardened, sorrow for having sinned. And the prayer which suddenly rises to the lips of him who thought he had forgotten it. And then the actual graces which they receive at certain moments and which sometimes slip perhaps into the great movements of the soul, natural in themselves, of which I first spoke. I am thinking also of the traces left by the grace which one has betrayed, and of the ambivalence of the effects which they produce: now remembrance, regret, nostalgia, now resentment which turns to hatred of this God and of this Church against the hidden attraction of whom one defends oneself (we know that hatred is sometimes an inversion of love, rage against that which one has loved and which one would like still to be able to love). And I am thinking above all of the secret pressure exercised by the collective charity and the collective prayer of the Church and of her saints, interceding unceasingly on behalf of all men, and especially of sinners.

7. It seems to me that after having meditated a little on all these things, one is ready to grasp, in its eminently realist truth, that which I consider to be the central intuition of Cardinal Journet concerning the "proper frontiers" of the Church, considered in her created soul and her life (sanctifying grace and charity) as in her uncreated Soul, which is the Holy Spirit. "These frontiers," he writes, "precise and real, circumscribe only that which is pure and good in her members, just ones and sinners, taking within her all that which is holy, even in the sinners, leaving outside her all that which is impure, even in the just; it is in our own behavior, in our own life, in our own heart that the Church and the world, Christ and Belial, light and darkness confront one another. The total Christ, Head and Body, is holy in all His members, sinners and just, drawing to Him all holiness, even that of His sinful members, rejecting from Him all impurity, even that of His just members."[12] It is thus that the Spouse of Christ is "wholly resplendent, without stain or wrinkle or anything of that sort, but holy and immaculate, *sancta et immaculata.*"

"The frontier of the Church passes through our own

hearts."[13] "The Church divides in us good and evil. She retains the good and leaves the evil. Her frontiers pass through our hearts."[14] Here we have the words which illuminate everything, and they refer to the secret of the hearts.

To the extent that a man acts in grace and charity, he lives by the life of the Church, his actions manifest in him the very life of the Whole of which he is a part. To the extent that a man is lacking in grace and charity, to the same extent, if he is a member of the Church, he withdraws from her life. And the evil actions that he commits are no stains on the Church, because the Church has no part in them; they do not soil the face of the Church, except as the spittles of the soldiers soiled the face of Jesus. The sins of Alexander VI related to his own person, from which they proceeded; they did not relate at all, except in order to offend her, to the person of the Church.

8. Here we are in the presence of the great question of the personality of the Church, that is to say at the very heart of the mystery of the Church. One understands nothing of this mystery if one does not discern in it above all the mystery of the person of the universal Church, *Una, Sancta, Catholica, Apostolica,* who transcends the persons of her members, who are all sinners, whereas her own person is holy and immaculate. The *Catholica,* as St. Augustine liked to say, the Church considered in her universality and her unity as to her invisible soul and her visible body at one and the same time, has a personality distinct from that of the members who compose her, and insofar precisely as Church she is a person. In order to convince oneself of this it suffices to read St. Paul, who speaks always of her as of a person.

It is this that I am going to venture to consider more closely, instructed by theology, but faithful to the proper concerns of the philosopher, I say of the Christian philosopher.

III

The Personality of the Church

Short Preamble

1. In order to consider the question more closely, it is necessary for us,—I apologize for it, but it will be brief,—to have recourse to some philosophical notions. A correct metaphysical analysis of the created being shows us that everything in the world has a *nature* (or essence) and an *existence,* and that nature and existence belong to two different orders, in other words are intelligible data distinct in the thing as in the mind which conceives them. Napoleon had a nature which made him such and such a man among all; once dead, this nature no longer exists, but the historians do not tire of scrutinizing it. When we look at the things which face us, we see in them, at one and the same time, but as separable by death or destruction, on the one hand, in the line of essentiality, that which constitutes them such or such, and, on the other hand, in the line of existentiality, the fact that they *are* purely and simply.

The nature of a thing is *that which* this thing is, or that *by which*[1] it faces us with such or such properties, whereas its existence is for it the very fact of facing us or of being *posited outside of nothingness.* In order to be able to exercise this act

15

(marvellous when one thinks of it a little) which consists in *existing*, it is necessary therefore that my nature (complete in its line of nature or of essentiality: what am I?—"a man," and "such and such an individual man") be that of a *subject*[2] able to unfold that which it is in the world of existence and of action ("I exist" today, "I act" today): in other words, it is necessary that the First Cause, in producing my nature, has conferred on it, at the same time as the determinations which characterize it, an ultimate determination of another order, which, in constituting it, no longer only as nature, but as *subject*, has enabled it, I do not say only to receive, but to exercize existence, and to act its part in the midst of all the other beings emerged outside of nothingness.

2. This ultimate determination, this seal imprinted on the nature, which puts it in state of exercising existence as its first act, is that which one calls *subsistence*.[3] The word offends no doubt contemporary ears, as much as the word substance. I can do nothing about it. I remark only that to tell the truth it is a question here only of a matter of style. The vocabulary of the ancients had no fear (not enough perhaps) of pure abstraction. Modern philosophical vocabulary is as baroque as the ancient, but it prefers words which in some way provide an image. Instead of "subsistence," could we say "freeing actuation,"[4] —which is demanded by every nature made in order to exist in itself, and puts the latter in state of reflecting in it, however little this may be, the infinite *by itself* of the First Cause? I shall continue for my part to say "subsistence."

And in every being endowed with intelligence and with liberty, in other words who possesses the privileges of spirit,[5] subsistence is the ontological foundation of *personality,* through which this being holds himself in hand, is a moral agent who posits free decisions according to a mode like no other, plays his role in the world with a visage, and an immortal visage, and with an immortal destiny,—in short, is a universe to himself, whereas all the rest in the great universe of here below shows us only structures in interaction destined to perish one day with the earth. Each human being, however wretched a fellow he may be, is thus a person before other men and before God, and possesses the dignity of person.

The Church as Person

1. In telling us that the Church is the Body of which Christ is the Head, and that she is the Bride of Christ, "for whom he gave himself up to make her holy, purifying her in the bath of water by the power of the word, to present to himself a glorious church, holy and immaculate, without stain or wrinkle,"[6] and that " '. . . the two shall be made into one.' This is a great foreshadowing; I mean that it refers to Christ and the Church,"[7] St. Paul teaches us that this great human multitude which extends itself through the whole earth and traverses all the centuries has a personality in the proper sense of the term; he teaches us that the Church is a person: not a person endowed, in a wholly analogical sense, with a "moral personality," but truly a person, and that this is her essentially supernatural and absolutely unique privilege.

This follows from the very fact that she has received mission in order to propose to us the truths revealed by God, and in order to continue until the end of time the work of Christ on earth. If a people,—the new people of God,—has received such a mission, it is because it is not only a people or a multitude, but also a supernaturally constituted common person who subsists from generation to generation, and who in order to accomplish her mission believes as having but a single heart, speaks as having but a single voice, acts as having but a single will, while being constantly assisted, as He promised, by Christ, her Head and her Bridegroom.

2. This is indeed what St. Irenaeus tells us: "Having received this preaching [apostolic] and this faith . . ., the Church, although disseminated in the entire world, keeps the deposit of it with a faithful care, as if really she had her habitation in a single house; and in these things she believes likewise, I mean as having but a single soul and a single heart; and it is with the same unity that she preaches them and teaches them and transmits them to the generations, as possessing but a single voice."[8]

This is why St. Thomas was able to say also: "The Lord's Prayer is uttered by the common person of the whole Church. If therefore someone who refuses to pardon those who have offended him recites the Lord's Prayer, he does not for all that tell a lie, although what he says is not true with respect to his own person: for this is true as to the person of the Church."[9]

It is this personality of the Church that we affirm implicitly each time that we declare: I believe *in the Church*, in the Church *one and holy, catholic* (in other words: universal) and *apostolic*.

The Church Considered in Her Unity and Her
Universality Has a Supernatural Personality
Which Transcends That of Her Members

1. No community of the merely natural order can be a *person* at the same time as a multitude of human beings. A nation subsists with the subsistence of all its individual citizens; it has a history, it has typical characteristics, common customs, it pursues a common end and has common interests: this history, these typical characteristics, these customs, this common end, these common interests are purely and simply those of its citizens, or of the great mass of them. And it has no divine mission, nor any promise of lasting always and of being constantly assisted by God.

It is altogether different with the Church. The Church has a double subsistence: a natural subsistence like every human community,—that of the human persons who are her members:[10] if all Christians were exterminated there would no longer be a Church here on earth. And she has, insofar precisely as she is the whole, one and universal, of the organized multitude of those who live with her life, a supernatural subsistence, which presupposes but transcends the natural subsistence of the individual persons who are her members.

2. It is clear, on the other hand, that subsistence and personality are, for the being which has them, something which informs it or perfects it intrinsically. Whence it follows that the supernatural subsistence and supernatural personality of the Church are of the created order as she is. However profound and however essential the differences between the two cases may be, she is a *person* (common or collective) as Peter or Paul is a *person* (individual).

How is this possible, when Peter and Paul are each an individual substance, whereas the Church is an immense multitude of human beings? Extraordinary paradox which marks the splendor of the mystery of the Church (supernatural mystery, mystery divinely revealed),—the Church, while subsisting naturally with the subsistence of her innumerable individual members, possesses herself, supernaturally, insofar as she is the whole—one and universal—of this multitude, a personality, truly and ontologically (and not in a wholly analogical sense, in the fashion of that which the jurists call "collective persons" or "moral persons"), she is herself a person in the proper and primary sense of the word, a person who renders a worship to God, who proposes to us the truths revealed by Him, who sanctifies us by her sacraments, who speaks, who teaches, who acts.

3. Let us take up again for a moment our philosophical set of tools.

Considered in the line of essentiality, the Church has a soul,—the grace of Christ,—and a life,—charity,—which are a supernatural participation in the divine life, and a body, the vast and complex visible organism which began to take shape as early as the apostolic age and the time of the great charismas: "God," St. Paul says, [11] "has set up in the church first apostles, second prophets, third teachers, then miracle workers, healers, assistants, administrators, and those who speak in tongues"—so that "through him [Christ the head] the whole body grows, and with the proper functioning of the members joined firmly together by each supporting ligament, builds itself up in love."[12] And according as they are moved by grace and charity, the members of this great organism are animated by its soul and live by its life.

Two points are to be noted here. In the first place, if grace must be regarded as the soul of the Church, it is because, as I shall explain in another chapter, the grace received by her is the plentitude of all the graces individually received, whereas distributed in all her "living" members, grace is given to each one only according to a measure more or less great but never full.

In the second place, unlike that which is the case for the body of each one of us, which its soul will leave at the instant of death and which will crumble to dust, the body of the Church is inseparable from her soul. Any member of the Church can lose grace and incur eternal death. This is impossible for the Church one and universal, who is for *always* the Body of Christ and the Bride of Christ. It is not only until the end of the world, it is for eternity that the body of the Church is vivified by grace and charity. There is already, and there will be eternally, a Church of glory composed of all the blessed, brought to the state of consummated grace, and having as leader Christ without there being there need of the mediation of His vicar. And of the body of this Church of glory the angels are also a part.

Considered in the line of existentiality, it is in her body and her soul constituting together a single and indissoluble living being, it is jointly in her soul (the grace of Christ) and her body, that the Church has, insofar precisely as one and universal, a supernatural *subsistence* and a supernatural *personality*.

It is so by reason of *the image of Christ* which God sees in this multitude distributed over the whole earth and traversing all the centuries, as He sees it also in the multitude of the blessed.

4. Is this an original and more or less arbitrary view proposed by a poor philosopher-man? No; it follows clearly from what St. Paul has written. In order to convince oneself of its truth, it suffices to meditate at one and the same time,—I say meditate, and not merely to bring together with a glance,—the teaching of the apostle on the Church as mystical Body and Bride of Christ (on this I have already insisted), and his teaching on the Christian as new creature transformed into the image of Christ.

What does he tell us on this subject? "If anyone is in Christ, he is a new creation,"[13] —"a new man, one who grows in knowledge as he is formed anew in the image of his Creator."[14] "The first man was of earth, formed from dust, the second is from heaven. . . . Just as we resemble the man from earth, so shall we bear the likeness of the man from heaven."[15] "Those whom he foreknew he predestined to share the image of his Son."[16] "All of us, gazing on the Lord's glory with unveiled faces, are being transformed from glory to glory into his very image. . . ."[17]

Where therefore and how do we become "a new creation," do we don "the likeness of the man from heaven," do we renew ourselves in the image of the Lord Jesus, and are we "transformed into this same image," unless in the Body of Christ and the Bride of Christ, and as members of His Church, living with the life of the latter? What St. Paul teaches us is that the image of Christ, of *this man* Who is God, is imprinted on His Church, that the Bride bears in her the image of the Bridegroom, or rather that she is herself this image,—presented to the Bridegroom, pure and "resplendent" from the very beginning, and growing from age to age in her terrestrial dimensions as in her resemblance to the inexhaustible richness of the features of the infinitely Holy One.

Considered in her unity and her universality, or insofar precisely as the invisible grace of Christ animates her vast human organism, the Church bears in her the image of Christ, and offers it to the gaze of God Who sees the invisible and discerns the grace at the bottom of hearts. Through this image the immense multitude of the members of the Church who live with her life is clothed with an individual configuration, so that by means of the individuality of the image of Christ it can receive a subsistence of its own as if it was an individual. The individuality of the image of Christ borne by the Church is an *analogue* of the individuality of the substantial nature possessed by each one of us; and just as in calling Peter or Paul to existence God confers on such and such an individual nature the subsistence which constitutes it subject or person, so also, in calling the Church of His Son to existence God confers on her, through this image which He sees in her, a subsistence which constitutes subject or person a multitudinous whole of human beings.

Such is the response suggested by St. Paul to the question which occupies us. It is by reason of the image of Christ, offered by her to the gaze of God, that the Church, according as she embraces in her universality all the members of her body who live with her life, possesses a subsistence and a personality as if she was a single human person: subsistence and personality which, like the soul of the Church and like the image of Christ which the Church bears in her, are of the essentially supernatural order, and make of the Church one and universal a person in whom is reflected "the Divine Being, the most universal and the most personal of all beings,"[18] and who transcends the personality of all the individuals who are her members.

An immense multitude, in space and in time, which has a personality in the proper sense of the word and constitutes really a person,—is it necessary to be astonished at the apparently irreconcilable conflict of concepts with which we have to deal here? It is the case before which we find ourselves with all the mysteries of faith: a God perfectly one in His nature in three different Persons,—an incarnate divine Person Who has two natures, divine nature and human nature, so that, insofar as human, He suffers an atrocious agony and dies on the Cross,—a bread which we eat and which is in reality the Body of the glorious Christ. . . . Bearing there upon objects transcendent by essence, our concepts are surpassed and seem in irreconcilable conflict, and nevertheless they are joined together without any contradiction.

That the Church of Christ is an immense multitude supernaturally endowed with a personal subsistence and constituting supernaturally a single and unique person, it is simply the sign that she is a mystery of faith.

Attributes, like actions, "are of the subject," of the *suppositum,* which, in the beings endowed with a spiritual soul, is a *person.* Let us say therefore that it is the person of the Church who is one, holy, catholic and apostolic.

It is the person of the Church who proposes to us the truths of faith.

It is the person of the Church who is constantly assisted by Christ and by the Holy Spirit.

* * *

5. It is necessary to remark again that in order to receive subsistence and personality in the line of existentiality, this intelligible structure which one calls a nature must be complete or whole in its own order, in other words not lack there any essential element. If a man lacks an arm, this does not at all prevent him from being a human person. But if all five senses were lacking in him, or the cerebral cortex, he would not be a human person, supposing that he could then exist.

We have just seen that by a unique privilege which is the proper mark of the mystery of the Church, the latter, while being composed of a multitude in space and in time, has by virtue of the image of Christ which she bears in her, received from God, and in the proper sense of the word, a supernatural personality. She is a single and same person in Heaven and on earth.

It is fitting therefore to consider that which, in the case of the Church of Christ, follows from the metaphysical distinction between nature and person.

Let us think for example of "dissident" or "separated" Churches such as the Greco-Slavic Orthodox Churches. At first glance they appear as possessing all that which constitutes the *nature* of the Church. It is true that their profession of faith does not include any of the dogmas proclaimed after the second Council of Nicaea, held in 787. But as this profession of faith (I am not speaking of such or such Orthodox theologian) does not deny expressly the dogmas in question, this lack, however regrettable it may be, from which suffer in their nature of Churches of Christ the Churches of which I speak cannot prevent the seal of the supernatural personality of the Church from being imprinted on them.

On the side however of the vast and complex organism that is the body of the Church here on earth, is there nothing more serious lacking, as it seemed at first glance, in these Churches in their nature of Churches of Christ? They have everything (or nearly everything) of this nature, *except that there is lacking in them* the leader or the head of the Church in her state of earthly pilgrimage: the vicar of Jesus Christ, the successor of Peter. And the head is clearly an essential organ. Since their separation from Rome, their nature of Churches of Christ here on earth is a decapitated nature.

A philosopher is indeed forced to conclude: however holy they may be (and this they are extremely anxious to affirm, rightly so moreover), they are therefore not integrated in the *person* of the Church. They are communities of individuals organized among themselves,—in the manner of a nation, of a people, of an innumerable army,—and they possess like these typical characteristics (among which, in their case, the grace of Christ) by reason of which the name of "moral persons" can be analogically applied to them. As long as they remain separated they do not bear the seal of the *real and properly so-called personality* conferred by God on His unique one, on the Bride of Christ, whom St. John saw as the Woman come down from Heaven, from God's home, and engaged here on earth in the struggle with the Dragon.[19] They are not the person herself of the Church under her earthly state.

I shall return to this subject in another chapter (Chapter X), in which, apropos of what one calls the elements of Church, I shall try to show that there is a virtual and invisible presence of the person of the Church in the dissident Christian confessions, and to a particularly eminent degree in the Orthodox Church and in the Anglican Church. I shall attempt also to discover the absolutely fundamental and universal element of Church by reason of which the person of the Church is virtually and invisibly present in the entire human race. The fact remains that among all the spiritual families of the world, the Roman Catholic Church, the *Una, Sancta, Catholica, Apostolica* of which the Vicar of Christ is the head on earth, alone bears here on earth the seal of the personality of the Church, in other words is the person of the Church under the peregrinal state in which she manifests herself visibly here on earth.

IV

The Infallibility of the Church

The Church Considered in Her Unity and Her
Universality Cannot Err or Fail

1. The Church considered in her unity and her universality, or as person, and person assisted by God, cannot err or fail,—Joan of Arc knew this well, and she knew also that the judges of Rouen were not the Church.

The person of the Church cannot make a mistake, although, there where it is not she who speaks and acts through their instrumentality,[1] Churchmen make mistakes as often and as gravely as men of the world (more gravely certainly, being given the importance of their responsibility), and although one sees them fall with as much facility as zeal into the traps put under their feet by each epoch of history,—Christ seeing to it always that through all human failures, and however badly our myopia may see there, the progress of His mystical Body continues here on earth.

But it is the Church taken in her unity and her universality that we have here to consider. In her mission of transmitting to us the truths revealed by God by instructing us in the doctrine of faith and of morals, of sanctifying men by the Sacraments, and of

24

pursuing herself the work of Christ by suffering with Him until the end of the world, she can neither err nor fail.

This follows immediately from this divinely received mission, and from the unceasing assistance which has been promised to her: "And know that I am with you always, until the end of the world" (Matt. 28, 20). This is why St. Paul tells us that she is "the pillar and bulwark of truth" (I Tim. 3, 15).

2. If we imagined that at any moment since Pentecost the Church could make a mistake in transmitting to us the word of God, how could we believe with an absolute certitude—because it is God Who has revealed them—in the truths which she proposes to us, how could we be ready to die for the least article of the Credo? On the side of the object presented to the mind, to believe that God exists and that He wills the good of His creatures is the first article of faith. But on the side of the subject who believes, it is *to believe in the Church* which is the first article and the first presupposition of faith consciously and explicitly professed. To shake in souls faith in the Church is to shake in them theological faith, and to lead them without their noticing it to slip away from grace.

Some Words on the Mythical Mode of Thinking and on Demythization

1. In current language the word "myth" has a pejorative sense and is synonomous with fable. In reality it is with much respect, and a kind of veneration, that it is fitting to think of the religious myths under the regime of which lived formerly for centuries the whole of humanity, and live today more or less vast portions of it.

Works of creative imagination through which passed great intuitions, they carried along, mixed with many errors, many great truths,—not grasped as such, to tell the truth, for the intellect still immersed in the senses had not yet disengaged the notion of truth in its intelligible purity. It is not surprising that God, while waiting until He will make Himself known through the Prophets, and until His Son will come on earth to announce the full truth, let the first education of men be accomplished under the regime of myth, nor even that in order to tell the chosen people the story of the creation He let the inspired writer use the mode of language and of thought proper to the primitive traditions, and instruct us by the means of a "myth which speaks the truth," as I noted in an essay on the second and the third chapters of Genesis.[2] What we read on the creation of Eve formed from the rib of Adam, and on the two trees which grew in the earthly Paradise, belongs still, in reality, to the mythical "literary genre," and presents to us under an imagery which it is not necessary to take literally, in other words under a fictitious form and in statements whose obvious sense is not the true sense, a content of truth of a sovereign importance, which it is asked of us to discover, or rather which it is asked of the Church to discover for us, as she did at the Council of Trent with regard to the original sin, its transmission and its effects (without any mention of the tree of the science of good and of evil, nor of the eating of its fruit; it is only Adam's betrayal of trust which is the object of the discussion,—as mysterious as it is immensely grave).[3]

I think that the case of these two chapters of Genesis, in which it is necessary to seek the true sense under an obvious sense which is not it, is unique in the Old Testament. For the Semitic mode of thinking, as soon as the genius of Israel became established, was a symbolic mode of thinking, not at all a mythical mode of thinking.

Be that as it may, when He Who is the Truth itself came among us in order to testify to the truth, to the point of dying for it between two thieves, that to which He testified as to be believed could include absolutely nothing fictitious to which it would be optional for us to give credit, His teaching could only be free from all trace of the mythical mode of thinking.

2. Let us remark here that the exegetes and the theologians who believe it their duty to demythize the Gospel and the Credo are victims of a prejudice current among the ideosophers of today, and according to which there cannot be any irreformable assertions.[4] This philosophical prejudice is worthless: it implies contradiction, for, in fact, those who say "there cannot be any irreformable assertions" utter there themselves an assertion held to be irreformable, just as those who say "there is no truth" utter there an assertion held to be a truth. And the prejudice in question is incompatible with the exercise of the intelligence; for each time that the intelligence utters an assertion which it holds as purely and simply consonant with the real, it states this assertion as irreformable. Even in contingent matter, if I say "in the moment that I write these lines, I breathe and my heart beats," that is an irreformable assertion. And in necessary matter, if I say "the

human soul is spiritual and immortal," that is an irreformable assertion. These assertions can be explicitated, completed, perfected indefinitely; they remain in themselves irreformable: because truth is the adequation of the intelligence and of that which is (of that which is either for an instant in time which passes, or always by virtue of the nature of things). The philosophers who declare that there cannot be any irreformable assertions do not believe in truth, or believe that truth is the adequation of the intelligence with that which changes, not with that which is: as if in order to change it was not necessary first to be.

On the pretext that any philosphy whatever can serve theology and exegesis, just as any condiment can be useful to a cook, and therefore that theology and exegesis must use the philosophy, whichever one it may be, prevalent in the intelligentsia of their time, some of those who would like to be, in sacred matters, the most intrepid pioneers of research have accepted with eyes closed the sophism to which I have just called attention. That is doubtless why they feel so at ease in the field of the demythization of the sacred.

All That Which Christ Taught Is, Such As He Said It, Eternally True

The parables to which Jesus had recourse have nothing to do with the mythical mode of thinking. They are stories, enigmatic tales which present themselves clearly as such, and as proposing to the intelligence some divine truth to be discerned,—and which were easy to decipher for minds sufficiently pure and enlightened, whereas they only astonished and disturbed the others. He took care moreover to explain them to His disciples when they did not understand them, and to disengage for them the meaning of them,—a meaning eternally true.

And each time that Jesus speaks openly,—"*ecce nunc palam loqueris, et proverbium nullum dicis,*"[5] —in other words each time that He declares something in direct terms and by absolute mode, it is clear for the Christian that His assertion—that which He says, such as He says it—is purely and simply true, absolutely true, true as no merely human assertion can be, at once by the light which it gives us and which lifts the veil, and by the sacred night in which it leaves the divine depths of the revealed mystery.

"*If you live according to my teaching,* you are truly my

disciples; then you will know the truth, and the truth will set you free."[6]

All That Which the Person of the Church
Transmits to Us As Revealed by God
Is, Such As She Says It, Eternally True

With regard to the Credo of the Church, the definitions of the Councils, or the dogmas, like that of the Immaculate Conception and that of the Assumption, proclaimed by the Pope, let us say all that which is matter of faith, the enterprise of demythization in vogue today is no less stupid than it is with regard to the teaching of Christ. Are there not demythizers according to whom Jesus returned from the dead only in taking life again in the preaching of the apostles (what they call "kerygmatic resurrection")? These people betray the faith by a kiss of their so-called charisma.

Let us repeat as many times as it will be necessary that which the irrecusable texts declare; is not the Church the "flesh of the flesh" of Christ,[7] "the Bride immaculate, without stain"[8] of error or of sin? is she not "the plenitude" of Christ?[9] the "Body of whom He is the Head"?[10] This human multitudinous person whom Christ has espoused, and whom He cherishes as Himself, is she not "the pillar and bulwark of truth"?[12] Does not the Spirit of Truth, come down into her in order to "guide her to all truth,"[13] dwell in her since Pentecost and for always?[14] Has not Christ promised her to be with her until the end of the world?[15] It is to the common person of the Church, in other words to the Church considered in her unity and her universality that this promise was made. When she speaks, Christ is the guarantor of her word.

The truths which she proposes to our faith and which she formulates in human words (she is fully free to invent words for this, like the word "consubstantial" for example, which are not taken from Holy Scripture, from the moment that these words make precise in a more exact and more pure manner the meaning of the sacred text) are truths revealed by God. They transcend time as God Himself does.

In other words, all the assertions which since the apostolic age the Church, in her unity and her universality, has stated as *truths of faith* are irreformable assertions, which it is necessary to understand as they are stated, by absolute mode, and according to their obvious meaning which is their true meaning,—a meaning eternally true. One can add to these assertions other assertions which develop them and complete them; one cannot change the meaning of them. "The dogmatic formula can be perfected and be made more explicit, it cannot *change meaning.*"[16]

To claim that these are only "settings-in-perspective," and to ask of the weak human head of such or such *laureatus* to unveil to us, by putting his eye to this telescope, the meaning (or the successive meanings, there will be as many of them as there will be of little prophets to come) supposedly hidden behind the obvious meaning of the assertions of faith, is to deny the infallibility of the Church, or to make of it an infallibility which does not know that which it says. One forgets then that in every *revealed* truth it is God Himself Who has lifted the veil. The Church knows that which she says. And this remains doubtless always perfectible, but this is *true,* irreformably true.

Supposing, in order to imagine for a moment the impossible, that no one of our human assertions is irreformable, those of Christ telling us that which He has heard from God[17] and those of the Church transmitting to us the revealed datum would still be irreformable, the only irreformable assertions which would be in that case offered as food to our intellect.

So much the better, a fideist will perhaps say, for at least we would be thus delivered from the incessant hullabaloo of a multitude of deceptive assertions which bombard our ears. Vain hope! The animal endowed with reason must endure the endless hubbub of the false doctors, as it must endure headache and toothache. And it is in placing confidence in reason and in its irreformable assertions, in reason comforted itself by faith, that he passes through the hubbub,—following the example of his Lord: *transiens per medium illorum, ibat,*—in order to attain to the regions of silence where the true makes itself heard.

Apropos of Prescriptions, Whether Doctrinal or Prudential, Concerning the Regulation of Morals

1. The teaching of the Church concerning the doctrine of morals is as infallible as her teaching concerning the doctrine of faith. She gives us furthermore prescriptions which concern the application of these general norms in given cases and at a given epoch, and which no longer relate to her doctrinal infallibility, but to her prudence.[18]

These prudential prescriptions have an eminently concrete character which seems to me very remarkable, and which confers on them a kind of prophetic value. They are given at a moment when, if they were understood and obeyed according to all their bearing, irreparable evils would be avoided for the future. Once misunderstood by men and neglected by them, the evil is done. And after many centuries it is in order to warn of other evils threatening human history that the Church will have to declare other prescriptions and interdictions, which will also run the risk of being neither understood nor obeyed.

I like to reflect (is this by malicious delight?) that the second Council of Lateran (1139) prohibited the use of the crossbow in tournaments (where a weapon which kills at a long distance is an unfair weapon). In actual fact the crossbow has disappeared from our tournaments, but in order to be replaced by the cannon. If however men had understood! We would not have today the atomic bomb.

2. But what prompts above all my admiration is the multiple condemnations,[19] declared of old against usury, which relate at one and the same time to the prudence of the Church, and, as to the very principle of usury (money itself and by itself must *yield,* or bring forth offspring) to her doctrinal infallibility. Later, by virtue of the same principle, instead of simply investing money in an enterprise in the fortune or misfortune of which one will participate, it is the enterprise itself which one will submit to the law of the greatest possible profit yielded by the money placed, at the cost of the misery to which, in the nineteenth century, the workers (even children) will be reduced, and which will with good reason rouse the indignation of Karl Marx.

If men had understood the whole bearing of the condemnation of usury by the Church, there would not have been any capitalistic regime or any society of consumption, or all that which ensues. . . .

3. It seems to me that it would perhaps not be without profit (intellectual) to think of the encyclical *Humanae Vitae* in the perspective which I have just indicated.[20] I have an idea that, as in the case of the prohibition of usury, the superior prudence of the Church and her doctrinal infallibility have each their part in it.

V

The Church, Plenitude of Christ

Pleroma

1. The notion of *pleroma* (plentitude), such as one finds it in St. Paul and the Greek Fathers, has given rise to many discussions and studies. I shall be content with noting here that, from the moment that it is a question of spiritual plenitude, which is the case when the word is employed by the metaphysician or the theologian, *all plenitude is overflowing.*

That is indeed what St. Paul tells us. Christ is the *plenitude of everything.*[1] And His plenitude overflows onto the Church. The Church is the plenitude of Christ.[2]

"It is he who gave apostles, prophets, evangelists, pastors and teachers in roles of service for the faithful to build up the body of Christ, till we become one in faith and in the knowledge of God's Son, and form that perfect man who is Christ come to full stature," εἰς μέτρον ἡλικίας τοῦ πληρώματος τοῦ Χριστοῦ.[3]

And thus this Perfect Man, which is the Church, will return to the plenitude of God, it "will attain to the *fullness of God* himself,"[4] which, in fact, has itself overflowed in the "whole" of creation (nature, grace and glory) of which Christ is the plenitude. Such is the admirable cycle of the overflowing plenitudes.

31

2. The Church is the plenitude of Christ. Impossible to indicate more strongly the character of supernatural mystery, of mystery of faith, which the Church bears in her very being.

That many Christians lose sight of this, and represent to themselves the Church as a mere natural community, a religious family merely constituted, like the other religious families here on earth, by the fact that it gathers together men professing identical beliefs, practising the same rites and living under the same moral climate,—this is the sign that they have been very badly instructed, and that in saying "the Church" they pass entirely by the side of the object of which they speak.

The Church Is Full of Grace

1. I said, at the end of the first chapter: there are three who are holy and immaculate, although each in a different manner and by a different title: Christ, the Blessed Virgin, and the Church. It is necessary to say likewise: through the effusion of the divine plenitude into the bosom of the created universe, there are three Persons who, by very different titles, are each full of grace:

Christ, Whose human nature is created, but Whose Person is the Uncreated Word, the Son eternally begotten of the Father in the perfect trinitarian unity;

the Blessed Virgin, whose purely human person was immaculate from her conception, by reason of the foreseen merits of the Blessed One whom she was to bring into the world;

the Church, whose collective or multitudinous person has from God her supernatural subsistence by reason of the image of Christ which she bears in her, and whose soul and life are grace and charity.

Between these three persons there is no common measure. The first is divine; the second is human; the third is not an individual person; she embraces in her,—in the unity of a single and same created subsistence supernaturally received,—innumerable human beings who subsist and exist already each with their own individual subsistence and individual existence.

But would one not say that in these three Persons whose degree of being is so different,—the Son incarnate, Mary his Mother, the Church his Bride,—God has willed to see, in the bosom of the universe of creation, a kind of mysterious and sublime reply to that holy and inaccessible Trinity which, but in this case in absolute identity of uncreated nature and of uncreated life, is Himself in His perfect and infinitely transcendent Unity?

When Jesus lived on the earth, the grace of which He was full, and which was infinite in the supraconscious heaven of His soul, did not cease to grow in the here-below of His soul,[5] in proportion to His age, to His trials and to the acts of His heroic love.

In Mary, as long as she lived on the earth, the grace of which she was full did not cease either to grow, until the moment when the Virgin was led, soul and body, close to the Father, the Son and the Holy Spirit, in order to become the Queen of the Angels and of the Church of Heaven and of earth.

And in the Church who proceeds on earth while carrying the cross of Jesus, the grace of which she is full will not cease to grow until the last trials and until the end of time; then, when time will be no more, she will be completely gathered up in the universe of the blessed (where from year to year, in proportion as here below time advances, the multitude of her members entered into glory increases constantly). And it is from there that the heavenly Jerusalem will descend into the material universe transfigured.[6]

2. I wrote a few lines above that the person of the Church embraces in her innumerable human beings. In order to be more exact it is necessary to say that she embraces in her,—in the unity of a single and same created subsistence supernaturally received (the same supernatural subsistence on earth and in Heaven),—innumerable beings who are not only men, her members here on earth, but also the glorious separated souls, and the holy angels (I have already noted that they also are a part of the Church). For it is a single and same person of the Church who finds herself under the state of glory, where she sees, and under the state of "way" or of earthly pilgrimage, where she believes.

Plenitude of Christ, how would the Church not be full of grace? Holy, immaculate, resplendent, as St. Paul saw her, "indefectibly holy," as the second Council of the Vatican has said. This is true of the Church in her state of earthly pilgrimage as of the Church in her state of eternal glory.

But in her state of earthly pilgrimage,—the one which occupies us at this moment,—it is in members who (except for the Blessed Virgin when she lived among us) are all poor sinners that the person of the Church is full of grace. Such is the case, as we have seen in Chapter II, because the soul of the Church is sanctifying grace itself, her life is charity itself; her personality is the supernatural personality which is conferred on her by reason of the image of Christ imprinted in her, and which seals with a unity as perfect as if they formed a single individual substance her soul and the organism with the multiple joints designated her body, and which invests each of her members in the very measure in which the grace of Christ vivifies the being and the action of the latter, whereas all that which relates to evil and to sin withdraws itself from this supernatural personality. The frontier of the personality of the Church passes through the heart of each one. There where the Father does not see the image of His Son, sanctifying grace and charity, there the personality of the Church cannot be; in the measure in which this or that one of her members slips away from grace and from charity, in this same measure he slips away from the personality of the Church.

This means that the "dead" members of the Church are still members of her body by their Baptism, by their faith ("dead" itself), their Confirmation, and, if they have received it, the Sacrament of Holy Orders, and still worked, although only from without, by the influences, the appeals, the stimulations and irradiations with which the person of the Church surrounds them; but that, as long as they remain "dead," their inmost being, having slipped away from the grace of Christ, has ceased at the same stroke to be assumed by the personality of the Church. If a Pope lives in the state of mortal sin, he can be moved instrumentally by the person of the Church in the acts in which he exercises his mission of Pope, and do then an excellent work. But as long as he lives in sin, he is in his own inmost being neither vivified by the grace of Christ nor taken into possession by the personality of the Church.

In the kind of circular meditation in which we are engaged, we shall be led, in the following chapter, to take up again, in order to try to extend them a little further, our reflections on the mystery of a person herself immaculate and of whom grace and sin dispute the members. This is the proper mystery of the Church of the earth. What was important to me here was to insist on the personality supernaturally received by the Church and which is a personality of grace.

An Iconographic Attempt

The images of the Church which abound in Holy Scripture are, as the second Council of the Vatican has noted, as varied as they are disparate,—this is consistent with the symbolic genius which characterizes the language of the Old Testament, as also that of St. Paul and of St. John. And it would be entirely futile to seek to reconcile in a same representation images such as the Field of the Lord, His Vineyard, His Temple, the Mother of the living, the Fold, the heavenly Jerusalem, the Body of which Christ is the Head, the Bride whom He has chosen for Himself,—images whose disparity testifies to the inexhaustible richness of the object designated.

The author of the present book is not however, alas, endowed with the genius of Israel. He is a philosopher born in the Greco-Latin climate, and who, in order to better grasp the intelligibility of the concepts which he assembles, has always felt the need to subtend them, in his imagination, with some symbolic representation which satisfies somewhat the eyes. He has therefore endeavored to unite in a same image the two great symbols which St. Paul uses in speaking of the Church, that of mystical Body and that of Bride, and he has asked, in order to be able to present worthily this image, the help of his friend Jean Hugo.

One will find therefore, on a following page, an illustration which I would have desired in colors, and in which the woman with extended arms who represents the Church is surrounded completely with a great nimbus (which I imagine of gold) formed by the face of the Lord Jesus; which recalls to mind that of the human person of the Church Christ is the human-divine Head, *caput supra omnem Ecclesiam,*[7] as St. Paul says in the Epistle to the Ephesians,—He is the Head or the Leader of the Church, but "above her."

And it is the Church of here below, the Church in her state of earthly pilgrimage, which is thus represented. The woman who symbolizes her is crowned with thorns, in order to show that all through the ages and until the end of time she "completes" (as to the application, not as to the merits) "that which is lacking in the sufferings of the Savior." And her eyes shed tears,—she is bathed in tears,—which indicates that the immaculate Bride takes upon her, in imitation of Christ, the offences of her innumerable members, and does penance for them.

Her head is the symbol of the highest authority in the Church of the earth, the authority of the Vicar of Christ, bishop of Rome, with, immediately below him, the world episcopate.

Her feet are bare because she is poor, bloody because of the thorns in the midst of which she advances here on earth, vigorous nevertheless because God assists her and protects her on the way.

The Universality of the Church
Is a Mystery, As She Is

1. As we have seen in Chapter III, the Church has a double subsistence: on the one hand the natural subsistence of the multitude of her members taken one by one; on the other hand a mysterious subsistence, and one unique in its kind, coextensive with the grace diffused through her members,—which she receives supernaturally from God because she bears imprinted in her the supremely one and individual image of the Word Incarnate. It is this subsistence,—subsistence of grace, at once collective and endowed with an ontological unity which derives from that itself of Christ,—which makes of the Church, unlike every other community, a person properly so called, supernaturally constituted, Body of Christ and Bride of Christ.

Concerning the universality of the Church,—and to the extent (and this seems legitimate to me) that one ascribes the word "universality" to the ensemble of the individual persons who compose this immense collectivity (it is their common faith which is her faith),— it is necessary to say likewise that there is for the Church a double universality: on the one hand a numerical or statistical universality, which apostolic zeal would like to see embrace all men, but which, in actual fact, leaves outside of it extremely vast parts of the population of the earth. It is in another sense that the Church embraces all men, according as she envelops them all in her prayer and in her love, and also, as we shall see, according as one can believe her *virtually and invisibly* present in all. In point of fact, her numerical or statistical universality extends only to all the baptized who are members of her organic structure or of her body with the multiple joints. Such a kind of universality is that which a system of calculators capable of counting all the members belonging to any vast human community would disclose. One can call it "universality of number." It has no interest for us, it is not the universality of the Church in the fundamental sense of the word.

Let us recall that the Church is infallible in matter of faith insofar precisely as she is considered in her unity and her universality. If the universality of the Church was understood in the sense of universality of number, then it is the thought, expressed thanks to I know not what universal Gallup poll, of the communities distributed in the ensemble of the local churches which would furnish the criterion of that which is of faith. And it is in that which is believed, at the base, by the unanimity or by the greatest number of the members of these communities in the entire world that what the Church holds to be true and revealed by God would consist. In order to see the absurdity of such a conception it suffices to think of the crisis of Arianism, and of the remark of St. Jerome about the stupefaction of the world noticing that it had almost woke up Arian. In the course of the great religious tempest of the fourth century many of the local churches had, at one moment or another, passed to Arianism or to semi-Arianism, and the faith of the Church was saved only by saints of an admirable grandeur and of an invincible steadfastness,—an Athanasius, a Hilary of Poitiers.

2. The universality of the Church in the fundamental sense of the word is that of all those of her members who are in the grace of Christ, and who do not hinder the assistance of His Spirit received by the person of the Church,—and in which each can participate either directly if he is himself interiorly illuminated by the *sensus fidei* proper to the "holy people of God,"[8] or through the agency of the teaching and of the decisions of the Church if he adheres to them willingly. Such a universality is a universality of grace, as such invisible to our eyes. But it becomes evident to us each time that from above the ordinary or extraordinary magisterium causes our ears to hear the voice of the person of the Church,—this by the Pope speaking *ex cathedra,* or by the ecumenical Councils bringing together in a single and same testimony, in union with the Pope, the episcopate of the entire world, or by the unity and the continuity through the centuries of the teaching everywhere given by the bishops. In each of the three cases which I have just mentioned, the unity and the universality of the person of the Church are sensibly manifested, and the Church considered in her unity and in her universality shows itself to us.

Thus therefore the universality of the Church is as mysterious as the Church herself. God alone knows its extensiveness, God alone knows who are those whom it embraces in act at each moment of history. To us others it becomes evident, as I have just said, only when the voice of the Church makes itself heard to us, in the sensibly manifested unity of the apostolic teaching,—either by the ordinary magisterium in the course of the centuries, or by the decrees and definitions of the ecumenical Councils, or by the teaching of the Pope *ex cathedra*. Then it is the Church considered in her unity and her universality who speaks to us, and who speaks to us infallibly.

3. Have I not however recalled just now that at the time of the great crisis which followed the Council of Nicaea, held in 325 (it is normal that the great Councils be followed by great crises), a great number of bishops found themselves one day or the other on the side of Arianism or of semi-Arianism? What would therefore have happened if in the very middle of the crisis Pope Liberius had found a way to summon the same bishops (perhaps in the majority) to an ecumenical Council?

In my opinion the answer is very simple: it was in the midst of the worst confusion, and of a chaos of events in which rivalries, cowardices, coalitions of interests and ecclesiastical court flatteries intersected with the intrigues of the imperial court, the decisions without appeal, the threats and the violences of the Emperor, and with a wave of persecutions, and it was by weakness, fear or ambition that the bishops in question slipped into error. Well, supposing that in the very middle of the crisis all had been brought together in an ecumenical Council, the assistance of the Holy Spirit promised to the person of the Church would have for a moment swept away in them the miseries of the old Adam;[9] and the same bishops, illuminated by the Spirit of Christ, would have condemned solemnly Arianism and semi-Arianism, as did later, in 381, the Council of Constantinople.

VI

The Church Penitent

1. *Veni columba mea,* come my dove, my all-beautiful,[1] without stain or wrinkle, holy and immaculate.[2] The Church is the Beloved of Christ, she is His plenitude. And yet this same Church is penitent. She accuses herself, often in very harsh terms, she weeps for her failures, she begs to be purified, she pleads unceasingly for forgiveness (she does so every day in the Lord's Prayer), she sometimes cries out to God from the depths of the abyss, as from the depths of his anguish one who fears damnation.

For us to take advantage of that to strike hard on *her* breast, when in reality we are speaking either of the failures of the hierarchy or of the sometimes atrocious miseries of the Christian world, the peasant of the Garonne saw there "a silliness in which many young clerics of today do not fail to take pleasure."[3] I think so still, but my language lacked courtesy. I should only have said that they are first-rate simpletons.

2. The fact remains that the penitence of the Church shows us that if, in the image of Christ immaculate, the Church also is immaculate, she is not so however in the same manner as He is. In other words the mystical Body of Christ is not in the same relationship with its members as the physical body of Christ is with its. Whereas the holiness of Christ renders the members of His

40

physical body holy as He is, the holiness of the Church, or of the mystical Body, does not prevent the members of the latter from being sinners.

Holy as Jesus Himself were the members of His body. In the members of this human body which walked on the roads of Galilee and whose voice announced the Good News, and which was crucified under Pontius Pilate; in these feet which Mary Magdalene covered with kisses, and which were pierced, in these hands whose touch healed the sick, and which were pierced, there was never the slightest trace of sin. In taking upon Him the sins of the world, He assumed something which was entirely foreign to Him, and which He made His own by pure love, pure will to substitute Himself as victim for sinful humanity; it is in this sense that St. Paul says that Christ was made sin in order to save us.[4] He never, in absolutely anything which was proper to Him, or which He had as His own, knew the taste of sin, had the experience of sin. It was solely by and in His love for sinners that He knew sin: *Darkness of the contemplation of sin, night truly implacable, experience founded in the charity and in the union of love of Christ with sinners . . . He tastes the infinite bitterness of our failures, as in the darkness of divine contemplation the poor saints taste the essential sweetness of God. . . .*[5]

Of the mystical Body, on the contrary, sinners are the very members. They are something of it. The Church "embraces sinners in her own bosom."[6] And thus the Church is not unacquainted with sin; "she is wholly mingled in sin,"[7] she knows the taste of sin, she has the experience of sin, in the innumerable multitude of the sinners who are her members, her head here on earth, her hands, her feet. She has sin in her members.

Is this not enough in order to be tempted to say with certain theologians that she is at once holy and sinful? Detestable formula, which blinds the mind as to that which the Church really is, and claims to make us kneel before a flagrant contradiction. As if in taking away the sins of the *world* Christ had not always at His side His Bride (who is not *of the world*); as if His mystical Body was at the same time His enemy; and as if she, the Plenitude of Christ, the one full of grace, "without stain or wrinkle," holy and immaculate, bore also in her that which gives death to souls, was soiled herself with all the crimes committed by those who bear the name of Christians.

3. It is fitting here to recall that the mystical Body is a collective body, and to be attentive to the ambiguity of the word

"member," which signifies now one of the constitutive parts of an individual living being, now one of the human persons who form a part of a community. If one of my "members" is sick, *I* am myself sick. But if a "member" of a learned society or of a political party catches the flu or the cholera, one cannot say for all that that this learned society or this political party has the flu or the cholera.

It is true, I have enough insisted on it, and I shall return to it again in a moment, that the Church is neither a learned society nor a political party nor any mere community whatsoever; she is a person. Yes, but a collective person,—whose unity (of grace) is of the superior and divine order,—and thus the sin of the human persons who are her members, and who each possess free will, and are each capable of following the instinct of grace or of resisting it, is not *her* sin.

"Holy" and sinful at one and the same time, it is in the members of the Church that the paradox resides, and that it resolves itself. Far from having, indeed, the plenitude of grace which in the person of the Church as in that of the Virgin Mary excludes all possibility of sinning, we others, members of the Church here on earth, and the best among us, live by grace and charity only more or less imperfectly (when we live by them); and it is therefore without any contradiction that we can be, in a measure, sanctified ones by the Blood of Christ, while remaining, in another measure, sinners and ungrateful ones.

As soon as one has understood that, by a unique privilege, the Church possesses, by virtue of the image of Christ present in her, a subsistence and personality of grace which in its supernatural unity transcends the natural personality of her members,—that which seemed an enigma becomes decipherable to the mind. That the Church has sin in her members and that she is wholly mingled in sin,—this does not at all make her to be herself sinful, because her personality transcends that of her members, and because they are invested with her personality only to the extent that they live by her life of grace and of charity. One understands at the same stroke that the Church in her own person is "indefectibly holy,"[8] and that she is nevertheless composed of human persons who are all here on earth sinners to some degree, whether it is a question of "living" members who in the measure in which they are living are assumed by the personality of the church while slipping away from it to the extent that they fail, or whether it is a question of the "dead" members more or less anchored in evil or more or less ready to live again, who have withdrawn from the personality of the Church and from her soul, but who belong to her body (and at the same stroke, virtually and initially, to the soul which informs the latter) by the faith ("dead" itself without charity) which they have kept, as also by the Baptism which they have received and the other character-imprinting Sacraments which they have been able to receive: inert shreds in which the blood no longer passes, but which the person of the Church considers still to be her own and for which she is more than ever sollicitous. For they were living by her life when she had received them from God in order to lead them to eternal life, and behold them now torn away from her life, and on the way to losing eternal life.

All of this,—it is the very mystery of the Church.

4. One sees, consequently, that of the person of the Church in her earthly state it is necessary to say that *by herself,* like Christ when He lived among us, neither does she know the taste of sin nor does she have the experience of sin; but that, unlike Christ when He lived among us, she knows the taste of sin and has the experience of sin by and in something which is proper to her and which she has as her own, *by and in her members,* her own members, who are a part of her without being herself.

She herself, who in her supernatural personality is free from every trace of sin, she "completes in her body," for all men, and all through the centuries, "that which is lacking in the sufferings" of her Bridegroom. And it is through love, like Jesus, that she takes on her the whole mass of sins which she has not committed. But if it is a question of the men *who have been made hers by the Sacraments,* then, unlike Jesus, it is sins committed by her own members that through love she takes thus upon her. This is why, then, she is not only coredemptrix, as was Mary; she is also *penitent.*

She does penance *for her members,*—who are not she, but who are of her and belong to her. She accuses herself, *in her members,* with whom she identifies herself through love; she weeps for her failures, which are the failures of her members, not of herself, and which she makes her own through love. She pleads unceasingly for forgiveness, for her members, whose sins she assumes through love. She sometimes cries out to God from the depths of the abyss, in making, through love, of the anguish of her members and of their distress her own distress and her own anguish. She is in perpetual labor of purification,[9] in her members and for her members, as if the *sancta et immaculata,* the one without stain had herself need of being purified. (She does not cease to grow in grace,—which is not the same thing. And that she calls purification this progress in grace, it is still by identification of love with the wounded and lame ones who are her members.) That is how the Church is penitent. And it is also because she knows that if there were more saints engendered by her, there would be more sinners who would return to God, more "sons who were dead, and who have come back to life, who were lost and who have been found,"[10] and whom the Father clasps now in His arms; and she knows that there is no greater joy in Heaven.

The Church suffers and prays for all men; but she suffers and prays especially,—as *penitent*,—for her members, and more particularly for those of them who have withdrawn themselves from her soul and who are dead to the life of grace. What a thirst in her, comparable to that of Jesus on the cross!

VII

The Church Considered in Her Integrality

(at once in glory and in time)

and the Church Considered Only According

As She Is in Time

A Preliminary Remark

1. One knows that the Church exists under three different states, that of Heaven, that of the earth, that of Purgatory. When one says "the Church glorious," "the Church in pilgrimage," "the Church suffering," one does not designate three different Churches, but the same Church, the same person of the Church, under the three states in question. The subject of this book has nothing to do with the Church suffering, I shall therefore say nothing about the latter, except that the Church of Heaven and that of the earth come constantly to her assistance by their prayers, as the Church of Heaven comes constantly to the assistance of the Church of the earth by her prayers and by her inspirations.

2. It is to the Church of Heaven and to the Church of the earth that the present chapter is devoted. It is essential to understand that they are, as I have just said, the same and unique Church of Christ under two different states. This is a classical doctrine[1] and one which I believe is recognized by all theologians. Jean Bréhal referred to it in the clearest terms at the trial of rehabilitation of Joan of Arc.

45

Being given the importance attached in this book to the person of the Church, one will not be surprised that I envisage this doctrine in the light of the central idea of the supernatural personality conferred by God on the Church.

3. We are going to try now to widen and to deepen our thought on the Church, in considering the latter not only in her state of earthly pilgrimage, but also in her state of glory in Heaven.

Heaven,—one finds today some students in the sacred sciences who seem annoyed by this word. No one however expected the cosmonauts to meet in their explorations the angels and the blessed souls; and one will continue always, by virtue of the most spontaneous and the most connatural of the metaphors which the eye suggests to the mind, to say "heaven" in order to signify symbolically the invisible world.

When Christ taught us to say: "Our Father, who art in Heaven," He made use, in speaking thus, only of a mere symbolic designation of the mystery in which the infinite transcendence of God envelops itself. And this symbolic designation was fully justified, and remains forever valid, from the sole fact that it is necessary for us to raise our head in order to look at the sky; sensible appearances are here alone in play, and they impose themselves on us irresistibly, when they show us the sky, along with the benefits which it pours upon us by its sun and along with the splendors with which it lights up the night, as the sign par excellence offered by our universe of the invisible kingdom where the spirits live with God.

I am fully aware that the cosmology of the ancients confused everything by masking with a physical sense this purely symbolic sense, and by causing the heaven of the blessed to be regarded as a physical place prepared on the celestial spheres for their residence,—the place of incorruption: that which gave the worst facilities to our imagination. But all of this has been fortunately swept away by modern science, so that the "heaven" of the elect has no longer anything to do with the "heaven" of the astronomers,[2] except with regard to the fact that the latter is and will remain always for the spontaneous instinct of the human heart the symbol of the former.

The Two States of the Church.
She Endures and Advances Not Only in Time,
But Also in the Duration Proper to Glory

1. The first point to be noted here is that the personality supernaturally received by the Church, by virtue of the image of Christ imprinted in her, is given to her for always. The person of the Church is imperishable.

Living ourselves in time, it is also in time that we are naturally inclined to consider all the existents of which we speak. It is the same with regard to the Church. At first, when we reflect that she is imperishable, this means for us that she is there among us, in time, until the end of the centuries and of the generations (and beyond, in the land of the resurrected, but then time will have ceased, such at least as we know it, and suddenly our reflections on the subject stop also).

In other words, our consideration bears upon the person of the Church considered in her state of way, or of earthly pilgrimage. This consideration is more normal and is necessary; but it does not suffice, for it refers only to a single one of the two states under which it is important for us here to consider the Church: duality which will cease only at the resurrection of the bodies, when the universe of matter, fully reconciled to the victory over death, will be itself transfigured in glory, and integrated in order to serve it in the beatitude of the spirits.

2. The other state under which the Church finds herself is that of glory and of beatitude. The duration in which she lives there, and of which theology has elaborated the notion, is not time, which is linked with the essential mutability of material being, substantially subject to becoming; it is the duration proper to pure spirits, which one calls *aevum* or eviternity, and which, as regards the very being of these, is mere fixation in existence, without mutation or succession, but is accompanied by mutation and succession as to the operations which they produce. Each time for example that an angel turns his thought toward a new object, he marks so to speak the indivisible aevum, in which he remains forever, of the initial point and of the final point of an operation which, in the immobility of an instant which endures, coincides with a certain flow of our time.

It is in this duration proper to pure spirits, and intermediary between time and eternity, that the Church in state of glory pursues her existence, and that there enter, one by one, once separated from their bodies, the souls of the elect. The holy angels had begun to see God for eternity from the instant, immediately upon being created, they chose to obey Him and separated themselves from the angels of pride. It is at the time of the Incarnation, Cardinal Journet tells us (III, p. 207),—I would prefer to say: at the end of the blessed trajectory Passion-Resurrection-Ascension,—that their grace (already virtually Christic by reason of Christ to come) became actually and fully Christic by reason of Christ come, and that the world of beatitude became the Church of Christ in Heaven. As to human souls, all those which since Adam and Eve repentent[3] were saved by the merits of Christ to come entered into beatitude only after He had come. They waited in "the bosom of Abraham." And it is "after the Passion and the death of the Lord Jesus," after the redemptive work was accomplished, that they "saw the divine essence face to face."[4]

But it is the Church *of Christ come* who is the object of our reflections. She began at Pentecost;[5] and the innumerable saints whom she has engendered since then and who see God and who praise Him, and who pray with men as one generation succeeds the other, compose with the angels that which one calls the Church of Heaven.

The person of the Church in her state of glory is essentially the same as the person of the Church in her state of earthly pilgrimage. She is a single and same imperishable person. But in Heaven her members are (along with the holy angels) blessed souls separated from their bodies, whereas on earth they are men wounded by the sin of Adam, and saved, if they do not refuse grace, by the Blood of the Lamb of God.[6]

Let us note in passing that the immortality of the human soul does not entail the imperishability of the human person, for the latter is soul and body together, and a separated soul is no longer, ontologically, a person. But the soul of the Church (that is to say, sanctifying grace, which in Heaven is glory or consummated grace) is never separated; it animates its body in Heaven as on the earth,—here people of human persons, succeeding each other from generation to generation, there people of separated human souls awaiting the resurrection of their bodies. This is why the ontological personality of the Church,—supernatural personality received by reason of the image of Christ which the Church bears in her,—knows no interruption. The person of the Church is a single and same person under the state of way here on earth and under the state of eternal glory.

Let us think of the human beings assumed by the personality of the Church who, in the fifth century for example, lived here on earth the time of a generation. They were consequently much less numerous than the multitude of souls, they too assumed by the personality of the Church, who since Peter had begun to feed the sheep of the Savior had already entered into eternal glory. Today, when Christians have behind them twenty centuries of history, the multitude of souls assumed, in glory, by the personality of the Church, is immensely more vast than that of the men, our contemporaries, who, assumed likewise by the personality of the Church, proceed here on earth with us. And it is the same supernatural person of the Bride of Christ who embraces in her these two multitudes, the one already in Heaven, the other yet a little time on earth, where the generations sprung from it are going to succeed it.

The Church in her state of earthly pilgrimage appears then as the advanced point,—living and enduring in time, generation after generation, under the government of the vicars of Christ succeeding one another,—of the Church in her state of glory, who lives and endures in eviternity, and under the direct government of Christ Himself (there the Popes have returned again into the ranks). And the personality of the Church invests at one and the same time, on earth her members in state of grace, and in Heaven, along with the multitude of the holy angels, that of the blessed souls, whose number does not cease to grow since Pentecost, and who from earth hurl themselves into eternal life like a torrent gushed forth from the wounds of Jesus.

The Person of the Church Considered in Her Integrality, According as She Advances at Once in Aevum and in Time, or Considered Only According as She Advances in Time

1. If one wishes to form for himself a complete idea of the person of the Church at a given moment of the history of the world, it is therefore thus that it is necessary to consider her: *both* according as at this moment she endures and advances in her peregrinal state here on earth and in the transluminous obscurity

of faith, and according as, all along what in the history of the world has been a more and more extended past, she has grown unceasingly in multitude in her state of glory, where she endures and advances outside of time, eviternally, beatified by the vision of God.[7]

I hold that this consideration of the Church in her integrality has a major importance, as does also the distinction which it implies: The person of the Church, of the Bride of Christ, presents herself to our thought under a double aspect; she can be considered either *only* according as she endures and advances on the earth and in time, or *both* according as since the day of Pentecost she endures and advances in Heaven and in eviternity, and according as she endures and advances on the earth and in time. The first manner of considering the Church is normal and necessary, but it is incomplete and does not suffice.

2. Epochs can arise (let us think of the crisis of Arianism) in which the greater number of the members of the Church of the earth are in the process of losing their way: very reduced in extension can be then the universality of grace and of divine assistance of those who do not err more or less in the faith. But in the Church of Heaven the immense multitude is there of those who see God, and they have not forgotten the earth, they pray unceasingly for their brothers making their way here on earth, they send to such and such of these their inspirations, they assist and illuminate the saints who suffer in this world, they have their own means of intervening in the affairs of this Church whom in leaving the earth they have certainly not left, since in Heaven and on earth there is but a single Church under two different states.

In short, the person of the Church being the same person here and there, it is necessary to consider her *both* in Heaven and on earth, in order to see that which the Church is at the worst moments themselves in which considered according as she is *only* the Church of the earth she seems to risk ruin, and in order to understand at the same stroke that the gates of Hell shall never prevail against her.

3. The Son of man, when He shall return, will He find faith on earth? It is He who has posed the question,[8] making allowance thus for human liberty. One can think that then, although the Gospel has been preached everywhere, a very small flock only will

have kept the faith,—a faith so ardent and so pure that it will compensate before God the apostasy of the great number.

It is this very small flock which will remain assumed here on earth by the personality of the Church. But it will have with it the whole multitude, assumed by the same personality, of the blessed souls gathered together in Paradise, along with those of Adam and Eve, since the Fall and the repentance, and of whom the incalculable number will have a hand in its accomplishment. The person of the Church, considered both in her state of earthly pilgrimage and in her state of eternal glory, will be more resplendent than ever.

And on the last day, as I have already noted, this duality of states will come to an end; the Jerusalem of Heaven will descend upon the earth, the souls will rejoin their risen bodies; and to the immense multitude of the resurrected will be united the small flock of witnesses of the faith still in life on the earth, who will pass into glory without having known death.[9]

It is thus that the Bride will go to meet the Bridegroom.

Digression on the Church of Heaven

1. Angels and separated souls, the blessed spirits are immutably fixed in the vision of God, by which they participate in the divine eternity itself. But in the eviternity which is their proper duration, they lead, outside of the vision, the highest life which the created being can enjoy,—that of the supreme activities of love and of truth in the unimaginable plenitude of the sovereign peace. They render to the three divine Persons a worship of praise and of thanksgiving, they each meditate in a sacred silence the mystery of the redemptive Cross and the other revealed mysteries, they adore Christ in glory, they pray for men and occupy themselves, each according to his office, with the things of our world and with the course of our history, and with each immortal soul created anew here on earth; they live among themselves in a mutual love which is the perfect communion of the saints, they converse among themselves (what marvellous confidences they must make to one another, and what marvellous stories they must tell to one another!), they do not cease to break together the bread of truth. And in all of this they rejoice in doing the will of the Father.

I note here that the vision of the divine essence is absolutely ineffable and incommunicable; that which is seen in it, indivisibly from it, cannot be expressed and communicated by any mental word, for this is infinitely above the capacity of every created spirit; it absorbs, it devours in it the gaze of the separated souls and of the pure spirits whom it beatifies. The concepts of which they make use in order to express to themselves that which they know, and in order to communicate to each other their thoughts, in the angelic manner,[10] —it is in the light of the infused science that they produce them in themselves; and it is in this same light of the infused ideas that the highest among them instruct the others, in opening themselves to them with the limitless generosity of charity.

2. In the Church of Heaven the blessed souls are equal with the angels, they have their place at the diverse degrees of their hierarchies,—indeed at the highest of all,—and through them also passes the flow of illumination which causes to descend through the immensity of the invisible world the communicable knowledge of the mysteries of nature and of grace, infused at first by God into the noblest created intelligence.

The noblest of all the created intelligences is that of Christ in his human nature. And immediately after this intelligence comes that of the human person who is the mere creature nearest to God, the Queen of Heaven and the Queen of the angels. In the soul of the Blessed Virgin in glory, the infused science, which she receives directly from Christ, is more universal and more perfect than in any other mere creature; it is Mary who in the Church of Heaven illuminates the highest of the angels (and perhaps, why not, certain human souls elevated like her higher than the angels; for there is nevertheless a privilege of man over the angel, merits which only he can gain: he can be a martyr, give his life for God. . . .)

I add that if one thinks of the infinite abyss of the divine transcendence, and of the fact that even *seen* in the beatific vision, the uncreated Essence will never be *comprehended* by a created spirit, one can think, it seems to me, that the illumination which, through the infused science, makes known to the pure spirits and to the blessed souls the depths of God, will never cease to grow,—in Heaven and then in the material universe transfigured at the time of the resurrection,—all through the endless duration which one calls eviternity: God alone enjoying eternity, unique instant without beginning or end which contains everything.

3. In order to envisage in its fullness the infallibility of the Church,—which is exercised not merely in matters of faith, but in

matters of morals, and also in the judgment which it bears when it canonizes a saint,—we must take under our gaze, in a single block, the Church of Heaven and the Church of the earth, the Church who sees and the Church who believes.

It goes without saying that the Church of Heaven is absolutely and wholly infallible, since she is fixed in the blessed vision, and since the teaching which is given there is an illumination of spirit to spirit in the light of God. Consisting in the impossibility of all error in that which is "seen" or intuitively grasped by all the intelligences of Heaven, one can say that this infallibility is an infallibility "immanent" in the immense assembly of the elect.

Infallibility is immanent also in the Church of the earth, who, through her theological life itself and, as the second Council of the Vatican says (Ch. II, Sect. 12), through "the supernatural sense of the faith" present in "the holy people of God" (in the *universitas fidelium,* or what I have called the universality of grace of the Church) "cannot err in the faith." But this infallibility *in credendo* has for condition, on the side of the object, the infallibility *in docendo* of the magisterium. So that the Church of the earth is infallible only because she has in her midst the Pope[11] assisted by the episcopate in union with him, whereas in order to be infallible the Church of Heaven has no need of pope and of magisterium.

I have said above that the Church of Heaven comes constantly to the assistance of the Church of the earth by her prayers and by her inspirations. It is necessary to go much further, and to say that the infallibility of the Church of the earth in matters of faith has for ontological foundation the fact that she and the Church of Heaven are but a single and same person, the person of the Church under two different states: which person of the Church, in her peregrinal state, can clearly, by reason of her unity, neither exercise, *in credendo,* the *sensus fidei* proper to the holy people of God, nor, *in docendo,* propose to us in human language the revealed truths of God, objects of our faith, except in believing and teaching that itself which in her state of consummated grace she sees in Heaven. Thus it is the Church herself, the person herself of the Church, who speaks to us through the instrumentality of her magisterium. I am not unaware that if the magisterium is infallible, it is insofar as it participates in the kingship of Christ and is assisted by the Holy Spirit. But this does not at all exclude the intermediary role played there by the person of the Church. The assistance of the Holy Spirit and the authority of Christ pass then through the person of the Church *speaking to us herself,* through the instrumentality of those of her members who are commissioned to teach us.

It is as voice of the Church *in her celestial state and in her earthly state* at one and the same time that (ordinary magisterium) the episcopate in union with the leader of the Church of the earth and (extraordinary magisterium) the Councils in union with the leader of the Church of the earth teach infallibly all the members of the latter. And if the Pope by himself alone, when he speaks *ex cathedra,* that is to say, according to the terms employed by the first Council of the Vatican,[12] "when, fulfilling his function of pastor and doctor of all Christians, he defines, through his supreme apostolic authority, the doctrine in matters of faith or of morals to be held by the universal Church," has the power to teach infallibly the whole Church of the earth, it is because then he is the voice of the person of the Church, who as Church of Heaven causes to pass through him her infallibility of Church who sees, when as Church of the earth she enlarges the field of her infallibility of Church who believes.

The Infallibility of the Church and the Infallibility of the Pope

1. It is especially with reference to pontifical infallibility that appears, to my mind, the importance of the distinction, on which I have insisted in this chapter, between the Church considered only under her state of earthly pilgrimage and the Church considered both under her state of glory and her state of way.

Let us consider indeed the Church considered *both* according as she is in the state of glory and embraces in her bosom a constantly increasing multitude of blessed souls, *and* according as she is in the state of earthly pilgrimage, and according as at a given time, let us say during a half-century, the multitude which she embraces is that of a generation which lives here on earth, while waiting to give way to future generations. Our gaze bears then on the person of the Church considered in her integrality. This person of the Church, who has for Leader, in the invisible world, directly Christ, and on earth His vicar, visible leader of the visible Church, is, in the celestial glory of all her saints, and of their Queen, and in the work of salvation which she accomplishes here on earth, that which is most sacred, most beautiful and most worthy in creation. The Pope is her servant, the most humble and the most venerable, the noblest and the most engaged, the most heavily burdened of her servants of the earth; the burden which he has to bear for her is the cross of his Master. His charisma of successor of Peter,—feed my sheep, feed my lambs,—it is from Christ,—insofar precisely as Head and leader, in Heaven, of the entire person of the Church,—that he receives it. He is head and leader of the Church of the earth in order to be able, according as he fulfills his function, and in the measure of the more or less lofty exigencies of the latter, to act here on earth under the inspiration and in the virtue of the Spirit of Christ exercising supreme authority over the person of the Church considered in her integrality.

It is on the relation between the Pope speaking *ex cathedra* and the person of the Church integrally considered, at once as Church of the earth and as Church of heaven, that I would like to insist here. If it is a question for example of a new dogmatic definition, I shall say that the content which constitutes the truth to be defined has had from century to century its witnesses in the Church here on earth, (witnesses also of the *sensus fidei* mysteriously diffused in the universality of grace of the "holy people of God") who have personally believed in this truth (it is the affair of theological and historical studies having reference to the preparation of the definition to show this); and that the infallible decisive discernment of this content is effected by the Pope under the assistance and the inspiration of Christ and of the Spirit, passing themselves through the person of the Church considered above all (this is the capital point to be considered) in her state of Church of Heaven,—I do not see why it could not be thus, since the Church of Heaven herself knows intuitively this same truth. (I remember moreover that Pius XI told me one day that he often received inspirations of major importance during his Mass,—and the Mass is always celebrated *in persona Ecclesiae*. . . .)

Likewise, with regard to the infallible authority with which the truth in question is defined as *of faith,* I think that it is always brought into play, not only under the inspiration of Christ and of the Holy Spirit as first and principal cause, but also under the motion of the person of the Church in her state of Church of Heaven and of consummated grace, because it is the *Church herself,* the very person of the Church, whom God wishes to have us hear through her earthly leader, and because the latter is then the instrumental agent of the person of the Church considered in her integrality, but principally and above all in her state of Church of Heaven, herself serving then as instrument to the absolutely supreme authority of her human-divine Head. The Pope speaking *ex cathedra* is the voice of the Church of the earth and also of the Church of Heaven, the latter bringing the former to enlarge the message which she transmits to us.

This is how I picture to myself the relation between the Pope speaking *ex cathedra* and the person of the Church integrally considered. The latter does not reveal to him the truth to be defined. She uses him in order that this truth, which in actual fact belonged already virtually (or rather *in actu exercito*) to the treasury of revelation received by the Church of the earth, be henceforth taught formally (or rather *in actu signato*) to the Church of the earth as truth of faith.

Thus the Pope is the voice of the person of the Church considered in her integrality, together as Church of Heaven (proximate foundation of the infallible authority with which the new definition is proclaimed) and as Church of the earth (to whom is now manifested as of faith that to which she adhered already in act lived by all those who in her followed on this point the impulse of the Holy Spirit).

It seems to me that when the Blessed Virgin appearing at Lourdes said to Bernadette: *I am the Immaculate Conception,* it was precisely in order to signify that the dogma proclaimed by Pius IX was sanctioned by Heaven, and that the infallible authority with which the Pope had defined it was the very infallibility of the Church of Heaven descending into him and passing through him. It is of the divine truth itself of the Immaculate Conception that the immaculately conceived one came to bring amongst us a sensible sign.

It follows from all of this that the Pope,—according as assisted by Christ and by the Spirit he is also instrumental agent and voice of the person of the Church considered in her integrality, as Church of Heaven and as Church of the earth together,—exercises his infallibility in sovereign fashion with regard to the Church considered only according as she is in the state of earthly pilgrimage. When he speaks *ex cathedra,* the authority of his infallible word imposes itself on the entire multitude of the members of the Church of here on earth. Those of them who on the point in question were in doubt or maintained another opinion know then the truth which they are held to believe. What the Pope has said in making explicit such or such a point of faith finds itself incorporated in the sacred deposit of revelation, and imposes itself on the faith of all the times to come.[13]

2. The views presented here are directly opposed to the conception according to which the Pope, when he speaks *ex cathedra*, would only express the accord, on such or such a point concerning the faith and morals, of all the local churches of the world grouped together in the Church (considered only according as she exists on the earth).

This conception, which results from a naive transfer of democratic themes (valid, if they are well understood, in the order of the temporal) to the order of salvation, and which in the end views the fold of Christ as governing itself by representatives of the human community deriving all their authority from the latter, forgets blithely that it is the Truth which saves us, and it is simply aberrant. It is not surprising that he whom one calls Pope becomes there the world president of a federation of religious clubs which one still calls churches, presided over by prelates whom one still calls bishops, and whose function consists in expressing the thought and satisfying the wishes of those at the base.

3. It seems to me, on the other hand, that in the perspective which I have proposed the notion of pontifical infallibility escapes the difficulties which it meets often in our separated brothers, for want of being adequately presented to them.

The Pope is not a human being suspended so to speak between Heaven and earth, and who by his charisma of infallibility would find himself above the Church. Christ alone is, as St. Paul says, *caput super omnem Ecclesiam*, human-divine Head *above* the entire Church. The Pope is a *purus homo* like the other members of the Church, and he is, in the Church and at her summit, but not above her, the head and the leader who, as vicar of Christ here on earth, directs her in her earthly pilgrimage. But, by very virtue of his function of supreme pastor and doctor here on earth it is necessary that in order to maintain intact the deposit of faith and to cause it to progress in explicitation, he be able in certain cases,—when he speaks *ex cathedra*,—to establish infallibly that which is to be believed.

It is not by making use of a privilege accorded to his person as proper or principal cause that he acts then; it is by making use of a privilege accorded to his person as instrumental cause,—according as then, under the first action and the inspiration of the Spirit of God, he is on earth the Voice of this person of the Church who is the same person in Heaven and on earth, and who as Church of Heaven is the proximate foundation of the infallible authority with which, in the progressive explicitation of the revealed datum, he manifests on such or such a point to the Church of the earth that which in this Church a great many were already inclined to believe through the assistance of the Holy Spirit.

The infallibility of the Pope is thus doubly at the service of the person of the Church integrally considered: it invests the leader of the Church of the earth with an authority which is each time that itself of the Church according as she is in the terminal state of vision, or of consummated grace; and it establishes explicitly as point of faith a truth which found itself implicitly contained in the revealed deposit entrusted to the keeping of the Church according as she is in the state of way, where she believes without yet seeing.

4. All that I have just said of the Pope speaking *ex cathe-dra*,—I shall say also of the ecumenical Council. It also has supreme and full authority.[14] Assisted and guided by Christ and the Holy Spirit, it extends the field of the infalliblity of the Church of the earth in causing us to hear the voice of the latter in the instant that, through the instrumentality of the episcopal college united with the Pope, she receives communication of the infalliblity of the person of the Church in the state of consummated grace.

And the teaching of the episcopate is likewise infallible when by the ordinary magisterium, and under the ordinary assistance of the Holy Spirit,[15] it transmits to us all through the centuries and in unanimous manner the deposit of the apostolic faith. It may be, I remark in passing, that in the faith of the Christian people such as they live it under the aegis of the ordinary magisterium there is included such and such a particular point which has not yet been defined by the Church or admitted by all her doctors. If it happens that the Pope, as Pius XII did when he proclaimed the dogma of the Assumption, takes into consideration the attachment to the point in question of popular faith, it is not at all because the latter has of itself the value of rule of faith; it is because *in the very exercise of his charisma of infallibility,* and therefore enlightened by the Holy Spirit, the Pope has seen in it a witness of the faith of the Church. And it is only by virtue of the solemn declaration of the Sovereign Pontiff, and of his extraordinary magisterium, that the point in question imposes itself then on the faith of all.

It remains nevertheless interesting to note that popular faith can thus find itself sometimes in advance of the new decisions of the magisterium. Is not this a mark of the *sense of the faith* present in the people of God, a sign showing that the assistance of the Holy Spirit is given in the universal Church, in the diffused state, to all the souls, those of the simple as well as those of the doctors, that—something that God alone knows—are inhabited by lively faith and do not obstruct the divine motions?

VIII

In Thinking of Simon Peter
Detached Thoughts

I shall note just as they are, in this chapter, the things which have come to my mind in the course of a musing on authority among men, and on some texts of the Gospel concerning either the Prince of the apostles or the Precursor.

I

ABOUT THE NOTION OF AUTHORITY

Authority and Liberty

1. Popular intelligence takes pleasure in the oppositions of words. And if it is a question of the words "authority" and "liberty," the opposition between them is rendered terribly easy by the multitude of abuses which in the course of history men invested with authority have committed against the liberty of others (whereas in other respects the devotees of liberty have above all cultivated utopia or flirted with anarchy).

In themselves, however, authority and liberty are twin sisters who cannot do without each other, and authority in some is *for* liberty in others. The authority of the master over the disciple has for its end to enable the latter to exercise freely his mind in the search for truth and to adhere freely to the truth. The authority of the State[1] and of its laws (if they are just) has for its end to assure the liberty of the citizens in the conduct of their life and the exercise of their rights. The authority of the Church has for its end to liberate each man in the Truth, and to deliver him from the servitude with regard to sin and to the Prince of this world, and to introduce him into the liberty of the sons of God, whom the Spirit leads.

Authority is the *right* possessed by someone to be listened to or to be obeyed,—for the good of those to whom he speaks or whom he commands. The misfortune is that this right requires normally a certain *power,* and that man asks only to confuse a responsibility heavy with anguish and with torments: the exercise of authority for the good of others, with the most tempting and the most blinding of pleasures: that of dominating another and of elevating oneself above him by a power which becomes consequently perversion of authority,—compensation for frustrations caused by some humiliating traumatism, or mere satisfaction of the desire for power and for glory.

We should congratulate ourselves that the notion of authority as *service* has become one of the favorite commonplaces of the contemporary intelligentsia. It is a notion that the Gospel has taught us—and with what nobility! Let us hope only that it will be well understood, and that a little demogoguery will not debase it, in having it be believed that in order to serve well those whom one is charged to command, one would not only have to take into account their wishes as much as possible, but to become the mere executant of the latter.

2. It is not always pleasant to obey authority. Moreover, it is inevitable, by reason of the wounds of nature, that the exercise of authority will be sometimes unjust, and that, even when it is just and benevolent, it will be subject to many practical errors. We must however obey legitimate authority, even at the cost of more or less great sufferings.

Nothing is more natural than to bear it a grudge then. But there are two very different ways of being subject to authority and of suffering from it. One can be subject to it slavishly, and suffer from it slavishly. A day will come then when one will revolt against it in letting explode a thousand long-repressed resentments, and when one will make it one's duty to overthrow the fundamental structures of authority, even of the most legitimate authority.

And one can be subject to authority as a free man, and suffer from it as a free man. It may be that then reason and courage require one to disobey an unjust order, or to rise up against an illegitimate authority, or to demand the change of certain poorly adapted secondary structures of a legitimate authority. Outside of these cases, however, someone who obeys authority—I say legitimate authority—as a free man does not try to set fire to the house when he has to suffer from authority. He no doubt does not deprive himself of inveighing against it, nor of seeking actively to change the situation with the means he has at his disposal. But in all of this it is in a kind of game that he engages with authority and around it, without thinking in the least of calling in question its principle or its fundamental structures.

At the time of Innocent II the means at one's disposal were rather harsh, and the game which one conducted rather brutal; people hurled at each other the most outrageous names, people were excommunicated, armies were raised, firm blows were dealt. If Anacletus was an antipope, he surely did not deserve obedience, and it was up to him to submit. It was necessary therefore that the sport around authority be harshly conducted, and intelligently. (The most intelligent of all was St. Bernard.)[2] But as regards authority itself, one revered it, and treated it with as much respect as humor. In the most profound fibers of their temperament these men remained, if I may so speak, *men of humor* (and of honor, it goes without saying). A civilization without humor prepares its own funeral.

Authority in the Temporal Order
and in the Spiritual Order

In the order of the temporal, 'divine right' monarchy has had its day. The regime of the totalitarian parties,—whether they be of fascist type or of communist type,—is still much worse; they push the principle and the methods of despotism to their extremes. In the democratic regime, which in the end is the best regime (or the least bad), authority comes from the people or "rises from the bottom." Still it is necessary to understand that, just as in giving to a friend a pipe or a bottle of whiskey I give him something of which I am not the author, so also, and with all the more reason, when the people confer authority on their rulers, while retaining through their elected representatives a serious control over them, they give to them something,—a *right*,—of which they are not themselves either the author or the principle; for every right is, as such, founded on the universal order which God had in view.

In the order of the spiritual[3] authority "comes down from above," which means that it not only has its foundation in God, but is conferred by the First Cause Himself on those who receive the fullness of the Sacrament of Holy Orders and are the successors of the apostles: it is so because it is God Who is the author of salvation through His Incarnate Son, Who is the Way, the Truth and the Life. "Christian life requires an organized community, a Church which is according to the thought of Christ; it requires an order, a free but sincere obedience; it requires therefore an authority which preserves and teaches the revealed truth (2 Cor. 10, 15); because this truth is the inmost and profound root of liberty, as Jesus has said: 'The truth will set you free' (John 8, 32)."[4]

II

FOUR TEXTS CONCERNING SIMON, SON OF JOHN

You Are Peter

" 'And you,' he said to them, 'who do you say that I am?' 'You are the Messiah,' Simon Peter answered, 'the Son of the Living God!' Jesus replied, 'Blest are you, Simon son of John! No mere man has revealed this to you, but my heavenly Father. I for my part declare to you, you are "Rock" (Kepha), and on this rock (kepha) I will build my church, and the jaws of death shall not prevail against it. I will entrust to you the keys of the kingdom of heaven. Whatever you declare bound on earth shall be bound in heaven; whatever you declare loosed on earth shall be loosed in heaven.' "[5]

The moment when these words were uttered, on the road of Caesarea Philippi, is the moment of the annunciatory dawn of the Church (of Christ come). She is still neither founded nor built ("on this rock *I will build* . . . "), it is at Pentecost that she will be founded and will begin to be built by Jesus—or (it is the same thing) to build herself[6] under His all-powerful hand, and to confess with Peter the savior God: *Te per orbem terrarum tota confitetur Ecclesia.* But the fundamental stone is already designated.

The absolute foundation, of the Church and of everything,—it is the Incarnate Word, Who transcends the Church and all things. But the immanent foundation, the created foundation of this living created edifice which is the Church,—it is Peter ("*you are* Peter, and *on this rock* I will build . . . ''): Peter not as individual person, but Peter *as confessing the Christ Son of God,* Peter *as illuminated by faith* (it is "my heavenly Father" who "has revealed this to you") and *as confessing the faith,* this faith which as soon as it gushes up in the soul implies the gift of self, this faith which will be that of the Church one and universal, *incorrupta, et casta, et pudica,*[7] and which Peter—as also those who will succeed him, and of whom the name-given-by-Christ will remain always Peter[8]—will have for mission to "confirm" or to "strengthen" in his brothers[9] and to maintain intact in souls.[10]

It is here the supreme authority, on earth, of Peter as *Doctor of the faith* which is above all affirmed and guaranteed by the Lord.

Vade post me, Satana

But, it was just after having constituted him leader of the Church of the earth, with these magnificent words: "Blest are you, Simon son of John; you are Peter, and on this rock I will build my Church," that Jesus hurled at him other words, singularly harsh this time; it is exactly at the same part of his Gospel that Matthew reports them to us. The text concerning the *you are Peter,* which I have just commented on, is found in Chapter 16, verses 15 to 19. A verse further on (verse 21), the Evangelist continues: "From then on Jesus [the Messiah] started to indicate to his disciples that he must go to Jerusalem and suffer greatly there at the hands of the leaders, the chief priests, and the scribes, and to be put to death, and raised up on the third day. At this, Peter took him aside and began to remonstrate with him. 'May you be spared, Master! God forbid that any such thing ever happen to you!' Jesus turned on Peter and said, 'Get out of my sight, you Satan! You are trying to make me trip and fall.[11] You are not judging by God's standards, but by man's.' "[12]

What is more striking than the junction of these two texts in the Gospel! Only Jesus could speak in such terms to the future leader of his Church, because He is the Son of God, infinitely greater than every *purus homo*. St. Catherine of Sienna called the Pope "our gentle Christ on earth":[13] and who would begrudge a word of love its excess? The Pope is not Christ on earth, he is only his vicar there; and he is, alas, a man like us, although constantly aided from above in his mission. I do not think that what the Gospel signifies to us here relates to the human weakness to which Peter was exposed,—the story of his three denials is quite sufficient for that. In taking into account the opposition which in reprimanding him Jesus makes between "man's standards" and "God's standards," it seems to me rather that that which is signified to us there relates to the dangers of every sovereignty here on earth, with the atmosphere of sycophancy, of authoritarianism and of love of prestige, of intrigues and of personal ambitions which it creates around it, in the ecclesiastical world no less than in the lay world.

The temporal power of the Papacy has made heavier this atmosphere. It was a historical necessity imposed by the defence of the independence of the Church against the incessant menaces of the princes and of the leaders of State (which had begun with the Emperor of Byzantium, then the Emperors of the West), but it put the Pope in the rank of the "powerful of the earth." There where I see especially the "man's standards" which clouded for a moment the mind of Peter,—it is the court manners and the court mentality which have long reigned in Rome, and to which certain popes have shown themselves complacent. Since the end of the pontifical States things have improved. I take the liberty of adding that from this point of view there is still in Roman circles a good deal of progress to be made.

Simon Joannis, diligis me plus his?
Pasce agnos meos

1. It was after the Resurrection, on the shore of the lake of Tiberias. There were present Simon Peter, Thomas, Nathanael, and the two sons of Zebedee.[14] "When they had eaten their meal, Jesus said to Simon Peter, 'Simon, son of John, do you love me more than these?' 'Yes, Lord,' he said, 'you know that I love you.' At which Jesus said, 'Feed my lambs.' A second time he put his question, 'Simon, son of John, do you love me?' 'Yes, Lord,' Peter said, 'you know that I love you.' Jesus replied, 'Tend my sheep.' A

third time Jesus asked him, 'Simon, son of John, do you love me?' Peter was hurt because he had asked a third time, 'Do you love me?' So he said to him: 'Lord, you know everything. You know well that I love you.' Jesus said to him, 'Feed my sheep.' "[15]

Here again is affirmed the primacy of Peter, and, this time, above all as *Vicar of Christ and sovereign Pastor here on earth of the people of God.* The Vicar of Christ and sovereign Pastor here on earth has not only supreme magisterium in matters of faith and of morals, he has also full and supreme authority of jurisdiction over the whole Church in order to direct and govern her amid the vicissitudes of history, and in the midst of the circumstances and contingencies of time, ceaselessly changing and requiring incessant particular decisions.

Nothing is more striking than the insistence with which Jesus Himself indicated the dependence in which this supreme authority, and all authority in the Church, finds itself with regard to the love of charity. The question addressed to Peter is posed three times. And no doubt this implies secretly, as Père Lagrange remarks,[16] so to speak an echo of the three denials which Peter has certainly not forgotten (this is why, at the third question, "Peter was hurt"),—and this is also a sign that they are entirely pardoned, and that the confidence of the Lord in His apostle is absolute. He asked the heavenly Father that the faith of Peter not fail, and He knows that His prayer has been heard.

But the insistence with which the question is put: do you love me? has above all as its aim to imprint in our minds this will of Christ that the love of charity, love of God above all, and fraternal love, be the essential character of authority in the Church. This is what the sovereign Master expects of His bishops and of His priests.

Authority in the temporal order as in the spiritual order is in order to serve the good and to assure the liberty of those who are subject to it. But in the spiritual order there is much more still: it is given by reason of the supernatural love of charity, and it is in this love that it has to exercise itself, in order to serve the eternal good of souls and in order to have them attain to the liberty of the sons of God.

2. The first of the three questions posed by the Lord was: "Simon, son of John, do you love me *more than these?*" It did not belong to Peter to know and to say whether he loved Jesus *more*

than the other disciples, so he replied simply, humbly: "Yes, you know that I love you." But the "more than these" was in the question, and Jesus knew that it was implied in the answer, He Who knew the depth of hearts.

May I be permitted a short digression here. Peter loved Jesus "more than these,"—*more* therefore than John himself, who was present at the conversation. And yet John,—*ille discipulus quem diligebat Jesus, qui et recubuit in coena super pectus ejus,*[17]—John was "the disciple whom Jesus loved," that is to say loved *more* than all the others. Shall I venture, after the admirable considerations of St. Augustine on this subject,[18] to attempt to compare the love of Peter and the love of John?

It seems to me that it is fitting to distinguish between the most characteristic quality of a love and its degree of ardor or of intensity. For, as regards the most characteristic quality, there is toward God and His Christ a love which is above all total gift of self in which the Faith exults, and which I shall call love *of devotion* (then the soul gives itself up wholly to its love for Jesus). And there is, on the other hand, a love (more elevated than the first as to the most characteristic quality) in which, in addition to the devotion of the Faith, there blossom out the highest Gifts of the Holy Spirit, and which I shall call of *mutual confidence and intimacy,* or of mystical union (then the soul is completely given up to the sovereign love of Jesus for it). And Peter like John, John like Peter, had each a sublime Faith and lived each under the regime of the Gifts. But cannot one think that the charity of Peter was above all love of devotion, in which his Faith exulted, whereas the charity of John was above all love of mutual intimacy and mutual confidence, and mutual tenderness, in which the gift of Wisdom and the other contemplative Gifts blossomed out?

And if this is true, cannot one think also that the love of John was, *considered in its most characteristic quality, or as love of mutual intimacy and mutual confidence and mutual tenderness,* greater in ardor and intensity, and, if I may say, in immensity than the love of Peter? Whereas the love of Peter, *considered in its most characteristic quality, or as love of devotion,* was greater in ardor and intensity, and, if I may say, in immensity, than the love of John? Peter gave his life for Jesus; at Rome he "extended his arms" and suffered martyrdom; he wished (if this is a legend, it shows at least what memories the first Christians kept of him) to be crucified head downward. John was certainly altogether ready to be crucified for Him Whom he loved,—Christ had expressly indicated His will, and that of the Father, that the occasion was not to be given to him.[19]

But it is a function of authority and of government, and of magisterium in the Faith, the function of supreme authority and government, and of supreme magisterium in the Faith over the Church of the earth, that Christ conferred on Peter. It was the greatest love of heroic devotion, which was required for this of the prince of the apostles, the most ardent love in which the Faith has ever exulted, together with the special help of the Gifts of the Holy Spirit that the exemplary exercise of such an authority called for in him.

Domine, tu mihi lavas pedes?

It was at the beginning of the Last Supper,[20] Jesus was at table with the Twelve. "Jesus rose from the meal and took off his cloak. He picked up a towel and tied it around himself. Then he poured water into a basin and began to wash his disciples' feet and dry them with the towel he had around him. Thus he came to Simon Peter, who said to him, 'Lord, are you going to wash my feet?' Jesus answered, 'You may not realize now what I am doing but later you will understand. . . .'

"After he had washed their feet, he put his cloak back on and reclined at table once more. He said to them: 'Do you understand what I just did for you? You address me as 'Teacher' and 'Lord,' and fittingly enough, for that is what I am. But if I washed your feet—I who am Teacher and Lord—then you must wash each other's feet. What I just did was to give you an example: as I have done, so you must do.' "[21]

"You may not realize now what I am doing but later you will understand." These things,—one is never finished understanding them, even after centuries. The second Council of the Vatican understood them in all truth, it had the assistance of the Holy Spirit. There are those who imagine, some in order to reproach the Council for it, others to congratulate it for it, that in recalling to mind that, in the Church, the more exalted one is in authority the more one must humble himself, through love, it meant that the more exalted one is in authority the more one must abdicate practically the latter, in falling into step with the good little or big lambs communitarianly gathered together whom one is thought to lead.

However it was in the very instant in which He had just washed their feet that Christ most clearly declared to His disciples His authority, over them, of Lord and of Master: *ego Dominus et Magister*. The matter has absolutely nothing to do with a juridical conception minimizing the role and the necessity of authority in the Church. It has everything to do with the inspiration which is in the heart of anyone who holds any authority in the Church, and, consequently, with the mode,—humble and breathing brotherly love, even to the point of showing that one would willingly wash their feet,—according to which this authority must exercise itself over those who are subject to it. The unction of good formulas certainly doesn't suffice for it. But if it is true love which is required, it is not for all that weakness.

As to those who are subject to authority, is it not desirable that for their part they do not think themselves dispensed from the duty of fraternal charity toward those who hold it? This would ease a little the difficulties of each day in which these latter are engaged.

III

JOHN THE BAPTIST AND THE KINGDOM OF HEAVEN

Et violenti rapiunt illud

The words uttered by Jesus, apropos of John the Baptist, on the Kingdom of Heaven, take us far beyond that which concerns authority among men. It is to the feet of God that they bring our minds, if it is true, as I think, that they evoke the great mystery of the divine law in the most universal sense of the word,—of this law whose authority imposes itself on us for our salvation, and which however seems to close to our misery the gates which the God of mercy wishes so much to open to us that He sent for this His Son to take our flesh, and to tell us the Truth, and to be condemned in the name of the Law by the authority of the High Priest, and in the name of political prudence by the authority of Caesar, and to suffer, and to die on the Cross.

"I solemnly assure you, history has not known a man born of woman greater than John the Baptizer. Yet the least born into the kingdom of God is greater than he. From John the Baptizer's time until now the kingdom of God has suffered violence, and the violent take it by force. All the prophets as well as the law spoke prophetically until John. If you are prepared to accept it, he is Elijah, the one who was certain to come. *He who has ears to hear, let him hear.*"22

Who would dare to say that he has ears to hear? Commentators however have not been in short supply, and this text of the Gospel has given rise to many interpretations. I venture therefore, in spite of my bad ear, to advance in my turn an opinion. It seems to me that if John is less great than the least in the kingdom of Heaven, it is that being the last—and the greatest—of the prophets, he scarcely commenced to see himself,—he died just at the threshold,—the age which he predicted, and in which the Incarnate Son revealed the love of the Father.

It seems to me also (and it is this I wanted to come to) that if this Kingdom of God, which is "within you,"23 suffers violence since the days of John the Baptist, it is because in order to enter into it it does not suffice to observe the Law; it is necessary also to pass beyond, by the violence of love. And if this is true of the Mosaic Law, it is also true, and more still, of the law,—the universal divine law in all its rigor,—which Jesus did not come to abolish, but to complete, and of which not one iota will pass away. In order to enter truly into the kingdom it is necessary and will always be necessary to force the gates of it by the violence of love.

"Jesus on the Cross, and very particularly at that moment of total dereliction, suffered the full rigor of the law of the transmutation of one nature into another—*as if* he had not been God; it was his humanity as such, taken from the Virgin, which had to feel the full weight of this law. For the head must experience the law that he imposes on his members. Because, having assumed human nature, he had to experience this supreme law to which human nature, called to participate in the divine nature, is subject.

"And if he had not suffered from the rigor of this law, it would not have been possible to say that the Word took a heart like our own in order to feel for our sufferings.

"This law of the transformation of natures—which comprises in it all moral and divine laws—is something necessary, physical, ontological if you like—God himself cannot abolish it, just as he cannot produce the absurd.

"But this law—the Law—is not He—He is Love.

"So when a soul suffers, and suffers from this inexorable Law of transmutation of a nature into a higher nature (and this is the meaning of all human history)—God is with this nature which he has made and which is suffering—he is not against it. If he could transform that nature into his own by abolishing the law of suffering and death, he would abolish it—because he takes no pleasure in the spectacle of pain and death. But he cannot abolish any law inscribed in being. . . .

"Thus Abraham, too, knew the hard law of the transformation of the natural man into the spiritual and divine man—but with a wide zone of human liberty in which many laws, left in shadow by God, were put in parenthesis.

"And, as for us, he has revealed to us all the terrible demands of the divinization of man.

"But in order to reveal them to us, he came himself—not with the blood of goats and bulls—but with the Blood of Christ through which his Love for us is made visible.

"Thus the new Law is harsher than the old Law.

"But at the same time the love of God (which softens everything) is more widespread . . .

"The law—all the laws—having become so clearly, and so terribly visible,
the face of the love of God thus risks being obscured.

"This is why it is more necessary than ever to distinguish between Love and the Law. . . .

"The law is just. The law is necessary—with the very necessity of transformation for salvation, that is to say, for eternal life with God.

"But the law is not God.

"And God is not the Law. He is Love.

"If God has the face of the law for men—men draw back because they feel that love is more than the law—in this they are wrong only because they do not recognize the salutary necessity of the law.

"But the observation of the Law without love would be of no avail for salvation.

"And love can save a man even at the last second of a bad life—if, in that second, the man has found the light of love—perhaps if he has always believed that God is Love. . . .

"Law is, in a certain manner, opposed to love. God has made it insofar as he is the Creator of being. But insofar as he is our end and our beatitude, he calls us beyond it.

"The law is proposed externally, it implies a subjection—in

itself it seems to have nothing to do with mercy—nor with the equality of friendship—nor with familiarity.

"It is truly a necessity; only a necessity.

"Love *gives over the head of* the Law."[24]

Because the violence of love enables one to pass infinitely beyond the Law, right to the heart of subsisting Love.

IX

The Structure of the Church

The Data of the Gospel
and the Prophetic Sketch Contained in It

1. Jesus, son of God, born of the Virgin Mary, wished, before beginning His public life, to receive the baptism of John, as a sign that He had come in order to take upon Himself the sins of all men.[1]

Then He began to preach and to teach, and to announce the good news of the Redemption. And He chose the Twelve for His apostles, among whom was Judas, who betrayed Him.

And Jesus designated Simon Peter as the prince of the apostles,—"you are Peter and on this rock I will build my Church, and I will entrust to you the keys of the kingdom of heaven,"—charged as such to govern the whole Church of Christ,—"feed my lambs, feed my sheep,"—and to be in her the supreme guardian of the faith,—"you in turn must strengthen your brothers."

Of Simon Peter I have already spoken in the preceding chapter. Concerning his primacy I shall come back further on (in Section 5).

This marvellously generous Peter was an apostle among apostles, although having a higher responsibility, and he was but a man

73

like them. At the time of the Passion he will deny his master. But his repentance made of him the greatest witness and hero of the faith.

I remark here that in order to replace Judas the Eleven had chosen Matthias,[2] who was therefore with them on the day of Pentecost; but that to the thus reconstituted apostolic group God willed that two extraordinary men be further added,—Barnabas (Bar Nabuah, the Consoler), that majestic one whom at Lystra the pagans took one day for Jupiter, and Paul, the persecutor convert (he had approved of the murder of Stephen, whose garments had been placed at his feet), Paul, the apostle of the Gentiles, the great elect of the Holy Spirit, the incomparable master in the doctrine of truth.

But from the apostolic times Peter and Paul appear as the two missioned ones par excellence of the Lord Jesus in order to establish His abode with us; and all through the course of history they will be inseparable, although their two missions are very different.

In marking this difference,—which is a difference of complementarity, not at all of opposition, as certain Protestant authors would like it,—one cannot forget that Paul, integrated by full right, through God and His Christ, in the body of the apostles, contributed by his martyrdom to found the Church of Rome, so that, as many have liked to proclaim, it is Paul at the same time as Peter that the Pope, bishop of the Church of Rome, succeeds. Such a fundamental parity in the apostolic and episcopal ministry being well recognized, the difference between the historic missions remains in my eyes striking. Peter is in the Church of the earth the supreme authority, the rock on which is constructed this immense temple of life, the Leader charged with governing until the last day; Paul is in the Church of the earth the holy liberty of the intelligence scrutinizing under the motion of the Spirit of Christ and causing to radiate the truth of the faith, instructing in this truth those who seek it, and urging them until the last day to deepen it.

Peter and Paul both cause the flock of Jesus to advance, each in his own manner,—Peter, together with his brothers in the episcopate,[3] constituting the Magisterium and the directing organ of the life of the mystical Body here on earth; Paul, together with those who follow him (without being invested for all that with any magisterial authority, even though they may be masters in theology) in the work of wisdom to be expanded unceasingly, being the ferment of the intellectual research and of the progress of the mystical Body through the ages.

And there is still a third to be a missioned one par excellence of the Lord Jesus, and to serve and to cause to advance the Church of the earth, in his own fashion, which is entirely hidden in God. He perpetuates himself, not, like Peter, by the succession of the holders of his powers, but, like Paul, by the line of the sons of his spirit. He is John, the adoptive son of Mary and the solitary of Patmos, the apostle of love and of contemplation, together with his friends who, as he, at the very heart of the mystical Body, support everything, compensate for everything, renew everything, in the intimacy of the union of love with the unique Beloved, and in the coredemptive participation in the sufferings of the Agony and of the Cross which continue in them.

2. The Gospel teaches us further that Christ not only commanded the apostles to preach from the housetops, and not only made Peter the first among them, in order to establish the meaning of the revealed Word and to assure the transmission of the latter, in order to govern the Church and in order to preside in her over the whole jurisdictional order. He also instituted the sacramental order on which His Church will live, by instituting, at the Last Supper, the Sacrament par excellence, which is indissolubly linked with the sacrifice of the Cross,—rendered present among us, every day and over the whole surface of the earth, by the Sacrifice of the Mass. The Eucharist is the center of the whole sacramental order, the supreme *raison d'être* of the other Sacraments, and very especially of that of Holy Orders.

And it is Christ Who, before rising above all the heavens, said to His apostles: "Go, therefore, and make disciples of all the nations. Baptize them in the name of the Father, and of the Son, and of the Holy Spirit."[4] This is no longer a baptism of penance, as was that of John the Baptist; it is the baptism of life and of resurrection.

3. Thus the Church was instituted by her divine Leader while He lived among us, before she began her own existence when having left the earth He sent upon the apostles the tongues of fire of Pentecost, and before consequently, under His heavenly direction, and "receiving harmonic consistency and cohesion from Him who is the head, Christ," she began to build herself, in the fashion of every living organism, "growing and building herself up in

love,"[5] in a vital progress which will continue until the day of the Second Coming.

And when the Incarnate Word was present here on earth, and traversed the roads of Judea with the little flock of His apostles and sent before Him the seventy-two disciples,[6] and announced to the people the coming of the kingdom of God,—the new times of the effusion of supreme grace and of the remission of sins,—it is the prophetic sketch of the Church which appeared already on the earth, and of which the most beautiful of human stories offers us the picture.

Christic Grace in the Age of Christ Come

1. Before the Incarnation all the graces received from God by men since the Fall,—beginning with Adam and Eve repentent,— were given to them by virtue of the merits of the Redeemer *to come;* they were Christic graces, ocean of love which during millennia spread over all the peoples of the earth; then, by a special title, over the chosen people.

But since the day of the Incarnation[7] these Christic graces have been the graces of *Christ come.* Let us say that the grace of Christ come is grace in the state of superabounding maturity: in what sense? In this sense that it is not only,—that which is essential to grace as such,—sanctifying grace deputing man to eternal life, but "architectonic" grace, I mean by that deputing the man sanctified by it to be a part of a multitudinous Body which will endure eternally and which is the mystical Body of Christ, the Church of Christ, His plenitude and His bride.

That one is a living member of this multitudinous Body, of the *Una, Sancta, Catholica,* who has received validly[8] Baptism and is sufficiently faithful to baptismal grace for it to bear in him its fruits of faith, of love and of union with God. He finds himself thus animated from above or "informed" himself, in his individual measure, and as part of the entire Body, by the soul of this immense and complex organism, which is made up of all the individually received sanctifying graces. Applied to the Church, the Aristotelian definition of the soul remains indeed always valid: first form or entelechy of an organized body having life potentially. Just as the soul informs matter in order to constitute with it a living organism, so also the grace of Christ in its plenitude,—the soul of the Church,—informs, in order to construct with them a single organized body equipped with all its joints and articulations, the human multitude gathered together in the unity, not only of a same Baptism, but first and above all of the profession of the true faith.

It is clear that this analogy must not be pushed too far, for the Church is not, as is each one of us, an individual substance, but a human collectivity endowed with a supernatural personality. Whereas the soul of a living organism is in its entirety in the whole and in each part, the soul of the Church is, as such, only in the whole, and is in each individual member only in the measure of the grace itself which he has personally received.

2. On the other hand, divine grace does not vivify only the visible members of the Church; it vivifies also, in the entire world, an incalculable number of men who are members of other spiritual families,—religious or areligious,—and who sincerely seek God, even without knowing it themselves: they belong invisibly to the visible Church.

But the grace received by each one of them is one of the constituent parts of the soul of the Church. By this very fact, they find themselves without suspecting it ordered to the immense and complex body of the Church. I shall deal with this question in Chapter X.

The Royal Priesthood of the People of God

1. It is to the age of Christ come, and to Christic grace in its state of superabounding maturity, it is to the Church of Christ, which took shape on the earth since at Pentecost He sent His Spirit upon His apostles, that relates the passage of the first epistle of St. Peter to which, in its Dogmatic Constitution on the Church, the second Council of the Vatican has particularly called the attention of Christians: "You, however, are 'a chosen race, a royal priesthood, a holy nation, a people he claims for his own to proclaim the glorious works' of the One who called you from darkness into his marvellous light. Once you were no people, but now you are God's people."[9] St. Peter, as the Council has explained, has here in view all of the believing people in whom the sacrifice of the Cross bears fruit.

Thus the royal priesthood of which St. Peter speaks is common to the clergy and to the laymen, to all the "living" members of the Church. This common priesthood of the faithful and the ministerial or hierarchical priesthood "differ from one another in essence and not only in degree."[10] They "are nonetheless inter-related. Each of them in its own special way is a participation in the one priesthood of Christ. The ministerial priest by the sacred power he enjoys, molds and rules the priestly people. Acting in the person of Christ, he brings about the Eucharistic Sacrifice, and offers it to God in the name of all the people. For their part, the faithful join in the offering of the Eucharist by virtue of their royal priesthood. They likewise exercise that priesthood by receiving the sacraments, by prayer and thanksgiving, by the witness of a holy life, and by self-denial and active charity."[11]

As Père Labourdette writes, "participating in the capital grace of Christ, acquired for the redeemed by the *sacerdotal* act of the Cross which is the great victory of the messianic *King,* Christian grace, in the whole of the Church and in each of her subjects, is a grace at once sacerdotal and royal: *gens sancta, populus acquisitionis, regale sacerdotium....* Every Christian, in this sense is a 'priest,' priest and king, like his leader: man or woman, having preceded Christ since Adam or having historically followed Him, every redeemed one has, by very reason of his grace, this priesthood." He possesses it "by the same title and to the same degree as grace," this priesthood is "inscribed in Christian grace. In Heaven, where the 'royal priesthood' will be in full bloom in the people of God and in all its members, the worship of praise and of thanksgiving will no longer be either a means of grace, or a symbol of a consummation still to come, but an expression of inner glory; nor will the sacramental sacrifice be celebrated any more, nor will the sacramental priesthood have to exercise itself, nor will the faithful have to participate in it. That the Christian is priest and king,—this will verify itself then as much for the elect who have never had either the baptismal or the sacerdotal character, as for the others. This 'royal priesthood' will remain for eternity as fruit of the sacrifice of the Cross."[12]

2. The great idea of the royal priesthood of the people of God is but one with that of the vocation of every Christian to sanctity. It is all the more urgent to recall it as it has been for a long time largely forgotten. Further it is necessary not to understand it wrongly, or to imagine that one is following the spirit of the Council in trying, in the name of the royal priesthood of the

people of God, to make pass a desacralizing detergent over the proper characteristics of the ministerial or hierarchical priesthood, which is the priesthood in the first sense of the word.

It is *in essence,* the Council has said, that the ministerial priesthood exercised by the priest and the royal priesthood common to all the faithful differ from one another.

Each one has to exercise the royal priesthood by his life, his prayer (*orate semper,* Jesus said), his love of God and of neighbor, his participation in the Sacraments, and his perseverance in tending, in spite of his weaknesses, to the perfection of charity; if he is in the lay and secular state, it is necessary for him to pass through the turmoils and the temptations of the world as a lame man supported by the angels, and with a confidence and a hope all the more firm.

The ministerial priesthood is that by virtue of which certain men, consecrated, by the Sacrament of Holy Orders, to the service of God and of the Church, have for their proper mission to celebrate the Eucharistic sacrifice, to distribute the Sacraments and to instruct the Christian people, to assist the sick and the dying, to aid and console the afflicted, to intercede for all, and to devote themselves completely, above all things, to bearing witness to the Truth which is Christ, and to the realities of the hereafter.

It is appropriate and normal, and especially required by the present age, that while remaining himself, the priest join freely in the common life of men, break the network of conventional customs which isolated him, take part in the social and cultural activities of his time. In the measure in which certain ones feel themselves called to it (and have the necessary time at their disposal), nothing is opposed to his earning his living by the work of his hands, which however is not his proper and primarily necessary work. For his *job* is the service of souls, a work as useful to men as—and more useful than—other works; and Jesus said, in sending His disciples before Him, that he deserves his recompense like the others: *dignus est operarius mercede sua* (Luke 10, 7). St. Paul was a tentmaker; one must believe that this trade left him much time to travel.

But by very virtue of his ordination the priest belongs to the sacred, to the kingdom of God, he is a *man of God;* the City which he serves above all is the Church; and by this title he is not 'like everybody else'; if he wished to be like everybody (without realizing that as a matter of fact he would be then a masquerader), he would lose all his force, and that "efficacy" so much and so futilely sought these days. What men expect of him is precisely to *not be* "like everybody. . . ."

The Hierarchical Ministry

The Church is a great living being whose invisible Leader is Christ, "seated at the right hand of the Father," and whose visible organization on the earth has in a Sacrament, therefore in the author of grace, the principle of its hierarchy.

1. *Some words on the laity.*—In the earthly city, and according as it is engaged in the affairs of the world, the innumerable people of which the Church is made, the laity, is a free people only if the temporal authorities who in the diverse nations of the globe have the charge of directing it give themselves for a goal (that which is normal de jure, but de facto rather rare) to assure the liberties of the citizens. This same people is, in the Church, and according as it is engaged in the things of eternal life, a free people, because the end divinely assigned to the spiritual authority which has the charge of directing it has in itself (except through its agents when they go astray) nothing to do with domination. It is at the service of souls in order to aid them to free themselves from the old servitudes of sin, and to live with the liberty of the sons of God. The spiritual authority in question is nothing other than a participation in the authority of Him Who came to deliver us by His Blood. And the men in whom it resides can certainly abuse it (they have not failed to do so in the course of history, and the Church has severely paid for it, although she herself was innocent of their errors), but their master will be more severe with them than with the others when He will settle their accounts; and they know it.

Laymen are so to speak the flesh and the blood of the body of the Church. At Baptism they were cleansed of the sin of Adam and made participants in the divine life; the three theological virtues were grafted into their soul, together with grace; at Confirmation they received the seal of the Holy Spirit; they are the flock of Jesus, and through the Sacrament of Matrimony they are commissioned to perpetuate it. The bread which nourishes them while they travel here on earth is the Body of the Lord. And like the Eucharist, the Sacrament of Penance and that of Anointing of the Sick are the pledges of the help of God for them as for their priests. Together with the latter they are called to constitute the chosen race, the holy nation, the royal priesthood, the people of God, to live by His truth, to do His work in history. The work by which the Church bears fruit and progresses on the earth is the common work of the layman and of the priest.

2. *The priesthood.*—I have just mentioned six Sacraments; it is by the seventh, the Sacrament of Holy Orders, that is constituted that which in the body of the Church is so to speak the nervous system; it is from the Sacrament of Holy Orders that the hierarchical organization of the Church proceeds.

This organization came into being from the apostolic age. It is to the Twelve that the institution of the diaconate goes back, when the seven were chosen in order to wait on tables.[13] The apostles imposed their hands on the first of their successors.

For the Church, a century is as a year for the human being. Her infancy lasted three or four centuries. In the course of this first growth there progressively took shape and consistency in her the two great functions of which the episcopal consecration confers the responsibility—those which concern the Sacraments and those which concern the magisterium and the jurisdiction.

The Sacrament of Holy Orders includes essentially three different degrees: the diaconate, the simple priesthood, and the episcopate. The episcopate is the plenitude of the priesthood. By this title, the bishop has full authority in his diocese or local church; but because the universal Church is the mystical Body of Christ, Body perfectly one, the very unity of the Church and her common good require that the questions which in themselves concern the Whole depend by right on the authority of the one who is the head here on earth of the Church in her universality. It is Christ Himself Who instituted this primacy of Peter, and it is from Christ Himself that it comes to the Pope.[14]

For the Sovereign Pontificate there is no special sacramental ordination, the Pope is Pope by the sole fact that he is elected bishop of Rome and placed on the see of Peter. He is Peter, as Paul VI said in his address to the ecumenical Council, at Geneva, on June 10, 1969. The Pope has also many other titles: supreme pontiff of the universal Church, patriarch of the West, primate of Italy, archbishop and metropolitan of the Roman province, sovereign of Vatican City. Those who complain about them show only that they have no historical sense.

Of the infallibility of the Pope, I have already spoken above (Chapter VII).

The Church of the earth is in time and accomplishes her growth in time. When it is a question of her it is very important to have some understanding of history. Many things which astonish us and sometimes shock us today had their necessity, of the wholly human order moreover, at the time of the diverse historical periods which she has traversed. Such is the case for example with the temporal power of the Popes, which had enormous drawbacks (the pontifical armies, the battles they engaged in . . .), but which in actual fact was required for the independence of the Church, in a Christendom whose kings and emperors had themselves anointed but were generally only anxious to submit everything to their power, even the Bride of Christ. And that there exists still, however small and however unarmed it may be, a Vatican State,— this remains clearly necessary. The Pope, in reality, cannot be the citizen of any nation, with the particular obligations implied by that toward this nation; and the supranationality which he enjoys as humble sovereign of a tiny territory is the sign and the guarantee of the absolute independence of the leader here on earth of the universal Church vis-à-vis those masked monsters in perpetual conflict which the sovereign States are.

One can remark, likewise, that the interventions of the great ones of this world (beginning with Constantine), of their ambitions and of their coteries, in the affairs of the priesthood were terribly frequent in that Christendom of long ago which the spectacle of the present world inclines us to idealize too much. However deplorable nevertheless and odious they may have been in themselves, they were the ransom, permitted by the Master of history, of a good first required by the exigencies of time, and which consisted in the spiritual unity of civilization; and, on the whole, the assistance of Christ enabled His Church to traverse all this human sludge not without grave losses undoubtedly, but in progressing always in her own development and in the accomplishment of her mission.

3. *The designation of persons.*—What matters above all in authority in the Church is the graces and the spiritual powers conferred by the Sacrament of Holy Orders, and by the charisma linked with the mission of Vicar of Christ. The mode of designation or of choice of those who are invested with an authority whose source is in Heaven is in itself secondary, and it has varied with time. In the primitive Church it seems that the very first bishops themselves designated their successors. After that, it was

either by popular acclamation, as for St. Ambrose, or by the choice of the episcopal chapter, that the new bishops were designated. At present, among the Catholics of oriental rites, it is by the Synod, around the Patriarch, that this designation is made, before being ratified by the Holy See. The rule which entrusts to the Pope the care of their nomination established itself quickly enough in the Latin Church, and there are certainly great advantages to having the one who has charge of the universal Church designate himself the pastors of the local churches.

What appears questionable is that this designation, at least in the countries in which the Holy See is diplomatically represented, be generally made at the suggestion of the Apostolic Nuncios: for these have sometimes seemed inclined to appreciate above all diplomatic prudence and to fear too vigorous temperaments and too exacting intellects,—all of which gave a chance to mediocrity, and did not prepare particularly firm and vigorous episcopates for eventual times of crisis. It seems certainly desirable that the nuncio be consulted, but also and above all the bishops of whom the new designee will be the colleague, and the diverse personages familiar with the ecclesiastical world but not being necessarily a part of the hierarchy, in the judgment of whom, for one reason or another, the Sovereign Pontiff expects to find some useful indication. In my humble opinion, such a consultation should remain wholly private, and be all the more extensive as it would be more free and less juridically fixed.

With regard to the Pope, it is by the College of Cardinals (of whom Paul VI has greatly increased the number) that he has been elected for centuries, and I think that the suggestions made here or there in order to abolish this mode of election do not take into account the central point to be considered. The College of Cardinals is composed of those whom the predecessors of the new Pope to be elected have chosen from all the countries of the earth in order to be their brothers and to collaborate in their universal mission, and who have been elevated to the cardinalate in the Church of Rome as a representation in her of the universality of the Church. This college has thus of the things of the Church an incomparable experience; and it seems to be better able than anyone else to appraise the persons among whom to choose the supreme leader of the latter.

I have already noted that if this college elects the Pope in electing the bishop of Rome, it is neither from it nor from the universal Church that the Pope holds his powers; he holds them from Christ Himself. I note further that one imagines sometimes that it is a rule that the Cardinals elect to the Sovereign Pontificate a Cardinal like them. This is a gross error. Any Christian is *papabilis,* any man professing the Catholic faith can be elected bishop of Rome, whether he be a priest or a layman; in this last case (which was—so much the worse for the reputation of laymen—that of Alexander VI, that famous Borgia) he receives the episcopal consecration immediately after his election.

Collegiality

1. With regard to the diverse powers in play in the government of the Church, those of the episcopal college, or of the episcopal body considered in its ensemble, have been well elucidated by the second Council of the Vatican. I cannot do better than to summarize here the statement of decisive clarity which Cardinal Journet has given to us on this subject.[15]

Insofar as they were, except for Paul and Barnabas, the companions of the Savior in His earthly life, and, all, His "envoys" (*apostoloi*) in order to lay the first foundations of His Church and to cause her to arise here on earth, in other words as regards *the advent of the Church in time,* the apostles were invested with an intransmissible authority in which they were all equal, each had received the entire grace of the apostolate, and Peter was only *primus inter pares.* But insofar as they exercised the *transmissible* function of feeding the flock of Christ, and insofar as Jesus designated one of them, unlike the others, as universal pastor, they were unequal in the powers relating to this function, and bequeathed by them to their successors in order to govern the Church, in other words as regards the *conservation* of the latter and her permanence in duration: in this respect it is Peter who holds,—and until the end of the world,—the highest authority.

"A single one of them, says the *Dogmatic Constitution on the Church* (III, 22) is constituted *pastor* of all the sheep and of their lambs (John 21, 15-17). A single one of them receives the keys of the Kingdom and is established as *rock,* that is to say as ultimate visible base upon which the Church will not cease to rest (Matt. 16, 18). A single one of them will, 'in turn,' have special mission to *strengthen* his brothers (Luke 22, 32)."

Supreme authority exists thus either in the Roman pontiff

alone (*seorsim*), or in the Roman pontiff *joined* (*simul cum*) with the bishops collectively taken, in other words with the episcopal college. "The Pope is subject of the supreme and full power over the universal Church. The *episcopal college*, in union with the Roman pontiff, its leader, and never without this leader, is also subject of the supreme and full power over the universal Church."

"When one asks the reason for which the Savior has willed this double subject, this double exercise, personal and collegial, of a single supreme power, the answer will be, it seems, that such a disposition is required by reason of the tension existing in the Church between on the one hand her *unity* and on the other hand her *catholicity*. The personal exercise seems charged to safeguard, not certainly exclusively, but at least principally, the *unity* of the universal Church; whereas the collegial exercise seems charged to safeguard, not certainly exclusively, but principally, the *catholicity*, that is to say the insertion into each of the clans of the world,—and according to modalities which in some way become connatural to them,—of the single and indivisible Church who is the Bride."

2. The collegiality in question here is that of the episcopate of the whole earth. It is the entire episcopal college or body which, in union with the Pope, its leader, has supreme and full authority over the universal Church. In bringing to light thus the relation between the Pope and collegiality, and the supreme power likewise possessed either by the Pope alone or by the episcopal college united with the Pope, it is therefore the relation between the Pope and the Council, object of so many theological battles in the past, which the second Council of the Vatican has definitively elucidated.

It is clear however that the principle thus disengaged by Vatican II, that of a closer cooperation between the Pope and the bishops, goes further in application than these "extraordinary" occasions that are the Councils; it must also apply, albeit, as it is indeed the case, in an altogether different manner, in the ordinary course of the government of the Church. One thinks here, on the one hand, of the episcopal conferences in which the bishops of a given country come to an agreement on the suggestions which they desire to submit to the See of Peter, on the other hand of the episcopal Synods in which do likewise,—chosen some by the bishops of their countries, others by the Pope,—representatives of the international episcopal body, but it is equally clear that, outside of the case of the Council, in which the Pope and the episcopate of the entire world exercise together the supreme power, the Pope, as long as he does not convoke a Council, alone exercises this power, without the cooperation of the episcopate with him, however close it may be as with the Synod evoking questions relative to the universal Church, being able to run the risk of compromising or shackling in any way his liberty of action. This means that the role of the representative organs to which I have just alluded must of necessity remain a consultative role, [16] except, naturally, when it is a question of decisions to be reached concerning only an ensemble of local Churches, and of processes of government which the bishops, by virtue of their ordinary power, and in the ordinary subordination to the Pastorate of the Pope, institute on the plane of their particular Churches.

A Few Indiscreet Questions

1. *On a change of vocabulary and a change of clothing appearances.*—It is a question here of things entirely secondary, but which, like all external signs, have however their influence, and not wrongly, on the mental reflexes of the human being.

With regard to the name which one gives to the persons who in one degree or another hold spiritual authority, it seems desirable that the simplification which began after the Council be extended as far as possible. It is good that all that which seems to elevate the servants of Christ above other men be eliminated, that one call now "Cardinal" those who were till now "Your Eminence," and that one dispense with the "Excellencies." It is not so long ago that a bishop was "Your Grace." They prefer now for themselves the name of "Father." It would be good also that there be eliminated the expressions in which words belonging to the order of the sacred are employed in a merely honorific sense which offends the ear. Why say "the *Sacred* College" when one could say "the College of Cardinals," and the "*Holy* See" when one could say (as Paul VI often does) "the Apostolic See"? Why call the Pope "the *Holy* Father" or "His *Holiness*" when one could call him for example (which would simply be conformable with reality) "Revered Father of all" or "Revered Vicar of Christ"? (In the Eastern Churches, the term in use goes still further,—is not the Patriarch "His Beatitude"?)

With regard to clothing appearances, it is otherwise that the question presents itself, for here one cannot forget that the disappearance of every distinctive sign, be it only, at least when it is possible, a small cross pinned on one's sweater or on one's jacket, would itself be the sign of a serious cultural lowering.

2. If it is a question after this of worship, in the Roman basilicas in particular, I understand well that the astonishing hotchpotch inherited from the Renaissance has begun to leave forever the solemn processions and the great ceremonies. Gone already are the long trains of the Cardinals, as also the trainbearers who held up the end of them. (Did they not suggest to us, in order to rejoice our eyes, both a high transitory dignity and the queue of importunate favor-seekers which every dignitary drags after him?) Gone also, or about to go, are the "tied" trains which the canons of St. Peter's held in rolls under their arms, and the pompons of their cinctures and of their birettas, and their furred gowns of ermine and the silver buckles of their shoes, and their purple mantillas over their rochets (which themselves will finally indeed seem too pretty with their lace ruffles). I confess that I miss the very wise drollery of all of this, which during a long time, thanks to the pleasure of the eyes, was able to maintain with regard to the pomp of religion, in the good people of Rome and in that of the pilgrims to the Eternal City, the sense of respect together with that of joviality.

Today it is the ritual of science, with the enormous enchantment of its machines and the pompous accoutrements of its cosmonauts, which has passed under the sway of the Punch and Judy show. But who notices it? We no longer respect much at all, and at the same stroke joviality as well as gaiety have left us.

One would like that the joyful picturesqueness to which I have alluded be replaced by new appearances, more simple undoubtedly, but also pleasing to the sight. It is a question of imagination; and it is a pity that Churchmen have today so little taste for this faculty which the Cartesians foolishly scorned, but of which philosophy and the human sciences recognize better and better the value and the dignity. And there are still great painters whose assistance one could ask. Beauty is one of the attributes of the Church, platitude is her enemy. Such remarks do not concern only the Roman ceremonies; they are true, analogically, in all latitudes, and for village churches as for cathedrals.

3. I have just spoken of that which relates to the eye. What to say of the poor ear, and of the miserable hymns which chase from our churches the spirit of prayer and produce nostalgia for Gregorian chant? I understand that young people are looking in the direction of jazz, which unfortunately has nothing to do with recollection. But one can find (as Father André Gouzes does) a precious source of inspiration in the Byzantine treasury; and there are admirable Negro spirituals, which could aid us, with the help of good musicians, in finding hymns truly appropriate.

4. *The labors of the episcopate.*—Let us pass on to still more indiscreet questions. The first one relates to the labors which the conditions of the epoch cause to weigh upon the bishops. These complain rightly that as a result doubtlessly of the demographic growth, but above all of the congresses, of the commissions, of the reports to be read and to be drafted, and of the enormous administrative task which is incumbent upon them, a crushing work load prevents them from giving the necessary time to their mission. Would it not be possible for them to shift the responsibility of a multitude of things onto delegates and auxiliaries more numerous than those which they have at their disposal at the present time?

The establishment of the episcopal commissions has certainly been a necessary progress and one that is consistent with the spirit of collegiality. One can nevertheless ask oneself what is their principal end: would it not be that the bishops of a region or of a country may have the occasion to meet periodically, to better know each other personally and to exchange their views? How much preferable to assemblies of a more or less juridical character, and burdened with a program elaborated beforehand, would not doubtlessly be mere reunions of mutual information in which one would talk around the dinner table or while taking walks together? At the end of the week secretaries could summarize in memorandums what was said that was most notable in these free conversations. But the idea of a work to be done would be entirely left aside. Is it not a well-known dictum that if one wants a work to be poorly done one should give it to a committee to do?

Finally, is not the essential point that the episcopal commissions, in whatever way one conceives them, remain merely consultative with regard to each bishop as the episcopal synod with regard to the Pope, and be clearly recognized as not being able to dispense their members from exercising each for his own account the power of decision? A bishop is by divine mandate the pastor of his diocese; it belongs to him alone to make, upon his responsibility before God, the decisions concerning the souls who are entrusted to him. If he became in a manner, not de jure, certainly, but de facto, the executive agent of a committee, is it not his very mission of successor of the apostles and the evangelical prescription itself which would find themselves injured?

5. In the months during which this book is being written the urgent problem which the bishops have to face is, if I am not wrong, that of their relations with their priests; a problem of first importance, clearly. But this is a family affair which will doubtless resolve itself quickly enough, in spite of defections to tell the truth scarcely regrettable when they indicate in certain clerics the absence of a true vocation.

What is terribly serious is the crisis of faith which is rife in the Christian world, and the need of an authentic doctrinal renewal, in other words one which causes the intellectual treasure of the Church to grow and does not destroy it. Too many theologians apply themselves today to throwing it to the four winds; blessed be the others. Let us recall here that the bishops are not solely pastors, or rather that this mission itself requires them to be also doctors of the faith. It is normal that they surround themselves with experts in theology, but it is normal also that they not put too much trust in them. Experts are useful and necessary informants; they are not worth much as counselors; they are not worth anything at all if they claim to present themselves as doctors.

6. *Theological pluralism.*—These words, of which one makes today such frequent use, give rise to a strange confusion which it is very important to clear up.

If it is a question of the magisterial authority exercised by her, the Church has charge of matters *of faith,* and can impose on the adhesion of minds only that which is *of faith.* But theology, while being rooted in faith, is in itself an affair *of reason,* not of faith; it is therefore evident that the Church cannot *impose* any theological doctrine. Hence a *de facto* pluralism which is inevitable *as to the exercise by the Church of her magisterial authority.*

While being able to turn out very badly through the fault of theologians whom the noises of the world stupefy and who obey the philosophies of the day, this pluralism has moreover its proper utility, up to a certain limit at least:[17] for in fact we are not in the presence of finished doctrines (it is the property of a doctrine founded in truth to progress endlessly), nor of philosophical and theological doctrines in the pure state; even a doctrine entirely founded in truth is, like the others, taught by men subject to the common limitations and to the common weaknesses: they can become encrusted more or less in their teaching, fail in the essential tasks of research, neglect or ignore many of the truths with which the progress of time enriches thought; and on the other hand we know also that in the most badly founded doctrines there is always some badly seen or distorted aspect of the real which asks to be rightly seen and put in place, or some captive truth which asks to be liberated.

Thus therefore, by the very fact that she has charge only of that which is *of faith,* the Church cannot impose on the adhesion of the mind any theological doctrine. All that she can do in this regard is to recommend a theological doctrine which has shown its mettle. And she has not failed in such a care for human truth (for she loves the intelligence, and has need of it). She has even gone as far as possible in this direction, by making her *Common Doctor* a master-thinker chosen among all.

7. But from this de facto pluralism, concerning that which in the exercise of her magisterial authority the Church imposes on minds, to a *de jure* pluralism, concerning *that which the intelligence requires* by its very object and for its very work, there is an abyss, which fickle minds cross moreover briskly. They declare to us then that a plurality as large as possible of theological doctrines and of theological hypotheses is as necessary to the Christian intelligence as a plurality of courses in a good meal: tastes differ, do they not? What is it that the minds in question really think,—it is difficult to say, for they think little. Supposing in them a coherent thought, it appears that for them what God has revealed to men is a divine Unknowable to which the faith of the charcoal-seller adheres in order that the latter may conduct his business in a more consoling manner, but to which our intelligence is so dispro-portionate that it can attain to absolutely nothing of it or receive absolutely nothing of it except deceptive images, and with which it can occupy itself only in order to render it acceptable to the taste and to the mentality of men, in adapting it according to the diverse recipes which at such or such an epoch flatter most their

palate. In short there is no theological truth,—nor, of course, any philosophical truth either,—nor any truth at all, because history teaches us that truth is a myth inherited from the Greeks. Who therefore has said: "I am the Way, the Truth, and the Life"? To hold theological pluralism to be necessary *de jure* is a sin against the mind, innocently committed by persons who do not know that which they say.

8. *Laymen and the temporal work which belongs to them.*—It is one of the great accomplishments of the Council to have decidedly awakened the Christian conscience to what is required of it in the temporal order. Contempt of the world is an old commonplace of which the saints understand the true meaning, but of which for too long a time and in too many people an unworthy resignation to evil and an unworthy indifference to the witness which the Christian must render here on earth to justice and to the Gospel have made the worst profit.

We should thank God that such a grave omission has become henceforth impossible, and that the Church has clearly recalled to us our duties. But human stupidity is always present; and the kneeling before the world of which many Churchmen afford us at this moment the spectacle is no better than the spittles formerly cast upon it by zealots of the same stamp.

Those Churchmen who bend the knee before the world, fabricate for it a religion made to measure, and believe themselves dedicated to the social progress and to the happiness of man here on earth know moreover very badly the world; and the command optimism displayed by them with regard to the future of a civilization which in fact, and for the moment, finds itself in full decadence is nourished by as many illusions as by holy desires.

9. The evangelical witness to be rendered and the task of Christian inspiration to be effected in the temporal order are the affair of the laymen. And this task will be well done only if being themselves true Christians, enlightened by serious theological, philosophical and historical knowledges, and possessing in social and political matters a tested competence, it is they who, grouped according to their affinities, take the initiative of it and conduct it at their risks and perils. That priests can join with them is evident. Let us mistrust however organizations created and directed to this end by members of the clergy anxious to exercise in this manner their renewed apostolate. In regimenting laymen and employing

their activities for certainly generous ends but also in order to compensate the frustrations of clerics become finally men of their time and temporal leaders, they seem good above all to engender a new form of clericalism as little desirable as the old one.

The work through which our civilization has a chance to right itself, and the temporal city a chance to proceed to the radical changes, of an order at once structural and moral, through which it would pass beyond both capitalist materialism and communist totalitarianism (rendered more formidable, and more similar, by technocracy), it is Christian laymen, in cooperation with their friends of the other spiritual families, who alone can strive to accomplish it,—but laymen as such and acting under their own responsibility.

The priesthood is dedicated to another work, more necessary still, and for which it has promises which will not fail.

X

Invisible Presence *IN* the Visible Church and Invisible Presence *OF* the Visible Church

I

PRELIMINARY REMARKS

**No Salvation outside the Church
A Formula with a Double Meaning**

1. "No salvation outside the Church,"—this is a formula of unparalleled ambiguity. According to the sense in which one takes it, it is either a misleading assertion which immures the mind in a dungeon where it believes itself forced to despair of all those who are not *our own*,—or the statement of a holy truth in which we can nourish our hope toward all those who are not *our own*.

2. In the first sense, the formula in question signifies: "No salvation for those who do not belong *visibly* to the visible Church." Unfortunately this first sense has prevailed for a long time. It is said that St. Francis de Sales wept at the thought that all Protestants would be damned. It was to confuse the man, the human subject member of a non-Catholic spiritual family, and the sin of heresy abstractly considered in itself.

In the second sense, the formula in question signifies: "No

93

salvation for those who to the visible Church do not belong visibly
or *invisibly.*" And these last ones are doubtless innumerable,
among non-Christians as also among non-Catholic Christians: because the Church of Christ extends invisibly beyond her visible
limits, and embraces in her bosom all those who are saved by the
grace of Christ, even if they do not know Him, or if they know
Him poorly, or if, for any reasons whatever of which sad human
history is not avaricious, their ancestors separated themselves from
the Church of which Peter continues in his successor to be here on
earth the leader, in other words from the person of the Church
under her earthly state.[1]

Some Words on
Three Great Non-Christian Spiritual Families

These few words are a second preliminary remark,—a kind of
preface, longer than I would have liked, in which, in order to
know a little bit of whom we are speaking, I shall try to sketch the
significant traits, in my own perspective,[2]—of certain great spiritual families about which the studies of comparative religion
expand today in a precious manner the knowledges of the Western
world.

It is toward the primitive religions, and the most primitive
ones among them, that I would have doubtless liked to turn first
my attention. But I confess to be poorly informed concerning
them. Besides we have few data on the cavemen. We know however that they "were great artists, remarkable observers, clever
artisans" and—Norbert Casteret affirms—"men preoccupied with
spirituality."[3]

Be that as it may, what interests me here, when I think of the
non-Christian religious families, is not the primitive religions; it is
above all the three great families constituted by Brahmanism,
Buddhism, and Islam.

Brahmanism

1. It is essential to a *religion* to *link* men among themselves,
and with God, through a common "faith" in sacred truths (the
word "faith" covering there many analogical diversities). Brahmanism[4] is a religion in the strict sense of the word, and the most

exalted religion at which man has arrived without the help of the Revelation inherited from Abraham and from Moses,[5] by virtue therefore only of the thirst for the Absolute, Cause of being, which he carries naturally in him,[6] and of the effort thus aroused in his mind in order to rejoin in some way this Absolute.

This means that at the origin of the Brahmanist religion there is the élan of "natural mysticism" with its highest aspirations.

A parenthesis here, in order to settle vocabulary. First, the word "mystical." I call "mystical" experience, in general, any experience *fruitive of the absolute.* Afterwards the expression "natural mysticism," which is doubtless not too felicitous a one. Let us recall that there is a "supernatural mysticism,"—that one in which, through the gifts of grace and of the Holy Spirit, the soul enters into the depths of God: one could call it also mysticism of the union of love. In contradistinction to this supernatural mysticism, the "natural mysticism" of which I am speaking here is due to the sole forces of human nature surpassing itself, beyond any concept and beyond any work of reason; it would be better perhaps to call it mysticism of deliverance, or mysticism of the evasion of time.

I have dealt with it in an essay in which, in my eyes at least, there are some important views, and in which my attention was wholly turned towards Hinduism. The mystical experience in question there has nothing to do with the entry into the depths of God.[7] I described it as a wholly intellectual experience of the pure substantial *existence* of the *self,* in which, returning by a persevering exercise the ordinary course of mental activity, the soul empties itself of every particular operation and of all multiplicity, and through this abolition itself of all ideative act attains and knows in night, beyond all concept, that metaphysical marvel, that absolute, that perfection of every act and of every perfection, which is existence,—its own substantial existence.[8] The abolition of every act of thought of which it is a question here is itself, let us note this well, an act of the soul, unique in its kind and intensely vital.[9]

2. Such a mysticism of deliverance, tending toward the divine Absolute and attaining,—mediately but without any rational inference,—the Cause of being through and in the supraconceptual experience of this finite absolute: the pure *existence* of the human self,[10] —this is what, in my opinion, is for the philosopher (I do

not say for the historian) the first element to be considered in Hinduism, as accounting for its deepest élan.

The second element to be considered is the metaphysical speculation traversed by this élan, and which builds its great systems with a view to consummating itself in the experience to which it tends (even though the latter were then to assume new aspects, as it happens with the bhakti).[11] Although the Veda and the Vedanta are held to be revealed, this "revelation" (scruti),—in which figure also the writings of sages who came later (it was prolonged in the Upanishads) and which does not present itself at all as the word itself of God transmitted to us, but as an intemporal truth perceived by inspired ones,—lends itself to interpretations so fundamentally different that the "theology" of Hinduism takes on its dimensions only in the metaphysic or rather the metaphysics of the latter:[12] metaphysics higher than those of Aristotle and of the Mohammedan falsafa, but which, being religious in essence, and using concepts with a view to passing finally beyond them, were able, in actual fact, to climb their Himalayas only by traversing shadows and receiving the more or less secret support of Imagination and of Myth.

They advance thus without the rigor required in itself by a work of pure reason. Not having, moreover, the idea of the absolute liberty of the creative act (the universe is for them a necessary manifestation of the generosity of God), they tend no doubt to recognize the transcendence of God but do not attain to it truly (the human soul is a mode of the divine Being; insofar as spiritual it is of the same nature as He; He has a cosmic body . . .). The Self (ātman) is fundamentally the same in God and in man, although free in God of all imperfection and of all relativity.

3. Lastly we know that metaphysical speculation is something difficult in itself. On the other hand, in order to attain to a mystical experience of the natural order such as that of deliverance, it is necessary to employ very exacting techniques and disciplines, and to require of the powers of our nature a constantly prolonged effort of contemplative concentration, which is not within the reach of the multitude.

The great thinkers of Hinduism have carried this effort too high for it to be able to be lived at this level by the majority of men. Let us not be surprised that in the popular masses it has quickly become an idolatrous cult in which gods and goddesses abound and which holds very low the human being.

Buddhism

1. Buddhism is a religion only in the expanded—very expanded—sense of the word.[13] It is above all a discipline of behavior and of mental therapeutics, a regime of disaffection from everything to be practiced in a nondiscontinuous manner (at least by the *bikkhus,* if not by the multitude which gains merits upon merits by making to them its offerings). There are required in it the more and more profound persuasion that all things are illusory appearance, very long empty meditations, meticulous rules, and, in the Buddhism of the "Great Vehicle," a universal compassion due to the perfect experience of the vanity of everything: all of this with a view to withdrawing the finally delivered one not only from the sufferings of life in time, but, in the final analysis, from the human condition, and even from the condition of existent. *Save us, we beseech you, from the ocean of existence,* as it is said in a Tibetan hymn.[14]

Just the opposite of the Brahmanic experience of *mukti,* or deliverance (which I have described above as a nocturnal experience of the pure *existence* of the *self,* through and in which—mediately therefore, but without any concept or rational discursus—there is perceived in night the existence of the Cause of being, or of the divine Self), the Buddhist experience of deliverance, the accession to *nibbana* (this is the Pali word) or *nirvana* (this is the Sanskrit word), must, in the perspective of our essay on natural mysticism, be described, by very reason of the radical phenomenism professed by Buddhism, as a nocturnal experience of the nonexistence of the self.

And this changes many things. I noted a moment ago that in the Hindu experience the abolition of every act of thought was itself *an act,* an intensely vital act through the means of which the soul attains in night the pure *esse* of the self. Now such an act, in which the reality of the self culminates, is clearly out of the question, since there is no self. And as to the flux of the captive acts-pure-phenomena of the illusory becoming, it is precisely it which it is necessary to transcend. How so? A philosopher is entitled to pose the question. It seems indeed that what is required can be only a total vanishing of the Spirit. And one does not experience the vanishing of the spirit.

2. The assiduous exercise of meditation on anything, be it on a single word indefinitely repeated,—and above all on the imper-

manence of things,—can lead to a good dose of wisdom, of detachment, and of courage, sometimes of heroic courage. One finds thus among the Buddhist monks great figures who do honor to humanity.

But what to say of the final term to which all this effort of meditation tends? The entry into nirvana, supposing that one reaches it by the prolonged use of the appropriate techniques, can be a mystical experience of deliverance only at the cost of a lived contradiction: for it is by an act in which, in actual fact, the reality of the self culminates that the soul is enraptured then in the nonexistence of the self.

I shall certainly not venture to try to discover in what *Zen* consists,—which all the veils of the Orient protect from indiscreet glances. Moreover how could one ask oneself in what consists that which refuses to anything all consistency? Michel Perrin risked it; in a conversation with a Buddhist nun of high degree, at the monastery of Suji-Ji, he asked, "What is Zen?" Answer: "Zen is everything, and yet it is nothing; but it is also something." Then, after a moment of meditative silence, and a subtle smile: "To speak of it is to say false things; to think is a hindrance to intuition; one can only practice it. . . ."[15]

What one succeeds nevertheless, however "obtuse" one may be, in perceiving in it, is a kind of judo in which by dint of disconcerting the disciple, the master leads him, not certainly to any theoretical conviction (that which would suppose that one attaches importance to something: the truth rationally grasped), [16] but to a mental state (or rather vital, psychophysical) testifying even in the slightest reflex that nothing is worth the trouble of anything. Then there will come—perhaps—suddenly the illumination, the flash of wonder in the *hic et nunc* absolutely liberated from all thought.

It would indeed be futile to seek there unfathomable metaphysical depths. It would be futile also to leave in oblivion the strong seasoning of inevitable mystification which flavors with pimento these great secrets of spirituality.

Islam

1. Islam is a religion in the strict sense of the word, like Hinduism, and of a certainly more elevated and more pure type than Hinduism, for it has an extraordinarily strong sense of the

divine Unity and of the divine Unicity, as also of the infinite transcendence of God,—an extraordinarily strong sense but which remains too dependent still upon the human measure: Islam does not know the trinity of Persons, which shows more divine still the unity of the divine Essence; and it does not know the generosity with which God makes Himself known, and which shows more divine still His infinite transcendence.

The fact is that on the one hand Islam rests upon the Revelation inherited from Abraham and from Moses, through which human thought has been fortified and superelevated in its élan toward God; and that on the other hand it is totally subject to another "revelation," which issues only from a merely human fire (and not without fumes) with which the heart of Mohammed was inflamed when he was struck as if by a clap of thunder by faith in the unique God,—supernatural faith, may one think,[17] preyed upon from the outset by the merely human fire in question. It is this other revelation which in the sons of Ismael took the place of the supreme accomplishment brought by the Incarnate Word Himself to the whole teaching which Israel had received from the Holy Spirit.

There are for Islam five great apostles: "the first is Noah, who embarks in the Ark 'in the name of God,' and with whom, after the flood, God renews the pact."[18] The second is Abraham, ready to immolate the son whom God had granted to his prayer. The third is Moses, to whom God spoke in the burning Bush on the mountain. The fourth is Jesus, whom God "cast into the womb of Mary," and who, according to the Koran, was only in appearance crucified and put to death.

And it is Mohammed who is chronologically the fifth, but "qualitatively he is the first of all, since his message is called to complete all messages." The revelation received by Mohammed is recorded in a book, the Koran, which Islam holds to be the very Word of God supernaturally dictated to the Prophet, and upon which it is entirely centered.

2. The God of Islam is a God Inaccessible in the mystery of His proper life, and Unparticipatable, a God Unknowable, or, as Louis Gardet prefers to say,[19] Impenetrable in Himself. Of Him the Islamic faith knows "the most beautiful names" which designate Him,—and, in the relation which creatures have with Him, His Omnipotence, and His Mercy toward men; but only that. So that by a strange paradox, it is in the *falsafa*, in the great metaphysi-

cians (Avicenna in the first place) steeped in Hellenistic thought,—which was held to be suspect and heterodox by Algazel and the doctors of the *Kalam*,—that it is necessary to seek the riches of Mohammedan thought in that which concerns not only the universe of creation, but Being through itself.

Let us note finally that for strict Islamic orthodoxy those attribute—blasphemously—to God a human passion who admit between Him and His creature a union of love through which He gives Himself to him and transforms him in Him, for his supreme accomplishment and His eternal, consubstantial joy. (It is faith in the Incarnation and in the Holy Spirit which enlighten a little the Christian on this matter.) And it was because he believed in this love ("God whose Essence is Love," "I have embraced with my whole being all Your love, O my Holiness! You have manifested Yourself to me to such an extent that it seems to me that it is Yourself Who is in me!") that Hallâj was condemned by the public powers, scourged and cut up, and put to death on the gibbet in 309/922.[20]

II

INVISIBLE PRESENCE *IN* THE VISIBLE CHURCH

**All Non-Christians and Non-Catholic Christians
Who Have in Them the Grace of Christ
Are Invisibly in the Visible Church**

1. They are in the visible Church *invisibly*,
either from the fact that (non-Christians) they belong visibly to a spiritual family originally other than the Church,
or from the fact that (non-Catholic Christians) they belong visibly to a confession in more or less profound dissidence with the Church.

The non-Catholic Christians, by the very fact that they all have faith in Christ (a faith not diminished in the regions of the dissidence least removed from the center) must clearly be placed in another category than the non-Christians. Moreover, as we shall see in the third part of this chapter, the degrees to be considered in the more or less profound dissidence of the confessions to which they belong raise, with regard to the latter, a problem (that of the "elements of Church") which does not present itself, at least at first sight (it presented itself only after the Council), with regard to the non-Christian spiritual families. Finally the diverse degrees of dissidence in question require that one make, with regard to the non-Catholic Christian confessions, distinctions which matter greatly to the theologians, but which are extraneous to the subject-matter of this book.

Let us make another preliminary remark: unless he is completely dehumanized by *business*[21] or by the life of pleasure, every man, by the very fact that the human soul is spirit, worries about religious matters and has *his ideas* concerning them, which, if he does not profess the faith which the Church professes, can be more or less near to this faith or more or less opposed to it.

And let us understand that, in this last case, a man who for example is firmly attached to a non-Christian religion or even makes profession of atheism[22] (I have known some whose greatness of soul I envied) can have in reality the grace of Christ in him, if, while not knowing or not recognizing in his head Christ and His divinity, he has without knowing it, at the bottom of his heart, and in the *supraconscious* and *supraconceptual* state, faith in Him, through the most profound élan of his moral being and of his volition of the good.

I have just employed the words "supraconscious" and "supraconceptual." They relate to a higher psychological sphere, to a "heaven of the soul," in which the latter knows in a wholly intuitive manner, unformulated in concepts and in words, things which it does not know itself that it knows, because this knowledge is supraconscious. In the presently envisaged case it is also a knowledge of volitional type, in which "the appetite passes to the condition of object," but which includes a speculative element due to the *lumen fidei*.[23]

As soon as one has to do with the supraconscious of the spirit, the words "implicit faith" and "explicit faith" are to be rejected in like manner: because, drawn from current language which concerns itself only with the conceptual register, they enclose us in this register. If one believed for a long time that in order to have in oneself grace it was necessary to believe "explicitly" the two articles containing virtually all the rest ("to believe that God exists and that he rewards those who seek him") which the Epistle to the Hebrews (11, 6) mentions, it is because one remained solely at the plane of conscious and conceptual thought, and because one neglected thus a good half of the human psyche. What is necessarily required is not a faith (in these two *credibilia* at least) formulated in concepts at the plane of conscious thought; it is a faith (in these two *credibilia* at least) which is present in the soul and has a hold on it *actually* and formally, even if as a result of one of those blockages which are not rare in human psychology, it cannot pass into consciousness and be formulated there in concepts and in words.[24] An atheist can have such a faith completely unbeknownst to him. It is the secret of God.

This is why we are not obliged to admit that for a man who professes atheism to be saved it is necessary that an Angel come and instruct him and teach him to recite the two first *credibilia;*— nor are we obliged to send into Hell a great atheist like Nietzsche (this atheist,—one can indeed believe that it was through thirst for God, in the supraconscious of the spirit, that at the plane of conscious thought, obstructed by modern philosophy, he announced the death of God in the words which he uttered).

2. By the sole fact that he has in him the grace of Christ, a man, to whatever spiritual family he may belong, or without any spiritual family, is *in* the Church, even if (contrary to what would have been normal in itself) he is not in it visibly: because to be vivified by the grace of Christ and to be vivified by the soul of the Church is the same thing; in other words, because, as I have said in Chapter II (note 11), the soul of the Church is the pleroma of all graces (the word 'grace' designating here sanctifying grace, principle of divine life which inhabits a human soul or an angelic spirit). It is made up, in that which concerns the Church of the earth, of all the graces (sanctifying graces) individually received by men since the repentance of Adam, according as they are all likewise, although to different degrees, participation in the divine life, and according as all of them, by virtue of the dynamism of charity which emanates from them, are interconnected and constitute a single and supreme common good in the unity of the love of God, and of all the beings created in His image. It follows from this that the soul of the Church informs the body of the latter in an indissoluble union with it, but that it is not, as is our soul, prisoner of the body which it informs. For grace is free like the divine generosity. So that the soul of the Church, while being the "form" of the body of the Church, is also in all those among the other spiritual families to whom, without their being visibly part of this body, Christ has granted His grace: each one of these individual graces being *in itself*[25] one of the constituent parts of the soul of the Church. Thus, at the same time as in the body of

the Church, which it informs, the soul of the Church exists
also,—like a sowing of stars,—in a multitude of men dispersed in
the entire world who do not belong visibly to her body, and to
whom she brings supernatural life.

I hold that there is perfect coextensivity between the soul and
the body of the Church, if by "body of the Church" one understands the structures of this visible complex organism, the articulations required in order to assure the service of its collective life,
and the organs and the acts (sacramental and magisterial) through
which the person of the Church acts among us (cf. further on,
Chapter XI). All of this is informed by the grace of Christ which is
the soul of the Church, whatever may be in other respects the
possible shortcomings of such or such Churchmen.

But if one applies it to the individual persons (who are the
object of our present considerations),—whether individual members of the Church, or individual persons belonging visibly to other
spiritual families,—I do not think that the maxim: "where the
body of the Church is, there her soul is; where the soul of the
Church is, there her body is" remains correct unless it is suitably
nuanced.

It is thus as regards the first part of this maxim: a baptized
person brought up in the Church and who has installed himself
decidedly in a life of mortal sin has lost grace; he remains a
member of the body of the Church—on condition that he has kept
the faith ("dead faith" since it is now without charity); but the
soul of the Church is no longer in him, no longer actuates his soul.
It is true that belonging to the body of the Church, the faith, even
"dead," which he has kept remains in him an *initium* of the
supernatural order which has a chance of aiding him to recover
grace, and that, on the other hand, everything is ready around him
in order to aid him also to recover it; his brothers pray for him;
and if one day he decides to change his life, he has only to make a
good Confession. Yet it is necessary that he decide to do this. Let
us say that as regards him the soul of the Church is still "there,"
but *in a wholly tendential and virtual manner* (or rather *initial,* by
reason of the faith which has remained in him).

Likewise, in its second part, the maxim in question is correct
only on condition that it is suitably nuanced. For the body of the
Church is not only the visibility—at least for the angels—of the acts
accomplished by a non-Christian under the influx of the grace
which is in him. The body of the Church is her whole complex
organism, with all the structures, the articulations and the joints of

which St. Paul speaks,[26] and with at its summit the earthly leader of the Church. And it is indeed clear that in the case of a non-Christian who has grace in him this complex organism is not "there"; it is elsewhere. This non-Christian is neither visibly nor formally a part of it. (*Mutatis mutandis,* it is necessary to say as much of a non-Catholic Christian: in his case the complex organism of the Church is not "there" in its integrity.)

But the grace which sanctifies this non-Christian (or this non-Catholic Christian) is not given to him only as salutary for him; insofar precisely as grace of Christ (every grace which He gives to one or to another,—He destines it to the royal gift, to the sharing of the divine life with which He wishes to overwhelm His Bride), the grace which sanctifies this non-Christian (or this non-Catholic Christian) is given to him as being *in itself* (or "by birth" if I may say, and from its infusion into the soul) one of the constituent parts of that plenitude of all the individual graces in interconnection which is the soul of the Church. It is the soul of the Church which is through one of its constituent parts rendered present in this non-Christian (or this non-Catholic) by the grace of Christ.

But every soul is in itself architectonic: made in order to inform a body it tends toward this information, it demands it ontologically. Received from God by the non-Christian (or the non-Catholic Christian) in question, the soul of the Church contains already in it, in its architectonic virtue, this body itself in its entirety. It is "there," *but in a manner wholly tendential and virtual,* or rather *initial.*

This, in my view, is how one can declare that, through the individual graces which God spreads everywhere, the soul of the Church exists, in innumerable and invisible dispersed ones, beyond the body itself which it informs and to which it causes them to belong initially, and overflows immensely this body (which it does not however leave) in the non-Catholic and non-Christian regions of the entire world, without contradicting for all that the maxim: "where the body of the Church is, there her soul is; where the soul of the Church is, there her body is," on condition that this maxim is suitably nuanced. Through the architectonic virtue of the soul of the Church present in him, a non-Christian who has grace belongs invisibly, in an initial and wholly tendential manner, to the visible body of the Church.

And this is how every non-Christian (or non-Catholic Christian) who has grace in him is invisibly a part of the visible Church.

He is *in her* because the grace of Christ by which he lives supernaturally is in itself one of the constituent parts of the soul of the
Church, and because living by the grace of Christ he lives, at the
same stroke, by the soul of the Church. And he is in the visible
Church *invisibly* (*voto, non re*), since he belongs visibly to a
spiritual family which is originally other than the Church (or
which, while being Christian, finds itself in more or less profound
dissidence with the Church).

May I be permitted to insist upon a point briefly indicated
above: the views which I propose here[27] do not weaken in any
way the thesis of the coextensivity of the soul and of the body of
the Church. In reality it is the pleroma of all the sanctifying graces
individually received,—by all the dispersed ones who belong only
invisibly to the Church, as also by all the ones gathered together in
her unity who belong to her visibly,—which constitutes the soul of
the Church and which informs the organism with the multiple
joints which is her body. And it is to the body of the Church in its
full and complex integrity that the grace of Christ received by a
non-Christian, and which is one of the constituent parts of the
soul of the Church, deputes this non-Christian, joins and articu-
lates him virtually and initially, makes of him one of the members
of the great body in question, but an invisible member, hidden to
the eyes of all and to his own eyes, and whose belonging to the
body remains initial and in the tendential state.

However lofty may be in itself the grace received by him, it is
in him under an incomplete or imperfect mode, since he is not
formally and in act, but only through the architectonic virtue of
the soul of the Church present in him, a part of the body of the
Church, is not aided by the Sacraments and the other means of
salvation which she dispenses, does not participate in her worship,
does not proclaim with her the kingship of Christ; in other words,
since the grace received by him, and which makes him a partici-
pant in the capital grace of Christ, to a very high degree perhaps,
does not unfold in their formal expansion all the demands and the
riches which it contains with regard to the body of the Church as
also with regard to fully explicitated faith. This non-Christian who
has the grace of Christ is in the house of the Bride and enjoys her
intimacy,—and he is there as a friend and blind servant, he does
not see the face of the Bridegroom nor the treasures of His house.

But he is really although invisibly a member of the Church and
of the communion of saints, he lives truly by her life of grace and

of charity, he is assumed by her personality, he participates by this fact in her coredemptive mission, and he can be much more exalted in sanctity than many of her visible members.

That in Order to Be Saved It Is Necessary to Belong Visibly or Invisibly to the Visible Church,— This Is Because the Person of the Church Is Already Here on Earth the Plenitude of Christ, His Body and His Bride, and Because in Heaven She Gathers Together in Her, Until the Last Day and for Eternity, All the Saved

1. Another question presents itself finally, and one which it is important, I believe, to bring to light. It has for object the *reason for which* no one is saved if he is not visibly or invisibly a part of the visible Church.

Why is this so? It is not by reason of the *means of salvation* which the Church offers to men. Alone here on earth the Church of Christ, of Christ come, offers to us in their full integrity the means of salvation which the divine wisdom had in view from all eternity and which Christ entrusted to His Bride. But it is not for this reason that in order to be saved it is necessary to belong visibly or invisibly to the Church. In no domain do the means at our disposal suffice to enable us to attain the end which we are pursuing: we must *use* these means, and use them well. And to use the means of salvation which the Church offers to us is the affair of our liberty aided by grace. And it depends on our liberty, faithful or unfaithful to grace, to use or not to use these means, and to use them well or badly.

2. The reason for which there is salvation only in the visible or invisible belonging to the Church does not stand in the perspective of the means of salvation. It stands in the perspective of salvation itself. Salvation is in Christ. To be saved is to be in Christ, in Him Who in saving by His death assumes into His life all the saved. But, on the one hand, already in her peregrinal state the person of the Church is the Plenitude of Christ, His Body and His Bride. How is it possible to be *in way of being saved* if already here on earth one does not belong visibly or invisibly to His Plenitude, to His Body,

to His Bride? On the other hand, in her state of consummated grace or of eternal glory, the Church gathers together in her, since the repentance of Adam, and she continues in the course of time,—until the day when Purgatory and this earth will come to an end, and when the dead will come to life again,—to gather together all the saved in her glory. How is it possible *to be a saved one in eternal glory* if one is not a member of Christ in glory, and of the person of the Church in her state of glory? That which supposes that from here on earth one belongs already visibly or invisibly to this same person in her peregrinal state?

3. Such is, in my eyes, the true reason which founds the maxim "No salvation outside the Church" and permits one to understand it in its proper meaning. I believe that if during too long a time one has understood this maxim in an erroneous sense (no salvation if one does not belong *visibly* to the visible Church), it is because for too long one has assigned to it a reason which was not the true one, in seeking the *reason why* of it in the perspective of the means of salvation, which only the Church offers to us in their integrity (no salvation therefore if one does not have at one's disposal these means in their integrity).

Let us add that on this question of the *reason why* it is important for us to keep ourselves always on guard. If, even today when no one believes any longer that in order to be saved it is necessary to be visibly in the visible Church, we continued to envisage the problem of salvation in the perspective of the means of salvation, would we not run the risk of being led to think, be it subconsciously, that the *number* of the saved is a dependent variable of the more or less perfect and more or less complete means of salvation which men have at their disposal? Who would dare to say however that there are more saved among the Christians than among the non-Christians? Who would dare to dream of establishing (with what theological supra*computers*?) a statistics of the elect of God? The Christians have at their disposal more means of salvation than the others. But, as I indicated above, there is always human liberty which can slip away from grace and misuse the better. And there is also this terrifying saying: *"When much has been given a man, much will be required of him. More will be asked of a man to whom more has been entrusted."*[28] And there is also what Jesus has showed us: His severity toward the Pharisees, so studious to use (badly) the means of salvation prescribed by the Law, and His refusal to condemn the adulterous woman, like so many of those who came to Him without having used these means of salvation.

4. The fact remains that in everything every man has need of being aided by others; and that in order to attain an end we have always to use some appropriate means: a boy who wishes to become a doctor or an engineer must pass through the schools and the formation which are befitting.

If it is a question of the supernatural order, of attaining salvation and eternal life, then we have fundamentally need of an aid—incomparably stronger—which God sends to us through our human brothers. And we have fundamentally need of the means of salvation which come to us from the Church, whether visibly present to us (because we are visibly in her), or invisibly present to us in some manner (as we shall see later on).

This is why preaching, apostolic activity and missionary activity,—in order to cause to radiate more here on earth the glory of God, and in order to bring the means of salvation in their plenitude to more men on the earth,—have in the Church a role of such essential importance: which however is not the primary importance absolutely speaking. For the primary importance absolutely speaking belongs to the aid brought to our brothers by things which relate, no longer to the means of salvation which these latter have to use, but directly to their salvation itself and to the exercise of their liberty: the love (to tell the truth it is an "extravagant love") which God asks of us for Him and for them, prayer, and the participation,—in suffering for them, if it is necessary, to the point of dying for it,—in the redemptive work which Christ pursues in and through His friends until the end of time.

I add that the Trappists and the Carmelites are precisely delegated to this order of things; and also that a simple presence of true love and of true prayer among men is a testimony which of itself has a chance of drawing them toward the Savior and of causing them to turn their eyes toward His Church (and this all the better as one does not know it oneself, and as one does not propose to oneself to exercise any apostolic activity). It is not unimportant, it seems to me, that Christian laymen become conscious of such realities.

III

INVISIBLE PRESENCE *OF* THE VISIBLE CHURCH
THE CHURCH, SACRAMENT OF SALVATION FOR
HER MEMBERS, AND FOR OTHERS

Catholic Ecumenism

1. It is the second Council of the Vatican which has given to the Church this name of "sacrament of salvation," *universal sacrament of salvation,*[29] whose import is in my eyes so great. It is it also which has called Catholics to enter into the path of ecumenism. Hence the general title which I have given to this third part, in which it will be a question of ecumenism in the proper sense (concerning the ensemble of Christians), but also of an "ecumenism" in the expanded sense (concerning the ensemble of men).

The word *ecumenism* is a holy and venerable word; it is not its fault if, betraying the thought of the Council, many incompetents stimulated by a small number of avant-garde thinkers (excuse me, I should say charismatic) call today ecumenism the search for a spurious universalism, whose first condition is indifference with regard to truth: the idea being to unite finally all Christians in spite of their dissidences,—and all men in spite of the diversity of their beliefs,—in a same "Church" gathering them together in the name of Jesus in order to lead them to our final plenitude on earth, without one knowing either that which is the one or in what consists the other. The duty of fidelity to the light is however a duty which one does not elude, without abdicating at the same stroke intelligence.

One can note in this connection, according to a remark of my friend Father Cottier, that the transcendentals play nasty tricks on us because they are too lofty for us. At the time of the wars of religion the idea of Truth rendered ferocious a multitude of brave people, who in its name massacred each other mercilessly. Today the idea of Unity causes a similar multitude of brave people to completely forget that which is due to truth, in other words stultifies them without recourse.

There is however, thanks be to God, an ecumenism which is an authentic universalism,—because it joins together complete fidelity to truth and fervent love of unity,—to be reestablished if possible among all Christians and to be recognized among all men. With regard to our dissident brothers, it is the merit of Father Congar to have called attention, in a work published as early as 1937, to this *Catholic ecumenism,*[30] to the progress of which the second Council of the Vatican was now to ask Christian intelligence to devote a vast effort of renewal in the pure flame of faith.

2. The problem presents itself first concerning dissident Christian confessions. It will be a question of them in the two following sections. For the moment I shall confine myself to two remarks:

In the first place, it is indeed evident that one cannot conceive an ecumenical assembly as the assembly of a kind of council of administration, of which the members represent and defend diverse interests and come to an agreement with the help of mutual concessions and of compromises. The truth of divine revelation is not divided into portions of each of which each Christian confession would have the particular deposit, so that unity would come about through the bringing together of these different portions into a single whole. The whole is already there, in the Church one, holy, catholic and apostolic. The Church of which the successor of Peter is the head here on earth has received the mission to propose to men the whole truth of the revelation consummated by Christ and of the doctrine of the faith, with the marvellous richness and the divine profundity of all the contrasting themes which it envelops and reconciles. Error comes from exclusivism, and everything is included in the immense and multiform unity of the faith of the Church.

Every Catholic is and ought to be conscious of this. This is why he salutes with joy and love every truth of faith professed by a dissident confession, while knowing that he also professes it already.

And this is why there is no question for him of asking a Lutheran or a Quaker to abandon the truths of faith to which he is attached. Let him attach himself to them more than ever! By reason of these truths one can say that it is *in* and (in a measure) *through* his spiritual community that he will be saved (account being taken of the substitutions due to grace in the supraconscious of the spirit). What the Catholic regrets is that this Lutheran or this Quaker does not recognize other truths of faith.

What does this mean, if not that,—as long as the dissidence will last (a long time certainly in many cases), and without brushing aside the hope of preparing from afar, and as much as possible, a global unity of faith and of jurisdiction (embracing absolutely *all* presently dissident Christians) which it is permissible to regard as a great utopian ideal,—what from this moment is required above all of Catholics is a work of fraternal friendship with men who do not think like them in religious matters, and who can be admirable Christians but do not profess the Christian faith in its integrity. Nothing is more stupid than to imagine that in order to be true and profound friendship requires identity of thought. There are many Catholics who are far from being my friends; there are non-Catholics who are for me blessed friends. The truest and most fraternal friendship can exist between men who think differently on essential matters. It includes doubtless, then, an element of suffering, but one which renders the friend more dear still. One prays for him, but far from bringing pressure to bear on him in order to convert him to one's own faith, one loves him such as he is, and one esteems, one respects, one strives to know better and to understand better that which he believes and that by which he lives.

It is curious to note that one uses abundantly today the word: ecumenical *dialogue* (in which one has to do with abstract ideas and notions,—to their detriment sometimes, when one planes them down in order that they may accomodate themselves or have the appearance of accomodating themselves to one another); but that one almost never hears anyone speak of ecumenical friendship (in which one has to do with men, and with human reality). And yet is it not this which is first required? Well-established habits of mutual friendship, strengthened by time,—are these not the indispensable condition in order that the ecumenical spirit may pass into reality, where it will take one day juridically constituted forms of unity? May I say that from this point of view, however useful may be, at their plane, the meetings of commissions, with their definite programs, their reports, and their speeches, more useful still would seem to me fraternal banquets, in which Catholics and members of such or such dissident confession would eat and would drink together, and would go then to smoke together in the drawing room, conversing at random, joking, passing from one subject to another, and forming unexpected relations of reciprocal confidence? I do not seem serious; I speak however seriously. The meal taken in common is a natural rite of human friendship.

Be that as it may with the banquets of my dreams, the fact remains that what it is a question of above all is to know one another better, to understand one another better, and to love one another better.

And at the same stroke it is a question also of exchanging goods of great value.

3. For if such an exchange is not at all conceivable in the domain of faith and of divinely revealed truth, in other words of the teaching which, on the one hand, the Catholic magisterium and, on the other hand, the diverse dissident confessions give,[31] it is possible and real with regard to the manner in which this teaching *is received and lived* by the members of all the Christian communities in question. There is thus,—this is my second remark,—a vast domain in which for Catholic ecumenism,—and on the basis of mutual friendship,—a fruitful exchange is desirable between all: I think for example of the fervor shown by this one with regard to such or such particular truth of faith, whereas that one is inclined to neglect it more or less; and of the diverse kinds of psychological attitudes and behaviors linked with the ethnic varieties; or of the varied types of spirituality and of religious experience which it is so instructive for each one to learn to know in the others; or of that reading of the Bible in the vernacular which has long been so to speak a privilege of our Protestant brothers, and which has henceforth passed into the Catholic people.[32] With regard to the whole vast domain to which I allude, one can speak of a kind of ecumenical complementarity, on condition that one is resolved to use each time his intelligence, in attention to truth *first served*. Did not St. Augustine say that heresies are thorns that prick us out of our torpor? And does not Cardinal Journet add that in these thorns there can be roses? Adding also that "in the measure in which the discoveries or experiences of the dissidents have occurred under the influence of heresy, they will need to be rectified before they can be integrated. . . ."[33]

A Catholic will be pleased thus to recognize the true values present in the dissidents. He will find much to learn from Russian spirituality, from this "Christianity of penitents, and of penitents who are not embarrassed to confess their grossest faults," from that sacred respect toward the humiliated and the offended, and toward suffering, which makes that for this spirituality, from the moment that a man suffers, and above all suffers unjustly, he becomes venerable, to the point that one has seen "examples of children or of other innocents" canonized by the people "for their unmerited suffering."[34] A Catholic will be able to profit from the tenderness of heart and from the zeal with which many members of the Church of England practice that *pietas anglicana* of which

Father Congar speaks with good reason. He will like to read the poems of Herbert, of Vaughan, of Traherne, of Crashaw. He will be grateful to the Lutheran Paul Gerhardt for those hymns full of love with which Bach nourished his genius. He will be able to appreciate the "theology of the heart" of Zinzendorf and of the Moravian Brethren.

And in the present epoch in which the fear of God is so briskly forgotten, he will seek to scrutinize, with a kind of sympathy, even the terrifying sentiment of the divine transcendence and of the glory of God with which the soul of Calvin was invaded, so blindly that the Reformer hardened and falsified it because in reality he formed of the divine transcendence itself a too human idea (it is not in His essentially mysterious and immensely generous infinitude; it is in comparison with man and with the abjection in which he is immured that Calvin conceived the greatness of this jealous God, Who when He justifies a man does not put in him anything holy, any grace which is inherent in him).[35] But it is above all,—and not only in order to understand better his Protestant brothers, but also in order to grasp in the entrails of history the development of modern thought,—it is above all the original experience of Luther that a Catholic will study with a passionate interest, that tragic anguish of salvation,—centered in the insurmountable misery of subjectivity,—which shows God as an enemy and which, while the whole of the human collapses, throws itself desperately into faith (while waiting to throw itself later into philosophical unreason).[36] Being well understood that in these two last cases one does not have to do with an "exchange," and it is not at all a question of purifying an experience in order to integrate it (one does not integrate the absolutely unique and personal experience that a man has had), but of trying to see how, and by what truths to be restored, the experience of a Luther or of a Calvin would have found itself transformed *if it had been pure.*

The Elements of Church

1. Before the second Council of the Vatican, it was the word *vestigia Ecclesiae,* the "vestiges of Church," which the theologians employed. They designated thus *that which remains still* of the Church in the dissident confessions, which were torn away from

her by schism or heresy, or "that which can subsist of the true
Church in the dissidence."

But it is not the word "vestiges"; it is the word "elements"
which the Council used. "Some, even very many, of the most
significant *elements* or endowments which together go to build up
and give life to the Church can exist outside the visible boundaries
of the Catholic Church: the written word of God; the life of grace;
faith, hope, and charity, along with other interior gifts of the Holy
Spirit and visible *elements*."[37]

Consequently, the theologians employ henceforth the expression "elements of Church."

There is here, in vocabulary, a very significant change and one
of great bearing, and which, in my opinion, marks a certain
progress. With the word "elements of Church" one has to do with
a mere objective declaration: *that which there is common* between
a dissident confession and the Church, without reminder, in the
background, of the scars of schism or of heresy.

It seems to me that this change in vocabulary is not without
relation with the so manifestly true declaration of the Council
which is found in the same section: "One cannot impute the sin of
separation to those who at present are born into these Communities and are instilled therein with Christ's faith. The Catholic
Church accepts them with respect and affection as brothers."[38]

2. These elements of Church exist *in act* in the dissident
confessions. It follows from this that, as Cardinal Journet
writes,[39] "the separated Churches and Communities can continue
to represent, to render present,—in a doubtless partial, deficient,
and affected-with-privation manner,—the indivisible Church of
Christ. The latter *subsists* integrally under the hierarchy, in whom
she has her nucleus, but she recognizes herself *present*,—it is a
secret joy for her,—everywhere that there is at work some authentic gift of this Christ of whom she is the Body." Let us say
therefore that through the elements of sanctification and of truth
of which it is a question, the Church *is present* in a certain manner
in the dissident confessions. This is an *invisible* presence of the
visible Church: I mean invisible to these other religious families,
although this same presence discloses itself in some manner to the
eyes of Catholic theologians, attentive to the elements of Church,
which are in act, and therefore discernible and visible in themselves, in the religious families in question.

And this invisible presence is a virtual presence. For through the elements of Church which exist in act in these dissident communities, it is the entire visible Church, it is the person herself of the Church under her terrestrial state who is rendered virtually present in them. Presence *virtual and invisible* at one and the same time, and more or less· vigorous in proportion to the number and to the value of the elements of Church discernible in the dissident communities,—in proportion above all, shall I say, to the value of *truth* of the said elements.

I add that in explaining the formula: "the Church universal sacrament of salvation," the Council referred to the classical theory of the sacrament as *sign and instrument:* the Church is *signum et instrumentum intimae cum Deo unionis totiusque generis humani unitatis,* the sign and the means of intimate union with God and of the unity of the whole human race.

The elements of Church, understood in the proper sense of the word, which render the Church,—the Church one, holy, catholic and apostolic, the Church of Rome,—virtually and invisibly present, unbeknown to them, in the dissident confessions, communicate to this extent to these the virtue of this universal sacrament of salvation; and at the same time, according as they are there in act, they manifest to our eyes the means of salvation which these dissident Christian confessions place themselves at the disposal of men. "It follows that these separated Churches and Communities, though we believe they suffer from defects . . . , have by no means been deprived of significance and importance in the mystery of salvation. For the Spirit of Christ has not refrained from using them as means of salvation which derive their efficacy from the very fullness of grace and truth entrusted to the Catholic Church."[40]

3. The change in vocabulary of which I have just spoken entails, it seems to me, a new question of great importance. Since the elements of Church which exist in the non-Catholic Christian communities designate *that which there is common* between these communities and the Church of whom Peter is the leader here on earth, is it not natural to ask oneself if there are not also such elements in the non-Christian spiritual families? Do not all the spiritual families of the earth, even those which are at the lowest degrees of the scale, and which are the most mingled with errors and with deviations, contain some seed of goodness? (For pure evil

cannot exist.) And is it not true that to nothing of that which is good in humanity is the Church a stranger? Have they not all *something common* with the Church?

We shall discuss this question in the following section. But right here I indicate that in my opinion it is necessary to answer: yes, *there is something common;* but can one—and when can one—see in it an *element of Church?* This is an altogether different affair.

The fact remains that in any case the word "ecumenism" finds itself henceforth singularly expanded,—as far as the limits of the earth: since the Church, as universal sacrament of salvation, is, as the Council says, *the sign and the instrument of the unity of the human race;* in other words, since all the saved of the entire world are saved by God and His Christ through the instrumentality of the Church.

This is the final object—profoundly mysterious one—to which our weak eyes have to turn their attention. Let us say immediately that the consideration of the diverse spiritual families, however important it may be, is, as we are going to see, far from sufficing when we seek to form for ourselves some idea of this great mystery.

The Elements of Church and the Diverse Spiritual Families

1. It is normal for a man to belong to a spiritual family. Let us remember, besides, the fundamental difference which, from the point of view of our present reflections, exists between the case of an individual man and that of his spiritual family. In the case of the individual man or of the human person there is, as I noted above, a supraconscious which it is very important for us to take into account. In the case of the spiritual family it is not at all the same. A collectivity as such, a family as such has no supraconscious activity which is proper to it. What one has to consider in it is only the visible notes which characterize it, above all the expressly formulated beliefs which it professes.

It follows from this, in particular, that a spiritual family can be itself very deficient, atheistic for example, and must consequently be envisaged as bearing this character. Whereas, by the supraconscious life of the spirit, which is something altogether personal, such and such individual members of this family can have in them the grace of Christ, and be saved.

2. I am going therefore to attempt here to consider, with regard to the elements of Church (which for a moment I take in the most indeterminate and most vague sense), some of the most representative spiritual families. I apologize immediately for the doubtlessly very imperfect vocabulary which I shall use: it is the vocabulary of an old philosopher who on the one hand has sought to simplify things, by not taking into account certain points of detail which are the concern of the theologian, and who on the other hand has chosen his words only in hesitating a great deal. I have taken great pains to propose a correct analysis. If I have not succeeded in this, another one more competent will succeed in it, I hope. And it will not be fruitless in any case to have raised the questions entailed by such an analysis.

It is according to the degrees of a descending scale that I shall conduct my inquiry. It is therefore the case of the dissident Christian communities that I shall consider in the first place.

The Dissident Christian Communities

1. One cannot conceive the Church without her leader who is Christ Savior.

I shall say therefore that there are *Elements of Church,* in the *proper* sense of the word, only in the dissident Christian communities.

These elements of Church, in the proper sense of the word, belong to the supernatural order, and they relate to the *means of salvation* according as the dissident communities in question offer them to their members, even though they be more or less diminished (they are entirely complete only in the Church).

Finally these elements of Church, in the proper sense of the word, being in themselves linked with the whole of which they are a part, and which is the Church, render, as we have seen, the entire Church mysteriously present, although more or less vigorously, in the non-Catholic Christian communities.

All that which was said on pages 114-115 concerns therefore only the dissident Christian communities.

2. I shall not study the characteristics of each of them (this book would not end). I shall be content with a few brief remarks.

Let us note that among these dissident Christian communities one finds above all the Greco-Slavonic Orthodox Church, the "Old Catholics," and the Anglican Church; then the Protestants (Lutherans or Calvinists), the Methodist Church, the Presbyterians, the Congregationalist Church, the Baptist Church, the Unitarians, religious groups like the Christian Scientists and the Quakers. . . .[41]

If it is a question of the Greco-Slavonic Church (or rather Churches) and of the Anglican Church, I think that in order to form for ourselves a just idea of them it is particularly important for us to take into account, in applying it to the Church, the metaphysical distinction between "nature" and "person." The elements of Church are in such abundance in the two Churches in question (above all in the first) that it is not only, as with the other dissident Christian confessions, the *virtual and invisible* presence of the person of the Church that we have then to consider; these two Churches appear, in diverse degrees, as possessing themselves *almost all* the nature (soul and body) of the visible Church. I said "almost all" the *nature* of the visible Church. This is why they are truly, more truly and more completely than any other dissident Christian confession, messengers and witnesses of Christ. There remains however the word "almost": and it refers to the absence of an element which one can certainly call capital, since in these Churches which do not recognize the head of the Church in her state of earthly pilgrimage, the successor of Peter, the nature of the Church of here on earth is decapitated, as I said in Chapter III.

But personality supposes a nature that is whole in its proper order (or to which there is lacking nothing essential) which it completes in the line of subsisting and existing in itself. This is why, as long as they remain separated from Rome, the two Churches of which I speak are not integrated themselves in act in the person of the Church.[42]

Photius, whom the Orthodox Church canonized, detached the latter from the person of the Church. The Greco-Slavonic Church or rather Churches are venerable collective bodies which have the episcopate and the apostolic succession, the doctrine of the faith, the Sacraments, the means of grace and of salvation, and many saints in Heaven and on earth; they are not the *person* of the Church under her earthly state.[43] Moreover one does not see in them either that movement of progression in time, even in dogmatic matters, or that apostolic radiance over the entire world which attest the proper life of the person of the Church here on earth.

The Church of England finds itself, roughly if I may say so, and with objective problems more difficult to confront, in a historical situation analogous to that of the Orthodox Church. I believe, besides, that on the subjective side, which is important in my eyes, there is in a good portion of its members a sincere regret of, and a real suffering from, separation, which one meets else-where only to a lesser degree. This is why it seems to me that it is, among the dissident Christian confessions, the one of which, with a fair amount of time no doubt, union with Rome appears as the least arduously realizable: in spite of obstacles of which the greatest is perhaps the fact that the love and the fidelity of the Anglicans toward their Church go along with a notable diversity in dogmatic matters,[44] which this Church itself regards rather as a privilege; without speaking of the question of authority, so de-bated among Anglicans themselves, and of the thorny question of the Anglican ordinations, which more thorough historical studies and a reciprocal concern of goodwill sparing of every susceptibility have, one can hope, a chance of resolving.

3. If we pass now to the non-Christian religious families, it is fitting to set apart those which, without recognizing Christ Savior, have faith in the transcendent God Who rewards those Who seek Him, and Who has revealed Himself to men (faith which, in itself, contains implicitly all the rest). Since they profess this super-natural faith in God, I think that that which they have in common with the Church merits still the name of Elements of Church. But since they reject faith in Christ Redeemer, of Whom the Church is the mystical Body and the Bride, it can no longer be a question but of elements of Church *in the improper sense* of the word.

It is the case of Judaism and that of Islam which I shall have to consider here.

Judaism

1. Judaism is the religion of the true God blocked one day in an impasse by the men who failed to recognize their Messiah: a holy religion with bandaged eyes which, after the war foolishly launched against the Romans by the Zealots had brought about in 70 the ruin of Jerusalem, the destruction of the Temple, and the extinction of the sacred flame of the daily sacrifice, has during centuries maintained the spiritual unity of the Jewish people entered into the Diaspora.

The Jews faithful to the Synagogue have, although wounded by their human tradition since Caiphas, the supernatural faith of Abraham, of Moses, and of David. They have the Holy Books, the written Word of God. They have the Law and the Prophets. They have the Psalms and the Song of Songs. These are the elements of Church which one finds in Judaism.

Of itself the Judaic faith inclines one to seek intimacy with God, as certain eminent witnesses of Jewish spirituality, the Hassidim for example, show. The great work of the rabbinate however developed in an altogether different direction, in which subtlety of mind attached to the letter strives to determine, scrutinize, comment upon, often extend in a strangely arbitrary manner the meaning of the latter. It is to the rabbis of the first centuries that is due the composition of the Mishnah, of the Talmuds, of the Targums.

But, without speaking of its significant incapacity with regards to the Messianic problems,[45] the rabbinical teaching, by its intellectual narrowness combined with its taste for imaginary exegeses, has certainly contributed, in modern times, to divert from any religious belief many Jewish souls. The fact remains that "it is in rabbinical Judaism, which has preserved the three essential elements of the Jewish patrimony (the Book, the Sanctuary, the Land), that eternal Israel has drawn its unlimited capacity of revitalization."[46] The fact remains also that the Jews of our day, however unbelieving a good number of them, especially in the West, have become, are still the sons of the people of the Revelation, and of the sublime Awaiting. The awaiting of the Messiah Savior has no longer any reason for existence, since He is already come. But may we be able, Jews and Christians, to await together his Second Coming!

2. The elements of Church which exist in Judaism belong to the supernatural order, but, as I indicated above, these are elements of Church *in the improper sense of the word*. They relate to means of salvation themselves *truncated* (in the Old Testament the sacraments like Circumcision prefigured, did not give grace; and, as far as I know, the idea of sacrament is absent from the Judaic theology. As to the Holy Books, they are cut off there from the New Testament.) And if in themselves the elements in question are linked with the Whole of which they are a part, and which is the Church, nevertheless an inhibition,—which proceeds from the fact

that this religious family, which believes in the most holy God, does not believe in Christ Savior,—prevents them from rendering the Church mysteriously present in it. Israel was formerly the Church in one of her preparatory ages. It would be futile to speak of an invisible presence of the visible Church in the Israel of today.

It is clear, besides, that if at a given moment of history the princes of the priests condemned the Son of God, and if the greater part of the people followed them in their refusal of the Truth preached by the apostles, nevertheless all the Jews who in subsequent times were born and were raised in the rabbinical community, and our contemporary Jewish brothers, are as innocent of the blood of Christ as our Lutheran brothers are innocent of the sin of heresy committed by Luther.[47]

Islam

1. Islam is the second of the non-Christian religious families in which, because it takes into account the supernatural order, it is fitting according to me to recognize elements of Church.

But if it believes in the unique and transcendent God, Who reveals Himself to men, it rejects like Judaism faith in Christ Savior. The elements of Church present in it are therefore elements of Church *in the improper sense of the word.*

2. I have spoken above of Islam, I can therefore be brief here.[48] I shall say that it professes to have, as the Council says, "the faith of Abraham," supernatural faith although less pure in it than in the Jews (it requires that one believe also in the diverse fables which strew the Koran), and not seeking in itself intimacy with God. Islam reveres also (without giving it the first place) the Word of God written in the Old Testament. It regards Jesus as a prophet, born of Mary without a human father.

Thus therefore, *elements of Church in the improper sense of the word.* And *means of salvation* in a sense which I shall call *as reduced as possible* (no notion of sanctifying grace; no sacraments, be they only figurative). And for the same reason as that which I indicated concerning Judaism, these elements of Church (in the improper sense), while remaining in themselves linked with the whole of which they are a part, cannot render the Church mysteriously present in this religious family. It would be futile to speak regarding it of an invisible presence of the visible Church.

Brahmanism

1. I have already said also some words about Brahmanism. I shall note that in considering it a new question presents itself from the outset. In reality, it has no doubt a certain notion of revelation, the latter however has nothing to do with revelation such as we understand it (the Sanskrit word is moreover *audition*). It is a question here of an intemporal revelation. If in the time of men the sacred texts have been gathered and communicated by inspired sages of whom the list is long, these sacred texts are themselves eternal and uncreated, "without beginning" and "not human." [49] The sages transmitted them to us after having in their meditation listened, not to God speaking to them at a moment of history, but to a syllable-less song which has neither beginning nor end.

Likewise there is for Hinduism a "salvation" procured either "by experimental knowledge of the absolute" or "by divine grace raising up on the part of the dependent soul a response of love." [50] But here again the words could deceive us: this salvation is liberation from the law of Karma and of transmigration, this grace issuing from one of the three supreme ones who crown the Brahmanist pantheon (Vishna or Çiva, closer to the Hindu heart than Brahma) is benevolence, favor or protection, but not gift which superelevates interiorly the soul and causes it to participate in the very life of God; and to experience the absolute is only a sublime attestation of the power of our mind concentrating in meditation. Finally the supreme God is so mingled with the cosmic energy of Brahman that one does not succeed in affirming clearly His perfect transcendence. And He is not the only God; there are other gods, who remain submitted to the servitude of transmigration, and who have merited for a time a suprahuman condition.

In short, with all the beliefs, the myths and the speculations of Hinduism, as with its mysticism and its yoga, man remains at the door of the supernatural order,—at the highest of his native forces when they cause him to surpass himself in order to attain to an ecstasy of natural spirituality, or to the dazzlement of a haughty metaphysical knowledge nourished with the obscure splendors of creative imagination.

2. The question which presents itself is therefore: when a spiritual family has in common with the Church things which do not belong to the supernatural order, but only to that of created

nature, can we say still that these are elements of Church? No doubt the Church is the guardian of the goods and of the truths which are at the foundation of the natural order. But her mission is essentially supernatural. That which she has in common with the spiritual family in question is therefore not truly elements of Church, neither in the proper sense nor in the improper sense of the word.

I shall say therefore that with Brahmanism we have to do with *preelements of Church;* and not with "means of salvation" in the Christian sense of this word, but with *preparations of the natural order,* more or less remote (and very mixed) of which grace can make use.

And more still than in the case of Judaism and of Islam, it would be futile to speak of an invisible presence of the Church in the Hindu religious family.

Buddhism

1. Of Buddhism also there was mention above. It keeps the common belief in transmigration, but in insisting less than Brahmanism on the fundamental rationality immanent in the universal order. Buddhism is above all practical, it is a question for it of delivering itself, more radically still than Brahmanism succeeds in doing, from the slavery and from the illusion of becoming, which cause suffering to abound endlessly. It is existence itself that it blames: it is necessary to reject absolutely all substantial being: neither God, nor soul, the experience of deliverance is an experience of the nonexistence of the self.[51]

Essential truths which relate to the capacities of our nature are thus ignored.

2. Here still there remain however things, and great things, which are found in common with the Church: the profound sentiment of the impermanence and of the nothingness which corrode all that which we see here on earth; the thirst for a definitive liberation, already in this earthly life, thanks to a plunge into spiritual experience (the latter totally different, moreover, from the experience of the Christian contemplative); and that universal compassion which makes the nobility of *mayahana* Buddhism, and which however does not come from love, but from

the supreme elevation of the delivered one considering in all things the misery of existence.

But it is clear that nothing of all this can constitute an element of Church. I shall say therefore that what we find here is *shadows of Church* (sometimes transluminous), and not "means of salvation," but *aspirations of the natural order to a spiritual deliverance* (ambiguous).

It would be clearly futile to speak of an "invisible presence of the visible Church" in this religious family ("religious" in a very diminished sense) which does not recognize the existence of God.

Marxism

1. In spite of the violent struggle which he carried on against religion, Marx himself gave rise in modern times to a new kind of religious obedience and of religious devotion, if one no longer understands by the word "religion" anything but the bond uniting among themselves a certain number of men on the basis of a more or less severe dogmatics and with a view to "absolute" ends,—the "religion" in question being entirely turned toward the earth, and completely atheistic.

I am not thinking at all here of the Communist Party (which insofar as political party does not concern my subject), but of the spiritual family constituted by those of the disciples of Marx who have, in my opinion, remained the most faithful to his original thought,—I mean to his lived contradictions which contribute for a good part to the seduction which he exercises (whereas on the doctrinal plane he despised every claim of justice as of a vain and empty ideology, his heart burned in reality with a holy rage against social injustice and the misery of the exploited, which shows us in him the same blood as that of the old prophets);[52] —of the problem of the relation between communism and man which always obsessed this heir of Western humanism;—of his idea (utopian) that the dictatorship of the proletariat will only be a transitory phase, and that communism will ensure the expansion of the human person, all alienation having definitively ceased, and will issue in the full realization of the first article of faith: *homo homini deus*, Feuerbach said; Marx will say: man is for man the supreme being, *das höchste Wesen;* in other words, communism will issue in Marxian "salvation."

I am full aware that the spiritual family to which I allude is (not without frictions) wholly entangled with the Party; but in itself it is distinct from it.

2. Between this atheistic spiritual family and the Church there are some common things: the claim, for the world of work, of conditions of existence really conformable to that justice which is an affair of praxis to be implemented but also—in the eyes of the Church, if not of Marx—an affair of moral exigency to be recognized; the clear view of the misdeeds of the adoration of profit; the consciousness that an economic and social regime become entirely dehumanizing must be fundamentally transformed,— without speaking of all the condemnations declared formerly by the Councils against usury (cf. Chap. IV, p. 30), and of the old medieval idea, still true in my opinion, that the fecundity of money is a thing contrary to nature.

It is indeed evident that by reason of an essentially atheistic doctrine, and for which there is nothing but the earth, these common things cannot constitute an element of Church. I shall say that there are here *traces* of Church, to which no "means of salvation" correspond, but *a call,* on the temporal and merely terrestrial plane, and however mingled it may be with errors and with illusions, *to a social condition more worthy of man:* traces of Church which, in the Party, turn into the worst counterfeit.

And it would be clearly futile to speak of an "invisible presence of the visible Church" in this atheistic spiritual family.

The Hippies

1. The hippies present to us a spiritual family particularly typical of our epoch. It is fitting to consider for a moment the family in question.

It is essentially *refusal:* refusal of the whole established system, refusal of the world of parents, refusal *en bloc* of the lies of civilization. This reaction of a portion of youth (there were 200,000 of them in their assembly on the Isle of Wight, 400,000 in that of Bethel, during the summer of 1969) is a worldwide phenomenon and one of great significance: according as it appears as a sentence of condemnation—merited, besides—brought against a culture proud of its idolatry of science and of money, and which is rotting from within. Such a refusal is not something bad in itself. The saints, when they decide to change their life, posit also from the outset an act of refusal: but because they have discovered a truth infinitely superior to the world, and to which they give themselves.

Nothing similar in the hippies. Their refusal is purely and simply *a flight,* a collective flight; whereas a refusal worthy of man is founded on the internal exigencies of the individual person, on his courage, on the effort of his intelligence and of his will in order to do a constructive work,—above all to save that which he feels noble and good in him, and then to work to change the world, to the extent that one can.

The flight of the hippies proceeds from a soft and forceless will, drowned in the troubles of adolescence, and from an intelligence which has remained childish through laziness, and which is thrown into confusion by all the slogans, Freudian and other, which the mass media of the adult world distribute. They are the victims of this bourgeois world which they are right in detesting. In their flight they carry away all its misery with them.

Flight into the gregarious (of this gregariousness one finds many other examples today: *to get together,*—it is the sole recipe of salvation for empty souls), flight into the irrational, into availability to the demands and to the mirages of instinct, into the hedonism of the full enfranchisement of the senses. I see there as if the reverse of Buddhism: instead of willing at any cost to deliver oneself from becoming, from its illusions and from its torments, it is a question of enjoying as much as one can the ephemeral, and of finding one's joy,—a collective joy, naturally,—in the instant which passes, while closing one's eyes to all the rest.

2. Such is, it seems to me, what from the first glance one perceives in the spiritual family of the hippies. But one discerns immediately another thing in it: that which I shall call a first threshold of human enigmatic and of stirring of the soul, or a first point of reflection. The flight of the hippies is possible only on the condition that they create for themselves a closed world, an artificial paradise in which they will lead their life. And consequently this world will have its own disciplines, and its own values.

In the first place they will be the values of the infrareason: a 'letting go' of nature, above all through a total sexual liberty, of which the greatest misdeed is to banish human love (which is permanent gift of self) by virtue of the decidedly effected dissociation between the pleasures of sex and love. Homosexuality plays also here its part. But here is the paradox, and where the stirring of the soul appears: this debacle of human nature (it is human only with moral rules) goes hand in hand with an ideal of *purity of nature,* of sincerity, of candid spontaneity. And, in actual fact, a certain purity can thus find itself present: vegetable purity (the flowers have no shame) which has its strange brilliancy, and which I am far from scorning.

And in the second place,—because in the hippies as in every human being there are present the radical aspirations of our soul, which is spirit, and because all the doors are open, including therefore those of the aspirations to the suprarational,—the closed world of which I am speaking will form its standards out of a general counterfeit of the values of the spirit: the sacred, mysticism, ecstasy, the flights of contemplation, the suprahuman (when it is not subhuman) element included in fraternal life, the ceremonial, the ritual, with its necklaces and its flowers, and all the signs which delight the imagination,—nothing is lacking there, all being brought down to the plane of nature and of the senses, and easily procured by rock-and-roll, L.S.D. and the hallucinogenic drugs, in a total confusion and without any human or divine criterion.

3. Finally let us take care not to fail to recognize the existence of a second threshold of human enigmatic and of stirring of the soul, and of a second point of reflection. For one cannot be content indefinitely with the counterfeit, and there are inevitable options.

On the one hand one can choose to go in the service of the devil: to seek what is worst in tantrism and the aberrant forms of oriental esoterism, to devote oneself to magic.

But on the other hand one can on the contrary, through the counterfeit, let pass spontaneous gushings which issue truly from the spirit: above all, and this is not rare in the hippies, the gushing of poetry,—I know that poetry is not grace, far from it; but when poetry is truly present, something of Heaven has shone nevertheless for a moment;—and the gushing of music,—in this respect the hippies owe much to the *blues* and to the *gospel music* of the Blacks. And along with this, why would it not happen sometimes that there gush up also obscure desires, however weak they may be, for the mysterious world which is that of the gifts of God?

In the midst of the blemishes of an anarchical and irregular moral life, such desires can gush up in a heart, and make there their secret way. We must take into account the complexity of the human soul, which the gaze of the angels can alone decipher. Personally I have not known any hippies, but I have known a good many people who resembled them. And among them I have been able sometimes to see, and to respect, that kind of vegetable purity of which I spoke a moment ago,—a sign perhaps, who knows ever, and prefiguration of another purity, worthy this time of the image of God. And I have been able to feel also sometimes the promises which the authentic sense of poetry, and the obscure desires to which I have just alluded, contained of a life really centered above reason, not below it.

I do not doubt that among the hippies there are *some* of the same human quality, and who, be it without their knowledge, have in their hearts a solicitude, sullied perhaps in other respects, real nevertheless, for the true things of which the spiritual family in question cultivates the counterfeit: solicitude for the true sacred, for true mysticism, for true contemplative humility, for a true life of fraternal devotion which charity alone can give, for the true enchantments of authentic liturgy. These ones, however few they may be, have something common with the Church, who cherishes in the light that to which they aspire in night.

4. Of course, there is no question here of "elements of Church," nor, it is evident, of "means of salvation." I shall say that it is a question rather of *tatters of Church;* and of a pitiable search, gropingly, for a *raison de vivre* which is founded in truth, and for what the hippies themselves call, without knowing that which they are saying, "the true liberation of the spirit."[53]

In Conclusion

1. In conclusion of this whole long analysis, we see that there exist elements of Church in the proper sense of the word, and by virtue of which the Church finds herself invisibly virtually present in a spiritual family constituted outside of her, only in the dissident Christian confessions, in particular in the Greco-Slavonic Orthodox Church and in the Anglican Church.

And it is only in two non-Christian spiritual families, Judaism and Islam, that there exist elements of Church in the improper sense of the word,—inapt, this time, to render there the Church virtually and invisibly present.

In all the other spiritual families which we have considered, the something common which they have with the Church is too weak and ambiguous in order to be able to be called element of Church. So that clearly one also cannot speak of a virtual and invisible presence of the Church in the spiritual families in question.

Let us not forget, on the other hand, that one finds in the modern world an appreciable number of men too immersed in the turmoils of the temporal in order to have, in that which concerns them, the slightest interest in any spiritual family whatever.

2. It follows from all of this that when one tries to understand a little the universality of the sacrament of salvation that is the Church, the consideration of the diverse spiritual families, however instructive it may be by way of complement, provides, as I indicated at the outset, only a very insufficient help.

It is necessary to turn our eyes toward something else. I have indeed my view on this subject, but it belongs to a domain which is not mine, and it would be the affair of a well-equipped theologian to judge decisively what it is worth. Believing it well founded, I am going to propose it nevertheless. Let it be well understood, however,—even if I do not express myself with all the oratorical precautions which would be necessary,—that it is conjecturally that I propose it.

The Absolutely Fundamental and Universal Element of Church

1. It is an absolutely fundamental and universal element of Church which we must discover. Where to seek it? In my opinion, in *man himself such as he comes into the world*. I think that the primitive and fundamental element of Church, and one which exists everywhere on the earth,—it is each human person who bears it in him, according as by nature he aspires to know the Cause of being, as also to a state of happy expansion of his being, and according as, wounded in his nature by the sin of Adam,[54] — to such a degree that in his first act of freedom he cannot choose the good (and therefore love naturally above everything the subsisting Good) without grace *naturam sanans*,—he has at the same stroke, if he does not slip away from the grace initially given, a thirst for God which is at one and the same time of nature and of grace (of grace, in other words "exceeding all created nature").[55]

And he has also, even if he slips away from grace, a desire to *save his being* which is consubstantial with him, because his being is wounded (he does not know it, but he experiences it since emerging from childhood through suffering and grief).[56] It is this desire to save his being, and to be aided by all the means which are necessary for this, however unknown they may be, which, in act in the supraconscious of the spirit, makes of each man an element of Church in the proper sense of the word, and it is through this desire,—*voto, non re* (I would prefer to say "truly, but by virtue only of desire, not of accomplishment"),—that in each of those to whom the Good News has not come, and by the sole fact that they are men born after the Fall, the whole Church is *virtually present,*—virtually and invisibly.

2. The philosophers tell us that the loved is in the one loving, the desired in the one desiring. But applied to the question before us this maxim assumes a meaning of an exceptional import and of an exceptional profundity.

On the one hand, indeed, with regard to the desiring subject, we have to do with a desire rooted in being, therefore incomparably more fundamental than all the ordinary desires which can pass in the soul. As long as a man exists, this desire torments him, conscious in those of us who have the religious sense, supraconscious in all.

On the other hand, with regard to the term of the desire, it is important to distinguish two very different cases. If it is a question of the object of the desire considered only *as object* of the latter, it is from the desire itself that it derives its being in the soul of the desiring one; the desired is in the desiring one, but it is in him only *ideally,* such as, for example, a journey which I desire to make. If on the contrary that which is object of desire is also,—with or without the knowledge of the desiring one,—*a thing possessing its own existence* outside of the desiring subject, the desired in question is then a real being in the world, which by the desire is rendered *virtually* present in the desiring one, and which as such finds itself virtually and invisibly immanent in his life.

Supposing that a woman exists somewhere in the world who is for such or such a given man the unique perfect companion possible, so to speak made-to-order for him, this woman, whom he does not know, exists virtually in him through the desire of human complementarity which dwells in him. She is mysteriously immanent in his life. It is she whom he loves through all the women whom he will be able to love. And it may be that one day he will meet her. . . .

3. Well! the Church of Christ exists, she is there, visible on the earth, and sovereignly real, together with all the means of salvation which she provides. Such and such a man "born in the forests" or in some primitive tribe does not know her; but through the desire to save his being, and to receive the aid of all the means necessary for this, which dwells in the man in question, this really existing Church is in her entirety *virtually* present in him, *virtually and invisibly* immanent in his life.

She attracts him without his knowing it to her reality. And in following the desire to save his being which dwells in him,—in other words, the desire which he has for her without knowing her,—he will have in his life, even if he be a sinner, and in the options which he will make, occasions to obey inspirations which come from above, to profit better from the good which there is in his religious family if he has one, to be guided in his path by the angels, and to open himself to the grace of God which in one manner or in another is offered to each, and of which no one is deprived except through his own fault. (And perhaps one day he will meet this true Church; and he will recognize her perhaps.)

This is how I conceive that man himself is the most fundamental and most universal Element of Church, in whatever region of the earth he finds himself, and whatever complementary help he may be able to receive from a religious family—Christian-dissident or non-Christian—in which he may have been born and may have been reared.

Every human being is thus, by the very fact that he is a man come into the world after the Fall, able to participate in some manner in the universal sacrament of salvation that is the Church; he can receive and is called to receive the effects of the *universal sign and instrument of intimate union with God, and of the unity of the whole human race.* He is already mysteriously a child of the Church.

4. And this is also how I understand,—but provided that one goes further than the consideration of the diverse spiritual families when one brings into play the notion of "element of Church,"— the theological text of an admirable richness of thought which has nourished the reflections of an old philosopher while I was working on the present section:

"Just as at the very interior of the visible communion of the Church, there is a very characteristic difference of incorporation between the just and sinners, so there is," Father M. V. Leroy writes,[57] "far beyond her visible limits, an immense domain in which it is [...] the holy Church of Jesus and of the apostles, the one and unique Catholic Church who realizes herself, immanent in the diverse Christian communions (and, beyond, in the other religious groups and in the entire human family), in the measure of the presence and of the action in them of the 'elements of Church.' So that those even who are officially non-Catholics, but Orthodox, Protestant, etc., are *already* her children, are already incorporated in her, doubtlessly in a manner still incomplete and therefore imperfect, but dynamic, open, requiring in itself a going beyond and a realization, and, for the best of them, personally salutary, 'spiritual,' although imperfectly 'corporal.' This presence, this immanence of the Catholic Church (—Roman!) in the other 'Churches,' this belonging to the unique Flock of all the faithful of Jesus (and, beyond, of all the men who in their hearts have received grace and opted for God and His Kingdom) cannot without caricature be interpreted in terms of possession: it is not a claiming of a power, but recognition of a gift. Those only will be shocked by it who, attracted to the dualism of the Reformation between visible Church (or Churches) and invisible Church, suspect instinctively the Roman Church of imperialism and of totalitarianism." " 'Thus the Church' " (the author concludes by this quotation from Charles Journet),[58] " 'the Church of Christ entrusted to Peter, is at one and the same time more pure and more vast than we know. More pure, since she is, not certainly without sinners, but without sin, and since the evil actions of her members do not stain her. More vast, since she gathers together around her all that which in the world is saved. She knows that from the depth of space and of time there attach themselves to her through desire, in an initial and latent manner, millions of men whom an invincible ignorance prevents from knowing her, but who have not refused, in the midst of the errors in which they live, the grace of living faith.' "

A Threefold Approach

1. If one tries to glimpse a little to what degree the Lamb who takes away the sins of the world wishes that His Bride be associated in His work and conduct with Him the affairs of salvation, not only as to the men who belong to her visibly, but also as to all the others, it seems to me that it is necessary to join together three considerations, or three different approaches.

In the first place the Church,—the visible Church,—is *the place of salvation:* all the saved are visibly or invisibly *in her.* It is this of which I spoke in the second part of this chapter.

In the second place, the Church,—the visible Church,—is *the universal sacrament of salvation,* and she is *herself present,* not only in her members in an actual and visible manner, but also, virtually and invisibly, in all other men, by the sole fact that they are men come into the world after the sin of Adam, and, by this title, absolutely fundamental and universal elements of Church. It is this of which I spoke in the third part of this chapter.

It is necessary to add now a third consideration or a third approach. The Church pays for the salvation of men, and in this sense she is *cause or agent of salvation,*—not only for those who belong to her visibly, but for the men of all the earth,—according as she is dedicated to that *coredemption* of love and of suffering through which Christ willed to unite to Himself, even in His redemptive sacrifice accomplished once and for all on the Cross, all those who have received His grace.[59] As Pius XII says in the encyclical *Mystici Corporis,* Christ "requires the help of His members," not certainly by way of complement, but by way of participation, in order that His Passion may bear its fruits on the earth.

It is a question here, no longer of the means of salvation, but of salvation itself and of the gifts from above to be obtained for men, in passing through the heart of God, His justice and His mercy, and in sharing the love and the sufferings of Jesus on the Cross in order that there be applied to the human multitude, all along the ages, the Blood of the Savior and Its infinite merits.

2. I think that concerning such a mystery a distinction must be made. On the one hand each soul in state of grace is called to it for his personal account, in the measure of his sanctity. There are hidden saints, immolated in prayer, upon whom everything rests. Did not Tauler say that a single act of pure love is more efficacious than all the works? Apropos of those whom he calls "the true friends of God," he says also that "their sole existence, the sole fact that they are, is something more precious and more useful than all the activity of the world."[60]

But on the other hand one thing matters more still: it is the coredemption of which the person of the Church herself in her peregrinal state pursues the work here on earth, and in which are assumed all her members,—however imperfect they may be, however often they may have to rise again from their falls,—from the fact that their belonging to the person of the Church carries off a little of themselves into the great coredemptive passion which she suffers here on earth until the end of the world. And this work of coredemption effected here on earth by the person of the Church goes as far as the redemptive work of Christ: it embraces all the earth and invokes grace upon all men. And it assumes in it, clearly, all that which the best among her members accomplish in the same coredemptive order in proportion to their personal holiness.

Let us note, further, that even if they do not belong visibly to the Church, all those who have grace, among dissident Christians or non-Christians, are also assumed by the person of the Church in her redemptive work. For by the sole fact that they are men come into the world after the sin of Adam the person of the Church is virtually and invisibly present in them; and by the sole fact that they have grace, the person of the Church, without their knowing it themselves, draws them to her and to that which she accomplishes. But then she draws them at the same stroke, without their knowing it, from their Christian-dissident or non-Christian spiritual family, which is not integrated in the person of the Church; and it is as being invisibly and unconsciously a part of the Church entrusted to Peter that they share in the redemptive work accomplished by the person of the Church. Whereas at the same time, to the extent that there is in them personal holiness, they bear testimony to the paths which the spiritual family to which they belong visibly leaves open to the grace of God.

3. It is by joining together the three considerations or approaches mentioned above that one is able, it seems to me, to best glimpse how the unity of the visible Church extends invisibly to the whole human race.

The Person of the Church Is Indefectibly Holy
Her Personnel Is Not

I
THE PERSON OF THE CHURCH

In Order to Complete Our Views
on the Personality of the Church

1. I have spoken a great deal already of the person of the Church; I would like to return a last time to this subject, in order to try to provide the final precisions which seem to me necessary, it being well understood that the concepts and the words which we have to use here are analogical, since they concern realities of the supernatural order.

The Church, we have seen, has a "created" soul, which is the grace of Christ diffused in her members and causing them to participate in the infinite grace which is in Him and in the very life of God. Considered in all those of her members who live by grace, and according as they live by it, one must say with Bossuet that the Church is "Christ diffused and communicated."

Let us think of the soul of Christ Himself: this soul, being created, is finite as to its being, but it had already on earth, at least according as at the same time as *viator* it was *comprehensor*,[1] and

135

it continues to have in Heaven, where it is only *comprehensor,* a grace *infinite* in its order or as to its formal effect, in other words to a point of perfection absolutely supreme and unsurpassable. Since the person of Christ is the uncreated Person of the Word Himself, it is connaturally that He sees God, in other words the grace which radiates in the soul of Christ *comprehensor* is as it were the asymptote toward which tends without ever being able to attain it the curve of ascending perfection of all the graces receivable by a mere creature. Thus the plenitude of grace is *absolute* in Christ.

Let us think of the soul of the Blessed Virgin: the grace which is in the latter is not infinite, Mary being a mere creature; but this grace (which increased during her whole life here on earth) is more exalted than that of any other mere creature, since Mary is Mother of God, humble woman at the confines of divinity. Plenitude of grace in the line of that which is accessible to the mere creature.

Let us think of the soul of the Church: this soul is the pleroma of all the graces which are given to men here on earth, in proportion as time advances, and which in Heaven, where they are consummated grace, constitute the glory of the holy angels and of the blessed. For the Church also, therefore, plenitude of grace (to an increasing degree as long as the Church of the earth has not completed her pilgrimage) in the line of that which is accessible to the mere creature.

2. The soul of the Church is the grace of Christ, which,— consummated grace in Heaven, informs there a multitudinous body of angels and of separated souls who see God,—and, grace in growth on the earth, informs there and builds for itself there an organized multitudinous body, composed of men who profess the apostolic faith, receive the Sacraments, and recognize the authority of the Pope and of the bishops.

Grace is given to each one individually. But it is one according as it emanates from Christ Who distributes to each a part of His infinite treasure, and according as it binds to each other, in the communion of saints, all those who receive it.

It is by virtue of this unity in its source (Christ) and in its term (the communion of saints) that the soul of the Church, and, forming but a single being with it, the multitudinous body which it informs and builds for itself, can, by reason of the image of Christ which God sees in the being thus constituted, receive supernaturally, as we have noted, a true subsistence,—perfectly one itself and sealing the whole in its unity,—which is the metaphysical foundation of the personality of the Church: case absolutely unique, which is the property and the mark of the mystery of the Church.

3. What is the place, what is the role of the Virgin Mary in the economy of this mystery? The theologians have much debated this point.[2] I am going to venture to propose what, in the perspective in which I am placed, seems to me to be true in this matter.

The Blessed Virgin is not above the Church, as Christ is, *caput super Ecclesiam*. She is *in* the Church, and *in* the communion of saints.

It is clear from the very first that the Immaculate One is in the Church as reigning, by virtue of her immense and incomparable holiness, over the whole human and angelic multitude which composes the latter, since she is queen of the angels and queen of the apostles, and *omnipotentia supplex*. In other words, she is, with all her personal holiness, member of the Church *by royal title*.

But she is also in the Church by another more important title.

Let us recall that she is universal mediatrix,[3] and that this function includes two aspects. On the one hand, Mary, by her personal initiative, or as "proper cause," prays, beseeches, carries our prayers and our complaints and our miseries before God.

And, on the other hand, God uses her prayers, her supplications, her love itself and the movements of her heart as an "instrumental cause" through the means of which He, who is the principal Agent, gives to the Church and to each of the members of the latter all that which He gives to them. This is why St. Bernadine of Sienna[4] compared her to the neck which joins the head to the body. Let us say—which seems to me a much better manner of speaking—that being the Mother of the Church and carrying her so to speak in her womb just as she had carried Jesus, it is through her that God and the glorious Christ cause instrumentally to pass all the gifts and all the graces with which they nourish the Church.

4. Well, once disengaged before our eyes, it is this aspect, the *instrumental* aspect which we have to consider, and no longer with regard to the prayer and the love of Mary, but with regard to her person herself. We shall say then that, more fundamentally and more intimately certainly than by her royal title, Mary is in the

Church *by an instrumental title* which is entirely unique. She is not in the Church, after the manner of the other members of the latter, as assumed by the personality of the Church. She is in the Church as *immanent* in the very personality of the Church, through the instrumental influx, always present in this personality, of the "model"[5] or of the sign by means of which God confers it on the Church. This "model" or this sign which God renders operative in making use of it instrumentally is the person of Mary immaculate, who is herself the living image of Christ, and whom God uses in order to imprint in the Church (soul and body forming but one), by reason of the image of Christ which He sees in her, the seal of a supernatural subsistence.

The Blessed Virgin being thus rendered, through the divine action, immanent in the personality of the Church, there is nothing in the latter which is not first in Mary. Mary is holy and full of grace before the Church. Was not Mary herself, at the foot of the Cross, the type and the figure of the Church, or rather, at that moment, the Church herself? It is through the instrumentality of Mary that the Church, the Church of Christ come,[6] is holy and full of grace in Heaven and on earth, and that on the earth her holiness and her plenitude of grace increase until the last day. When everything will be consummated, and when the Church will be completely gathered together in glory, then one can think that the holiness and the plenitude of glory of all her members taken together will be henceforth equal to those of their queen, who will have given everything.

5. That meanwhile, and as long as she makes her way on the earth, the person of the Church can be holy while being composed of members who are all sinners to some degree and keep all, to some degree, the wounds of nature left by the first sin,—we have seen how it is fitting to explain this: personality being a metaphysical completion of the soul and of the body joined together, and the soul of the Church being sanctifying grace itself, it is only according as we live by this grace that we are assumed by the personality of the Church.

The watershed passes through the heart of each man, the pure waters belonging to the holiness of the Church, of which the grace which operates in us makes us participants; the impure waters belonging to our weakness and to our strayings. In the very measure in which I yield to sin I escape from the personality of the Church.

How the Person of the Church Is Visible

6. What to say now of the visibility of this person of the Church who transcends that of her members,[7] and who includes in her only that which in each of her members on earth does not slip away from sanctifying grace?

"Person" in itself or as metaphysical entity is invisible, in the Church as in each of us. In the Church as in each of us it is visible to the eyes through its body, to the intellect through the signs which emanate from it and which manifest it.

Materially considered, or considered as mere human multitude, not as person, the Church is all the baptized,—whether they live in grace or in sin,—who are a part of the tissues and articulations of her body and who profess the Catholic faith. Such a multitude is indeed visible, but it is not the person of the Church.

Formally considered, or considered as supernatural person transcending the personality of her members, the Church is all those, in this organized multitude, who live by grace and by charity. This person of the Church is visible to the eyes and to the intellect, but *in confuso,* not distinctly (except in certain well-determined cases)—I mean that not knowing the depth of hearts we cannot trace any line which would mark the contours of the person of the Church in the midst of the multitude of Catholic denomination of which I have just spoken. However, without being able to trace the contours of her, we know well that she is there, since Christ said: "I shall be with you until the end of time." We know that for a large part, which remains indistinct for us (if not for the angels), and which is doubtless larger than we think, the members of the organized multitude of Catholic denomination are truly in act (and not only in a virtual[8] or potential[9] manner) a sanctified people, the people of God. We know that a Pope can be a great sinner, but that—a condition presupposed by his charisma (*"strengthen your brothers"*)—he will never lose the faith;[10] and that the episcopal body also will never lose the faith (although bishops individually taken can fall into heresy, at least through weakness,—one saw this too well, and very abundantly, at the time of Arianism). And all the holy works which are produced in the bosom of the Christian community; and all the testimonies which are borne in it to justice and to fraternal love; and the solicitude which appears in it to defend human dignity, to aid the weak and the innocent, to render the structures of human life more worthy of a being made in the image of God; and the light and the charity of which we have been able to receive personally the help close by a good priest or a Christian friend,—all of this renders visible *in confuso* the person of the Church.

7. Finally, if one asks by what ways and in what cases she manifests herself, no longer *in confuso,* but *distinctly,* so that we are absolutely sure of seeing her face, there are the canonized saints[11] and the Blessed Virgin above them all; absolutely sure of seeing her act, there is the whole sacramental order, and above all the Sacrifice of the Mass and the Eucharist; absolutely sure of hearing her voice when she speaks to God, there is the Divine Office;[12] absolutely sure of hearing her voice when she speaks to men, there is the extraordinary magisterium of the Pope speaking *ex cathedra,* and of the ecumenical Councils establishing and specifying the doctrine of the faith and of morals, as also the ordinary magisterium of the teaching constantly and universally given since the apostolic age by the episcopal body in union with the Pope.

If the preceeding considerations cause in some manner,—except in the cases which I mentioned just now,—the visibility of the person of the Church to recede into a certain shadow, I am far from complaining about it: on the one hand, indeed, this separates, as is necessary, and shelters this mysterious and holy person from the unreadable literature (pious or "contesting") of which the common run of Churchmen have the secret, and from the tumult of human words with which they think they have to gratify our ears under the pretext of leading us to God, and to the great silence in which He gives Himself.

On the other hand, and above all, this brings to light the difference which it is important to recognize between the person of the Church and her personnel.

II
THE PERSONNEL OF THE CHURCH

The Personnel of the Church Is Neither Indefectibly Holy Nor Always Inerrant

1. What I call the personnel of the Church is the men who, by the fact that they belong to the secular or regular clergy, are

recognized servants of the Church, and, in particular, those of them who from the top to the bottom of the hierarchy have the responsibility of authority with regard to the Christian people.

Their mission sets them apart, but as to personal behavior and to the wounds of nature they are men like the others, and members of the Church like the others, all exposed to falling more or less gravely into error and sin. And those who have the responsibility of authority can, in the very exercise of this responsibility, err more or less gravely, either in their conduct in matters of practical decision and of government, or in what they say and what they do in matters of doctrine (except when the ordinary or extraordinary magisterium of the Church is in play, and when they find themselves then protected from all error concerning faith and morals).

Of these failures and of these errors the historians can draw up very long lists. Some of them,—failures of omission or of commission,—have been very grave. To tell the truth, when one reflects on that of which men who hold such a formidable power as a power directly received from God would be capable, if they were left to their sole forces and to their sole instincts, what appears the more astonishing is that the failures and the errors in question have not been much more numerous still and much more grave.

2. The sins into which, with regard to their own moral behavior, certain members of the personnel of the Church happen to fall,—whether it is a question of pride of spirit or of the weaknesses of the flesh, or of the allurements of prestige and of riches,—have certainly repercussions on the flock which they are commissioned to tend and on the manner in which they lead it. However it is not these failures and these errors concerning individual morality which interest me here, but indeed those which concern the exercise of authority in the Church.[13]

For what poses a problem is the fact that through a personnel liable to err in the exercise of the authority which it has received from God,—for example when it holds as incompatible with the faith assertions which are not, or as guilty of moral aberrations someone who later will be canonized,—we could, in the cases which I mentioned at the end of the first part of this chapter, be put in the presence of the person herself of the Church, see her act, and receive from her the truths revealed by God which it belongs to her to propose to us.

Proper Causality and Instrumental Causality

1. The key which gives the solution of the problem is, shall I say, the distinction between proper causality and instrumental causality.

Let us recall first some metaphysical truths of an entirely general order. When a human creature acts as proper cause, or as principal agent, he has in the created order, under the motion of God Who inclines him to what is just and good, the full mastery of his act, and he can, through the liberty with which he is endowed, and according to a law of nature which God engages His honor to respect always, take an absolutely first initiative of nothingness which shatters this motion toward the good, and it is an evil or disordered act which he produces then.[14]

When this same human creature acts as *instrumental cause,* under a motion which comes from God, the act which he accomplishes as instrument[15] cannot clearly but be righteous to this extent.

2. It is the same, proportionately speaking, with the personnel of the Church. With regard to his private morality, a member of this personnel is in the same case as any other human creature. With regard to what he does as servant of the Church, and especially in the exercise of the authority which he has received from God, he is, according to the divine promise made to the Church of Christ, assisted by the Holy Spirit, Who inclines him to the right judgment and to full fidelity to truth, in short to the good for which he has been constituted servant of the Church.

But if he acts as *proper cause,* the assistance of the Holy Spirit is an aid which is offered to him and from which he can slip away through his fault.

It can happen also that without withdrawing from the assistance of the Holy Spirit, and without fault on his part, the limitations of human nature and those of the historical development, and the obstacles of every sort created by them, prevent him from having knowledge of such and such a particular truth which it would be necessary for him to see in order not to err, or in order to make a right judgment in such and such given circumstances.

In short, when he acts as *proper cause,* a member of the personnel of the Church is liable to error.

On the contrary, when he acts as *instrumental cause* in the hands of the First Cause, the assistance of the Holy Spirit is a divine motion which passes through him in order to produce its effect; then he acts, he speaks, but it is the Holy Spirit Who acts through him and speaks through him.

There are certainly many cases in which such or such members of the personnel of the Church speak and act through Him. But is is only in the cases which I mentioned above that we are *sure* that they speak and act thus.

I have just spoken of the cases in which a man acts, under the assistance of the Holy Spirit, not as proper cause, but as instrumental cause moved by the Holy Spirit.

What matters to me now is to envisage the same distinction between proper causality and instrumental causality with regard to this "principal agent" which is the person of the Church. I hold that every member of the Church, especially every member of her personnel, can act either as proper cause, or, if God wishes it, as instrumental cause brought into play by the person of the Church.

The thing is essential to my eyes, because it is only when someone acts or speaks as instrumental cause brought into play by the Church that it is the Church herself who acts or speaks (through him), in other words that we are then in the presence of the person herself of the Church, as it happens when the Pope speaks *ex cathedra.*

The idea that the Church can use the *instrumentality* of one of her members, so that through him it is she herself who speaks or acts, is, I believe, a new idea, which has therefore need of being explained and justified. Without entering into too many technical details, it seems to me that such a justification scarcely presents any difficulty, from the moment that one admits the central notion, upon which I am insisting so much in this book, of the *personality,* in the strong or ontological sense, supernaturally conferred by God on the Church by reason of the image of Christ present in her. Case absolutely unique, the personality of the Church is as really personality as that of an individual man, but,—and this is the proper mystery of the Church,—it is the supernatural personality of an immense multitude composed itself of human persons, or free agents, whose natural personality is transcended by this personality supernaturally conferred on the Church.

Consequently it is in two different senses that it is fitting to understand the word "member" of the Church. I shall say that a man is a mere "numerical member" of the Church according as he is a unity in the *multitude* which composes the latter, in the manner in which such or such an individual is a unity in the multitude of the citizens of a country. He acts then as proper cause.

And I shall say that he is a "functional member" of the *person* of the Church when the latter uses him in the manner in which I, an individual person, use one of my members or one of my organs in order to do that which I intend to do,—in the manner for example in which I use my hand in order to write. Then my hand is the conjoined instrument which I use in order to do that which I wish. Likewise when the Head of the whole Church of Heaven and of the earth, the Lord Jesus, wishes to use someone as a functional member or a conjoined instrument of the person of the Church, it is the action of the person herself of the Church which passes through the instrumentality of this someone.

The man in question is a free agent, and it is upon his liberty itself, as conjoined instrument of the person of the Church, that the all-powerful motion of Christ, Head of the person of the Church, exercises itself, without even his being conscious of it (for it is freely, as in his ordinary conduct, that he decides and acts); he is then acted upon in order to act; it is the person herself of the Church who speaks or acts through his instrumentality when he speaks and acts. And in such a case he cannot err; it is the infallibility of the Church of Heaven and of the earth, the infallibility of the person of the Church which passes through him.

The Sacramental Order

1. The sacramental order belongs itself entirely to instrumental causality. It is *God alone* Who is the cause of the efficacy of the sacramental words, as principal agent using them instrumentally.[16] This is why a Sacrament is as really effected by a morally bad minister as by a morally good minister, and by an inattentive minister as by an attentive minister; I shall return in a moment to this last point.

With this however all is not said. I think indeed that to this consideration on the effectuation of a Sacrament by God alone as principal agent, it is fitting to add another one bearing on the minister as human subject moved himself instrumentally when he utters the sacramental words: so that we have to distinguish between the instrumentality, with regard to God alone, of the sacramental words and of the human act which produces them *insofar as it has them for term,* and the instrumentality, with regard to God and to the person of the Church, of the man from whom they emanate, and of the act through which he produces them *insofar as it proceeds from his subjectivity.*

In this second consideration, I say that the human subject (and his act insofar as it proceeds from him as subject) is at one and the same time instrument of God and instrument of the person of the Church. It is necessary indeed to remark that if the person of the Church serves herself as instrument[17] for God and for Christ, she can however, in the sense which I have just specified, be at the same time, in the order proper to the mere creature, second principal agent, using as instrument such or such of her members, in particular such or such of her ministers.

This causality of the person of the Church intervenes in absolutely no way in the efficacy (it depends on God alone) of the sacramental words. But how would the person of the Church not be, in the created order, principal agent using instrumentally the priest (and his act insofar as it proceeds from him as subject), if it is true that the priest effecting a Sacrament acts *in persona totius Ecclesiae,* in the person of the whole Church?

Why is a Sacrament as really effected by an inattentive priest as by an attentive priest? Because, says St. Thomas,[18] it is indeed true that, the priest being an animated instrument, and moving himself in some manner himself, it is necessary that there be in him the intention to "do what Christ and the Church do." But supposing that this intention is absent from the mind of the priest, or that a distraction renders him inattentive to it, the required intention is there all the same, *quia minister sacramenti agit in persona totius Ecclesiae,* because the minister of the Sacrament acts in the person of the whole Church. Expressions such as *agit in persona totius Ecclesiae* or *ex parte totius Ecclesiae*[19] have an acceptable sense only if one understands that the person of the Church is then second principal agent.[20] It is necessary that the intention of the Church be *really* there, and truly active. It is the intention of the person of the Church which, through the instrumentality of the priest, informs and animates the act of the latter.

What does this mean, if not that when the priest effects the Sacrament, his act, insofar as it has for term the sacramental words, is certainly the instrument of God alone; but that this same act, considered insofar as it proceeds from the decision of the human subject, is at one and the same time the instrument of God and that of the Church, who, moved herself by God and by Christ, applies to act, through an instrumental motion, this human subject who is the priest, in other words acts herself through the instrumentality of the latter? It is the person of the Church who speaks through the priest, when the latter, be he inattentive or be he morally bad, utters the sacramental words.

I know that I am very rash in proposing thus a complementary explicitation to the classical treatise of the Sacraments. But since I undertook to write this book, it is necessary indeed that I omit nothing in it of what seems to me essential.[21]

2. Thus therefore it is necessary to say that God alone is the principal agent who accomplishes the Sacraments, in causing the efficacy of the sacramental words uttered by the priest. But let us not hesitate to add that the person of the Church is, in the created order, another principal agent (second) who uses as instrument the minister of the Sacrament in the instant that this human subject, be he distracted or inattentive, utters the words which God alone renders efficacious.

When a priest or a layman confers Baptism on someone, it is the person of the whole Church who confers Baptism on him through the instrumentality of this priest or of this layman. When a priest gives absolution to a penitent, it is the person of the Church who gives him absolution through the instrumentality of this priest. It is the same for all the other Sacraments.

And when a priest offers the Sacrifice of the Mass, it is the person of the Church who offers the Sacrifice of the Mass through the instrumentality of this priest. I recall here that the person of the Church is a single and same person in her state of glory and in her state of earthly pilgrimage: it is the Church of the earth who offers the Sacrifice of the Mass; but since she is the same person in Heaven and on earth, one can say that through the Church of the earth and the instrumentality of her priest the Church of Heaven also offers this Sacrifice, "carried to the altar of almighty God by the hands of his holy Angel," *per manus sancti Angeli tui.*[22] For it is also, and above all, Christ who offers it through the instrumentality of the priest and through that of the Church.

The Jurisdictional and Magisterial Order

1. Contrary to the sacramental order, the jurisdictional and magisterial order,—through which the personnel of the Church

governs itself, exercises its pastoral mission with regard to the people of God, and teaches the latter,—accords in general a very large part to the proper causality of the ministers of the Church. But, as I indicated a moment ago, instrumental causality has also its part in it: for it is very often as instrument of the Holy Spirit,—and of the person of the Church, as second principal agent,—that great servants of the latter, known and unknown, have spoken and acted in the course of the ages, and continue to do so. I note that then instrumental causality (and therefore inerrancy) and proper causality (and therefore possibility of error) find themselves intermingled.

It is that which happens for example with the holy Doctors, the holy preachers, the holy missionaries. And it is above all, it seems to me, that which happened with the Fathers of the Church; in reading them one feels oneself at many moments carried away by a divine breath, which comes from the Holy Spirit and passes through the person of the Church; whereas at other moments it is the phantoms of Plato or of Plotinus which one meets in them, or those of the contingencies of the epoch in which they lived, with the solicitudes of polemics and the hazards of battle which they included.

2. But when it is a question of the ordinary magisterium of the Church, then, if proper causality keeps its part in that which concerns the mode of distribution of the teaching, descending from degree to degree in order to attain *hic et nunc* the Christian people, it is wholly subordinated to instrumental causality with its inerrancy, which is alone in play in the teaching itself of the truths of faith universally given all along the centuries by the episcopal body, in other words in the "ordinary magisterium of the whole Church dispersed over the earth."[23]

And when one comes to the extraordinary magisterium, to the decrees of the ecumenical Councils in matters of faith and of morals and to the definitions made by the Pope *ex cathedra*, then (although, in that which concerns the redactional aspect, the style of the conciliar or pontifical documents bears inevitably the marks, sometimes quite pompous, sometimes very discreet, of the ecclesiastical style in a given epoch) the Pope speaking *ex cathedra*, or the bishops called together by him in ecumenical Council, act,—I mean in the strict measure in which there is aimed at in what they say the formal teaching to be given (whereas the side issues which do not fall under this aim are not matter of faith),—under the inspiration of the Holy Spirit as instrumental agents of the person of the Church integrally considered (herself acted upon by Christ and the Spirit) when the latter, in her essential unity of Church who sees and of Church who believes, but above all as Church who sees, expands the field of infallibility of the Church of the earth. They are thus the voice of the person of the Church integrally considered speaking to men,[24] and it is her infallibility which is communicated to them.

The Encyclicals of the Pope

1. A special question, quite difficult but one which I do not wish to evade, presents itself with regard to the papal encyclicals. They are not infallible documents; and yet they have an authority such that the assent of our intelligence to them is required. How to explain this? For the intellect is incapable of an adhesion which would be wholly honorary. It can adhere to that which is proposed to it on the authority of a word only if it is sure that through it it holds the truth between its hands.

I think therefore that it does not suffice to say that an encyclical *is not* an infallible document. It is necessary to add that always it brings us inerrancy or contains the *infallibly true*. In other words, proper causality and instrumental causality are intermingled in it. If it is not an infallible document, it is because for a certain part the one who wrote it acted as proper cause, liable, however wise he may be, to err in some measure. If it requires the adhesion of my mind, it is because, for a certain part also, and one which matters essentially, the one who wrote it acted as instrument of the Holy Spirit and of the person of the Church, and to this extent could not err. I shall say that when the Pope writes an encyclical, he expounds, explains and develops himself, in his manner, something long meditated concerning which a light come from above has divinely enlightened him. Could one not say, in this sense, that an encyclical is not *formally*, but is *virtually*, a teaching *ex cathedra?*

Let one apply oneself therefore to becoming aware of the infallibly true content which is there: the means to be employed to this end is to discern that which the encyclical has for positive objective and for essential intention to teach us.[25] Of the truth of this I cannot doubt, whereas I can doubt such or such reasons adduced, or desire complements of which the absence annoys me.

And if I am incapable of effecting the discernment in question, there remains to me always to tell myself that the Pope is more wise than I, so that of what he says my intellect lays hold as of a precious gangue of which it knows that it contains gold veins of indubitable truths.[26]

2. There are three manners of adhering to an encyclical. The first is to make to it a bow full of reverence, **while** inveighing against it and judging it inopportune and badly founded. I prefer, in order not to be offensive, to abstain from qualifying this first manner.

The second manner is to adhere to it *as if* from one end to the other it was an infallible document. He who reads thus an encyclical gives then more than what is asked of him. But as he does it in a spirit of faith, this can be for him the occasion of great graces. [27]

The third manner is the one which I have just indicated, and which I believe normal. It asks that one attempt an effort of the intelligence (is it possible to live by the faith, be one a village illiterate, without having to exercise one's intelligence?). But this third manner does not make of the success of the effort in question a condition of the adhesion which one gives to the pontifical document.

A Final Precision on the Notion of Personnel of the Church

1. I began this chapter by indicating in a few lines what I mean by "the personnel of the Church," and who the ones are who are a part of it. I terminate it by a few considerations concerning the men from whom the personnel of the Church derives its authority all along the course of history, without one being able however to regard them as having themselves been a part of this personnel.

In the sense in which I understand this word, it is necessary to say that the Pope and the bishops are at the summit of the personnel of the Church, as doctors of the faith and pastors of the flock of Christ: the Pope, successor of Peter; the bishops, successors of the apostles. Would it be necessary therefore to say that Peter and the other apostles were also a part of the personnel of the Church? I shall certainly be careful not to do this. If the Pope and the bishops constitute the high personnel of the Church, it is because their authority is that itself of Peter and of the other apostles *according as the latter is transmissible.* But there were also in the apostles an authority and a privilege *absolutely intransmissible.*[28] They were the men chosen and established by Christ Himself (be it after his Resurrection, like Paul), or (like Matthias and Barnabas) by the apostolic college itself, by the light of the Spirit of Christ, in order to be the historical foundations of the Church of Christ, her instructors for ever and her norms in the faith, and in order that for all the centuries to come their word would make known to the people of God the revealed truth brought by Christ in its plenitude. They were here on earth at the origin of the Church of Christ come; it is through them, under His all-powerful hand, that Christ founded her and caused her to come into existence.

And at the same stroke they were constituted in her the pillar to which is attached, in order to unfold itself in the course of time, the chain of those who form her personnel. How could they have been themselves a part of this chain? Instruments of Christ in order to cause to appear in time the person of the Church in achieved act,—of the Church of Christ come,[29] —how could they have been a part of the personnel which supposes her already constituted and pursuing her duration, and have been like it, in certain given cases, her instrumental agents? It is of Christ alone that they were the instrument.

They served the person of the Church of the earth more and better than anyone here on earth: but as her models for ever, companions here on earth, if I may say, of the risen Christ, and His instruments in the work of foundation of His Church.

2. If therefore, as I wrote at the beginning of this chapter, "the recognized servants of the Church, in particular those who from the top to the bottom of the hierarchy have the responsibility of authority with regard to the people of God," constitute the personnel of the Church, it is according as they came after this age of fire which was that of the foundation of the Church. In men whose function and authority were no longer assigned except for the conservation of the Church in existence and her permanence in duration, the part of proper causality, with the fallibility which it includes, quickly become much greater than in the giants of holiness pressed by the charismas of the 'to-cause-to-surge-into-being.' And as to instrumental causality itself, it is no longer as burning each with a heroic flame, as the apostles in the work of

foundation, that they were henceforth the instruments of Christ and of his Spirit; they were, by reason of human weakness and human mediocrity, capable of slipping away often from divine inspiration: it was necessary therefore indeed that of the person of the Church accomplishing here on earth her divine work they be also, in certain given cases, the instruments.

Finally the Pope and the bishops are not chosen and designated by Christ Himself (Whom however one of the Twelve betrayed) or by the college of His apostles, but by men for whom it can happen that, succumbing to the wounds of our nature or to historical circumstances, they slip away, to the extent that God permits it, from the assistance of the Holy Spirit, whether it is a question of the Christian community designating itself its leaders,—which was the case in the very first times; or, as today, of the cardinals electing the Pope, and of the Pope naming the bishops. As to the person of the Church, she confers upon the members of her personnel, through the Sacrament of Holy Orders, an authority which comes from God, but it is not she either who designates them and chooses them; they are chosen and designated by other members of her personnel. It is an inevitable and normal thing that this personnel recruit itself; so that the person of the Church is not by any title, even not by the title of designation,[30] engaged herself in what her personnel can do or say except in the measure in which it is instrumental agent in her regard.

XII

A Look at History

To speak broadly of the failures and of the errors of the personnel of the Church without saying clearly of what one is thinking would be, I believe, to fail in a duty of intellectual honesty. On the other hand, the slightest discussion of historical detail entails endless developments, incompatible with a book like this. I do not experience besides any pleasure in dwelling on a subject which recalls only too well the wounds left in us by the old Adam (as does history in general, history "with the hideous visage," as Julian Green says, history in which I also see "the nightmare of humanity"[1] in travel). I shall limit myself therefore, in this chapter and in the two following ones, to the analysis (impossible, alas, to make it as brief as I would have wished) of a small number of typical examples which I have grouped as best I could.

I
THE EXACTIONS OF THE CRUSADES
AND THE IDEA OF THE HOLY WAR

The Crusade and Its Executants

1. The crusade was an idea which, in itself, was pure, but, in actual fact, was immediately invaded and stained by an impure

idea. If one turns toward those who preached it, toward a St. Bernard for example, and toward those who assumed the chief responsibility of the enterprise (Urban II,[2] and the Popes who succeeded him in the course of three centuries), and if one thinks of the extraordinary élan of faith which gave birth to the latter, it is the pure idea which one sees first, as also the noblest religious motives, accompanied by temporal solicitudes themselves very noble, and by those great dreams of political wisdom—as activating as they are utopian—of which men have such a great need (to unify the Christian republic—in other words, the Europe of the Christian princes and of their sordid rivalries—for a supranational generous goal): let us not forget that the regime of mediaeval civilization was a sacral regime, in which the political is the ally and the instrument of the sacred. From the point of view,—itself utopian,—which I have just indicated, the history of the Crusades appears as a splendid epic.

But from the point of view of the reality of the facts, and considering the executants, this same history can appear only as at one and the same time heroic and terribly stained. In actual fact, the memories which the Franks left where they passed are those of their violence and of their exactions. In order to inaugurate the latter there had been the massacre of the Jewish colonies of the German cities by the unorganized popular bands which followed Peter the Hermit, and the havocs to which they had devoted themselves in the East. Other exactions were not lacking afterwards with the regular armies; pillages, rapes, massacres sometimes worse than those committed by the Mohammedans (such as the horrible massacre which followed the storming of Jerusalem in 1099: the blood of the massacred prisoners rose even to the knees of the horses[3]),—all of this is the lot of man unleashed in war. The "great white barbarians" did not go at it with dead hand in the matter of pillage and of brutality, and of the sacking of the treasures of a refined civilization. They excited the horror of the Islamic populations and caused them to hate the name of Christ; they insulted the Christians of the Greek rite; and what remains of the Crusades in the mind of numerous Christian Arabs of today, as of their Mohammedan compatriots, is the idea of an imperialist enterprise ferociously conducted by the West.

2. Louis Bréhier[4] remarks that the crusade of Louis VII and of Conrad III, launched by St. Bernard and Pope Eugene III, "had no other result than to augment the hatred between the Greeks

and the Occidentals." St. Bernard had intrepidly opposed the pogrom which threatened to annihilate all the Jews of the Rhineland when a populace inflamed by the crusade had wished to show how it also knew how to serve God. But St. Bernard was not in the East in order to evangelize those whom he had sent there in the name of the Almighty. After him, there was the unforgettable testimony of St. Francis of Assisi at Damiette,—the arms of his crusade were the word and love, and he succeeded in entering into the city and in having himself led into the presence of the Sultan of Egypt Malik-al Kâmil in order to tell him that he was ready to undergo the ordeal by fire,[5] refused formerly by the Christians; this conversation, cordial and courteous on both sides, took place three months before the capture of Damiette by the Crusaders (5th of November, 1219) and the pillage which followed, "so ferocious and so terrible" that Joergensen[6] sees in it the work of "wild beasts."

St. Bernard, St. Francis. . . . One will ask perhaps: And the high personnel of the Church? Did it raise its protest against the exactions of which I have spoken, and which dishonored the Cross? In the books which I have read I have found mention of the regret, expressed by Innocent III, of being constrained to shed blood.[7] But not a word, as far as I know, was uttered concerning the massacres and other excesses of which the Crusaders rendered themselves guilty. Valiant hearts without reproach, were they not, since they were (according to the common opinion) the instruments of the Church?—They were absolutely not the instruments of the Church, they were the missioned ones of the Popes of the Middle Ages,—whose intentions they betrayed. And these Popes themselves were in nowise the voice of the Church (in the whole affair, nothing, of course, which was said *ex cathedra*), they acted as proper cause invested with the highest authority in the Church of the earth: it is still the personnel of the Church which we have here before our eyes. The person of the Church,—it remained to her to weep, and to do penance for so many sinful missioned ones.

The Holy War

3. A still more grave omission concerns the idea of the holy war. It was necessary to wait for John XXIII and the general teaching of Vatican II for it to find itself *ipso facto* placed under interdict, and chased finally from the obscure subsoils where the phantoms of the past lie in the soul. Up until then I do not see

that the high personnel of the Church did anything in order to prevent the Christian conscience from being contaminated by the idea of the holy war, impure idea which poisoned centuries of history, and which is in itself an outrageous insult to the Gospel. To James and John asking Him for the authorization to cause the fire of Heaven to descend on a city which refused to receive Him, Jesus answered these frightful words: *"You do not know of what manner of spirit you are,"* adding: "The Son of Man did not come to destroy men's lives, but to save them."[8]

The pure idea of the crusade was invaded and stained from the outset by the impure idea of the holy war. In order to understand how this phenomenon too naturally occurred, I shall have recourse to a letter of St. Bernard to the Bishop of Spires,[9] in which, addressing himself to the "warlike natures," he says to them: "Why turn your zeal or rather your fury against the Jews? They are the living images of the Passion of the Savior. It is not permitted to persecute them or to massacre them, or even to expel them. ... It is not they whom it is necessary to strike, but the Gentiles. *These latter ones took the offensive.*[10] *It is fitting that those who bear the sword respond to violence by violence."* It is the notion of the *just war* which is here in play (notion morally well founded),—and of the just war haloed by the love of Christ; such is, according as it is allowable to disengage it from this text, the pure idea of the crusade.

But in the same letter there are other lines: "Admire," St. Bernard writes, "the abysses of His mercy. Is it not an exquisite invention and one worthy of Him to admit into His service murderers, plunderers, adulterers, perjurers and so many other criminals and to offer them by this means an occasion of salvation? Have confidence, sinners, God is good." Dangerous lines;[11] St. Bernard, carried away by his utopian idealism, *did not see* that the conclusion drawn by the sinners would be quite simply: "Let us kill therefore the infidels, it is the easy and sure means to gain paradise." He did not see that what he wrote opened the door to the idea of the holy war: war in order to chastize and to subjugate the infidels, or in order to convert them by force, or in order to defend by violence the faith threatened by the errors which they spread and by their arguments in controversy, even by their sole existence. He did not see that the very loftiness of the religious motive which inspired the crusade,—to deliver the Holy Places from the hands of the Mohammedans,—ran the risk, if one was not very careful, of effacing the sole reason (to reply by violence to one who has used it first) by which a war can be morally justified.

In actual fact this moral consideration was immediately forgotten, and the idea of the crusade confused with that of the holy war. Anxiety about the just war was not the affair of the Barons. They thought only of conquering the Holy Places in order to cause them to pass into the power of the Christians, and of gaining their salvation by triumphing over the infidels and by shedding blood for God. When Humbert of Romans defended the crusade, it was the idea of the holy war in its naked extravagance which he exalted. The Mohammedan nation was *summa culpabilis*. War against it was commanded *by divine authority*. Its combatants were the army of God, and the sword of the Church[12]....

4. The crusade of St. Louis was the last crusade properly so called. But from the eleventh to the sixteenth century the wars of the Spaniards against the Moors were a long crusade. And there were many other "crusades," in France against the Albigenses, in Bohemia against the Hussites,—one could extend the list. All of them conveyed the idea of the holy war. This idea played a role of psychological ferment—on the two sides—in the wars of religion of the sixteenth century. At the beginning of the present century it reappeared openly in the Spanish Civil War;[13] "blessed be the cannons," a bishop said then,[14] "if in the breaches which they open the Gospel flourishes." Under attenuated forms it had continued during a half dozen centuries to make its way in the subconscious of history;—without speaking of the secret stimulation which it had exercised in the choice of certain means of force and of constraint with a view to vanquishing the enemy, the unorthodox one.

The last crusade properly so called was the least stained. It was the pure idea of the crusade which inhabited the mind and the heart of St. Louis, and this great king (the sole great king in the history of France) conducted his crusade with pure hands. Did he not have however to accept a final purification? He died of the plague off Tunis (25th of August, 1270).

However fruitful in results *per accidens* they may have been for the West and for its culture the Crusades, as regards their essential aim, were a total failure. It does not seem that Providence wished to sanction the holy war and to seem to excuse the sins of the Crusades.

"God wills it!" shouted those who received the cross and

attached it to their clothing. May I be permitted a short digression on this.

The will of God is inscrutable. The sole events which we know to be purely willed by Him are the miracles which He performs Himself, and the actions accomplished by Jesus and by Mary. In good theology it is necessary to make, it seems to me, a distinction between the *pure will* of God and, I do not say the mere permission given (which concerns only evil), but what I shall call conjointly His *will-permission,* will which "countersigns" or marks "good for the event" that in which the free will of man, and that of the devil, have also their part. For its divine purposes, then, the will of God says *yes* to what is going to *happen* in history. This is why Léon Bloy said: "All that which happens is adorable." But that which happens on earth is very often frightful.

In Heaven there is no will-permission; it is the pure will of God which alone is done there. To tell the truth, in the third petition of the Lord's Prayer (Thy will "on earth as it is in Heaven,"—as in Heaven!) Jesus, in order that we may be simply Christians, has us ask God for the impossible. Through this petition itself we separate ourselves from the world, bear witness that, like Him, we are not of this world.

God wills it! God willed (willed-permitted) the Crusades as an event of this world, and terribly of this world, not as a thing willed by His pure will. This is a distinction which Humbert of Romans did not make.

II
THE INIQUITOUS LOT
INFLICTED ON JEWS IN CHRISTENDOM

The Teaching of St. Paul
Concerning the Chosen People

1. The mystery of Israel is inseparable from the mystery of the Church.

The Jewish people, and this is its glory, will always be suspect to the nations of the earth: because it is the chosen people, awaited through all the sufferings of history by Him from whom it turned away and to whom it is always beloved, and of whom the gifts are without repentance; the people of Moses and of the prophets, the people from whom Christ is descended, and from whom salvation comes, *salus ex Judaeis est.* There is here enough to excite the jealousy of people, of whatever strand they may be, and even if they are atheists.

One does not condemn a people for a judicial crime committed by a few at a given moment. St. Paul does not reproach the Jews for the putting to death of Jesus, a work, as to the second causes at play in history, of a high priest, of a band of Pharisees and of a Roman procurator of that time. Moreover, and as to the First Cause, Jesus had come in order to die thus, and He willed himself to give His life in order to take away the sin of the world. St. Paul reproaches the Jews for being deaf to the Good News and for refusing the crucified Redeemer.

With regard to Israel he has words both harsh and full of love. What does he say in the Epistle to the Romans? (One will excuse these too long quotations, I believe them necessary.)

9, 1. "My conscience bears me witness in the Holy Spirit that there is great grief and constant pain in my heart. Indeed, I could even wish to be separated from Christ for the sake of my brothers, my kinsmen the Israelites. Theirs were the adoption, the glory, the covenants, the law-giving, the worship, and the promises; theirs were the patriarchs, and from them came the Messiah (I speak of his human origins). Blessed forever be God who is over all!"

9, 18. "God has mercy on whom he wishes, and whom he wishes he makes obdurate. . . ." 30. "How, then, shall we put it? That the Gentiles, who were not seeking justice, attained it—the justice which comes from faith—while Israel, seeking a law from which justice would come, did not arrive at that law? And why did it not? Because justice comes from faith, not from works. They stumbled over the stumbling stone. . . ."

10, 19. "First of all, Moses says, 'I will make you jealous of those who are not even a nation; with a senseless nation I will make you angry.' Then Isaiah says boldly, 'I was found by those who were not seeking me; to those who were not looking for me I revealed myself.' But of Israel he says, 'All day long I stretched out my hands to an unbelieving and contentious people.' "

11, 1. "I ask, then, *has God rejected his people? Of course not!* . . . *God has not rejected his people whom he foreknew.*" [16]

11. "I further ask, does their stumbling mean that they are forever fallen? Not at all! Rather, by their transgression salvation has come to the Gentiles to stir Israel to envy. *But if their transgression and their diminishing have meant riches for the Gentile world, how much more their full number! . . .*" 15. "For if

their 'being set aside' [Tr.] has meant reconciliation for the world, what will their acceptance mean? Nothing less than life from the dead!"

What does this "being set aside" (ἀποβολή) mean, which is not at all a rejection?[17] It is, I think, a 'being set aside' in the history of the redemption. As long as they do not believe in Christ, the Jews are no longer members of the Body dedicated to the work of redemption, and which is henceforth the Church. But that the "true Israel" is henceforth the Church of Christ, and that the ancient Israel placed itself aside from the history of salvation, this does not mean in any way that God would have revoked the vocation and the election of this people, which are "without repentance," and therefore *for always*. In other words, the Church alone is henceforth the people of God, according as these words signify the people actually committed to the redemption of the world. But Israel remains for ever the people of God, according as these words signify that, even unfaithful to its mission, it is ever called and ever chosen, ever "beloved because of the patriarchs."

11, 16. "If the first fruits are consecrated," St. Paul continues, "so too is the whole mass of dough, and if the root is consecrated, so too are the branches. If some of the branches were cut off and you, a branch of the wild olive tree, have been grafted in among the others and have come to share in the rich root of the olive, do not boast against the branches. If you do boast, remember that you do not support the root; the root supports you ...." 23. "And if the Jews do not remain in their unbelief they will be grafted back on, for God is able to do this. If you were cut off from the natural wild olive and, contrary to nature, were grafted into the cultivated olive, so much the more will they who belong to it by nature be grafted into their own olive tree."

25. "Brothers, I do not want you to be ignorant of this mystery lest you be conceited: blindness has come upon part of Israel until the full number of Gentiles enter in, and then all Israel will be saved. ..."

28. "In respect to the Gospel, the Jews are enemies of God for your sake; in respect to the election, they are beloved by him because of the patriarchs. God's gifts and his call are irrevocable."

30. "Just as you were once disobedient to God and now have received mercy through their disobedience, so they have become disobedient—since God wished to show you mercy—that they too may receive mercy. God has imprisoned all in disobedience that he might have mercy on all."[18]

2. St. Paul did not foresee all the horror of the long persecutions which his people was to suffer. It is for the mind a terrifying mystery to think that all of this was permitted by God. Does an old vagabond without title have the right to express an idea on this? I think that in a unique will-permission God enveloped at one and the same time the obstinate fidelity of Israel to the awaiting, to the nonaccomplished, and this abandonment to the rage of men and to that of the demons which were in themselves the fruit of the refusal opposed to the Chosen One by the chosen people, after the death on the Cross: for it is a law of the order of the universe that every tree bears its fruit, and in not willing Christ it is the abandonment of which I have just spoken that Israel willed without knowing it. It is odious to say, but I believe that this is true: it has had that which it willed, this people whom God loves ever because of its fathers, and whom He has never ceased to love, and whom He awaits with what immense desire, and with the tears of whom He has made through the centuries pure jewels in Heaven.

God is not a furious lover Who takes to hating the one whom He loved and who has betrayed Him. It is to blaspheme Him to think that His hate and His malediction have fallen upon Israel and that He has revenged Himself on it like an insulted man.[19] He has respected, as He does always, the order of the universe, He has let the tree of obstinacy bear its fruit. But in loving more than ever Israel persecuted, and in sympathizing with all His love in its sufferings.

Christian Antiquity

3. In the course of the first century it was the Jews who persecuted the Christians.[20] And it was the fierce opposition of the princes of the priests, detesting that which they held to be an impious sect, which decidedly released that expansion of the Gospel to all the Gentiles which God wanted, and which had been prefigured by the Baptism of the Centurion Cornelius.

It is not surprising that the Christians kept an unpleasant memory of these persecutions. From this to becoming themselves persecutors, and to hating the Jewish people, there was a world.

One would err greatly if one took for hate really present in the heart all that which the Fathers of the Church were able to say against the Jews, even those who spoke of them in the most insulting manner. They were oratorical violences, due to the confrontation of two opposite proselytisms, and one knows that there is no more virulent eloquence than that which displays itself in religious quarrels: in actual fact one was in an immense spiritual battle, in which no one spared blows, and of which the stake was the fate of humanity and eternal life.

The Jews, in the first centuries, still enjoyed a great prestige, one admired their knowledge, and one kept mutual attachments, for in the Christian community the proportion of converts from Israel remained the largest. For the Fathers it was a question above all of averting the dangers arising for the faith from this mixture of customs and of beliefs which one calls Judeo-Christianity.[21] If St. John Chrysostom treated the synagogues as brothels,[22] and if St. Jerome, in a phrase unworthy of him (who owed so much to the rabbis), declared that if there was occasion to hate men and to detest a people, the Jewish people in its synagogues of Satan would be for him the object of a choice hatred,[23] I see there only strayings of polemics and verbal rages. They went nevertheless a little too far. Those of the Fathers of the Church who succumbed to them did not suspect that without wishing it they were opening the door to abominable ideas which under another historical and social climate were to invade the common consciousness in the beautiful periods of the Christian Middle Ages.

4. There had been for a long time a Jewish colony at Rome; others in Spain and in the south of Gaul. The Diaspora which followed the ruin of Jerusalem and the destruction of the Temple in the year 70 was more important; a great many Jews passed then through Asia Minor in order to disperse in Europe, toward the East, toward the North, toward the West.

Without forgetting that chronological divisions are always more or less arbitrary, let us say that during a first phase, of about three hundred years (end of the Roman Empire, in other words "Christian antiquity"), the condition of the Jews of Europe differed little from that of their contemporaries. For the Roman law the Jewish religion was *religio licita;* and in 313 the Edict of Milan prescribed religious liberty. Religious controversy was lively on the two sides, but except for the struggle against the Judeo-Christianity conducted by the Fathers and the episcopate in order to preserve the faith of the converts, no grave element of discord in the social domain and the ordinary course of life disturbed the relations between Jews and Christians.

It is true that the conversion of Constantine, about 323,

marked the beginning of a radical change in the situation of the Jews of the Diaspora as in the history of the world. Christianity became a religion of State, and the jurists also were going to employ themselves in defending the Christians against the Jewish attraction.

5. There will come soon the sacral regime in which religious faith did not constitute the body politic, as in the theocratic regimes, but in which it was the highest value recognized in the body politic, and asked (not without sometimes very lively resistances on the side of the princes) to rule and to move from above the social-temporal. In itself, the internal logic of the sacral regime tends to exclude or to subject the dissident. The Jews were therefore destined to become strangers on both religious and civil grounds, *alienigenae* whose presence was an affair of tolerance, not of right,[24] and who could enjoy only privileges graciously granted, and always revocable.

But the internal logic of a regime is slow to unfold, and the morals of people slower still to improve if they were bad or to deteriorate if they were good. There were needed the miseries of the whole of the High Middle Ages in order for the frustrations caused by them and the furious need of a scapegoat to give birth, by means of the rhetoric of the lower clergy, to a sordid religious hate in a Christian people composed henceforth almost entirely of the descendants of baptized pagans still half barbarian.

The High Middle Ages

One can start, approximately, from the second half of the fifth century (St. Augustine, who died in 430, is as it were the hinge), the second phase of the history of the Jewish Diaspora in Europe: a phase which lasted until the time of the first crusade, in other words, which occupied the whole of the High Middle Ages.

After the invasion of the barbarians the sacral regime which characterizes the Middle Ages is going to install itself. The Jews, already numerous in Spain, in Italy and in Gaul, and spreading little by little in Europe, will have from that time onwards the status of strangers (easily suspect at the same stroke to the common people) in a Christendom which expands and becomes stronger in the midst of tempests. During the period of which I speak they were often molested more or less gravely by Christian proselytism, while the abominable idea indicating in the Jew as such the enemy of Christ and the accursed one of God made little by little its tenebrous way in the uncultivated mass. But it is only at the beginning of the eleventh century that hatred and persecution will begin to break loose against them. Already however Baptism imposed by constraint or the threat of banishment was to become, especially in Spain, a frequent practice, in spite of the condemnation of forced Baptism by St. Gregory the Great[25] and Isidore of Seville. Nevertheless in this second phase of their history the Jews knew long respites,[26] and were not, in spite of the jurists, the object of a systematic discrimination in social relations. One had not entirely forgotten that they were the elder race.

It is very remarkable that then an authentically human convivium remained, in spite of all, normal between Jews and Christians. As Bernhard Blumenkranz has brought to light,[27] the relations of good neighbourliness were "greatly facilitated by the fact that, outside of religion, no important factor differentiated the Jews from the non-Jews: neither the language spoken, nor the professions exercised, nor the places of habitation. In a positive manner, good neighbourliness manifested itself by the armed service rendered in common, by familiar contacts in daily life, by frequent intellectual exchanges."[28] The missionary competition continues however, ardent on the two sides,[29] as also the religious polemics, accompanied "by intellectual exchanges pursued in a disinterested and gratuitous manner, instigated by the sole thirst to know," and attesting in a brilliant manner "the intellectual vitality of the High Middle Ages."[30]

The Jews are hawkers, merchants (who know the route to the Orient, and whom the ecclesiastical dignitaries appreciate very much), doctors, sailors, artisans,—and agriculturists (until the end of the tenth century they were able to acquire lands). In spite of the edict of Theodosius II (438) and the interdictions of the Councils one sees them often public functionaries (a right which will be later absolutely withdrawn from them). There are not yet any ghettos.[31]

The canonists, it is true, do not relax in their hostility, but their edicts remain long a dead letter. It was they however who won the game, the juridical apparatus codifying the legal disqualification of the Jews was ready when the brutal rupture in the relations between Jews and Christians occurs at the time of the Crusades.

The Last Centuries of the Middle Ages
Religious Hatred of the Jewish People Develops
and It Will Be a Good While before It Will Pass

6. One enters then into the third phase, a phase of calamity, of the history of the medieval Diaspora now widespread in the whole of Europe. The populace is ready for all the excesses against the scapegoat. It is over the blood of the people of Jesus that the Crusades make their way toward the Holy Land.

In the armies of the Crusades the Jews could clearly not take part; it is the end of armed service rendered in common, and from that moment onwards the Jews will be suspected of connivance with the enemy. The rights which they enjoyed are going to be abolished one after another (until there comes the expulsion from England in 1290, from France in 1306[32] and in 1394, from Spain in 1492).

The eleventh century inaugurated a long period in which what one is going to see is the regime of the ghetto,[33] and the discriminatory sign[34] —the small wheel in France, the sugar-loaf hat in Germany;—"it is the exclusion from a long series of trades, it is the accusations of violation of the Host, of ritual murder, of poisoning of wells, and the horrible theory of bloody persecutions which accompany these accusations, it is the skilfully organized religious discussions with the verdict in favor of the Christian prepared in advance, it is the autos-da-fé of the Talmud, it is the Jews slaves of the princes and lords, mere merchandise without will or right of their own, whom one exchanges at the best rate, whom one sells to the highest bidder, it is the usurers[35] impelled toward this activity by an economy which closes to them all other possibilities, reviled and execrated for this activity by the entirety of decent people. It will be a species of men definitively banished from society, exploiting for the greatest profit of the prince, exploited according to the good pleasure of the prince, money of exchange between the great, easy prey abandoned to the vile instincts of excited crowds, hypersensitized by a pious and sanguinary imagery, by an edifying and terrifying literature."[36] At the time of the Black Plague (1348-1350), it is they who will be held responsible for the scourge, one will massacre them everywhere.

Certain significant traits show the sentiments which animated the majority of the Christian people. Let us note first the abstention from the genuflection in the prayer *Pro Judaeis,* so beautiful in itself, of Good Friday.[37] For having been only local, other customs are nevertheless singularly revealing: at Béziers, for example, that one which was abolished only in 1160 (by the bishop Guillaume), and which authorized the Christians to stone the houses of the Jews from the first hour of the Saturday before Palm Sunday until the last hour of the Saturday after Easter; or elsewhere that one (wholly lay, and which seems to have been quite widespread) of the corporal toll required for Jews as for animals: "Upon each ox and pig, and upon each Jew, a sou"; [38] and again that one (quite late, I believe) of the homage given, the first Saturday of the carnival,—and what a wild carnival!—by the Jews of Rome to a civil dignitary who placed his foot on the nape of the neck of the chief rabbi, before he rises again at the word: "Go"; and again that one of colaphisation, which established itself at Toulouse at the beginning of the eleventh century, and which was the deed of the clergy: every year, the vigil of Easter, a Jew (he was at first the president of the Jewish community) was to be publicly slapped in the face by a Christian (who was at first the Count of Toulouse). Later the slap in the face was to become a more gentle but no less significant liturgical slap, on the condition of tax paid by the Jewish community to the venerable as much as shrewd chapter.

But what it is important above all to point out is the role of the imagery presented to the faithful during the readings in Church; (these images were traced on the back side of the scroll which the priest used, so that, while he read, the people could contemplate them). Let us not forget that, as Father Jean-Julien de Santo Tomas notes,[39] the religious Middle Ages was a civilization *of the image.*

"It is only through a slow evolution and one in correlation with the political and religious events of Christendom that the portrait of the Jew became stereotyped. Carolingian and Ottonian art possesses no iconographic attribute in order to distinguish the Jew from the Christian, so that it accompanied the image with a legend destined to identify the personages. After 1096, the date of the first crusade, therefore of an enterprise of Christendom from which the Jew found himself excluded, appear the distinctive signs";[40] either vestimentary (small wheel or sugar-loaf hat), or caricatural. And what do the miniatures studied by Blumenkranz show us? Roman soldiers (even Pilate himself) wearing the sugar-loaf hat when they scourge Christ or ridicule Him or nail Him to the Cross,—it is necessary that the Jew alone be guilty. The Jew "holds the role of the enemy of the Church, of the wicked person, of the profligate, of the heretic always in first place in the mouth of the infernal monster."[41] And how would the hatred of people against him not have blazed up, when these Jews whom they saw flagellate Jesus, nail His hands, and insult Him on the Cross, were "exactly dressed as the contemporary hawker, the contemporary shopkeeper, and the contemporary pawnbroker?"[42] The Passion of Christ was presented to the eyes of the spectators "as a crime eternally repeated in which one's Jewish neighbor finds himself always participating."[43] "The Gospel of love became, with the intense force of the image, a school of scorn and of hatred."[44]

7. What does this mean, if not that in the third phase, which occupies us now, hatred of the Jewish people decidedly took its seat in the heart of Christians? Hatred essentially religious (even when it addresses itself to the usurer execrated for other reasons,—he like the others is an accursed one who killed Jesus); "Christian" hatred which will be a long time ending. Let us recall the atrocious words of Bossuet, in 1652, in the cathedral of Metz: "He has dispersed them over the whole earth. For what reason? Just as the magistrates, after having executed some malefactors on the wheel, order that one will expose in several places, on the main roads, their quartered members, in order to instill fright in other scoundrels; this comparison horrifies you: the fact remains that God has acted approximately in the same way . . . He has scattered them here and there amidst the world, bearing on all sides imprinted in them the mark of His vengeance; monstrous people, which has neither hearth nor place . . . , now the laughing stock and the hate of everybody, miserable without being pitied by anyone; become the butt of the most reasonable. . . . And it is not for any other reason that God preserves the Jews; it is *in order to have the example of his vengeance last.*" If Bossuet was able to utter these words with a tranquil impudence, it is because he based himself upon a solid tradition, which dated back to the second half of the Middle Ages.

Essentially religious, the hatred of which I am speaking had a hearth at the bottom of souls, a sort of convergent mirror which nourished it with its fires; I mean the idea of the *deicide-people,*—the adjective "deicide" being an integral part of the substantive, and designating a mark of malediction imprinted for ever and become consubstantial: deicide people yesterday, today, tomorrow; it has deicide in its skin, it is deicide just as it is Jewish.

One finds the words "parricide"[45] and "deicide"[46] applied to the Jews in some Fathers of the Church, who had however, as I have noted above, no real hatred in their hearts. It was a verbal aggression—as extremist as it was eloquent—due to the vehemence of the missionary polemics,—that which I call a 'word-idea' or a 'paper-idea.' But finally the formula was virtually there, although deprived of the "consubstantial" sense which I have just indicated. It had to make a very long subterranean journey, in the lowest strata of the soul and through the horrors of history in order to end after five or six centuries in the 'vampire-idea'[47] which I have just mentioned and which carried in it homicide and hatred.

The heart and the mind are in interdependence. It needed that starting from the eleventh century the idea of the people for ever deicide poison even to the depths of the animal unconscious the mind of the Christian people, for its heart to be poisoned by hatred of the Jewish people. The idea of the 'deicide-people' and the religious hatred of the Jewish people are linked like flesh and bones.[48]

The Popes Condemned the Violence and Did Their Best in Order to Protect the Jews

8. The hatred of the Jewish people in the Middle Ages was the deed of the populace and of many in the bourgeoisie and in the nobility, and of many in the lower clergy. The high personnel of the Church, the Papacy above all, remained free from it.

The conduct of the Holy See with regard to the Jews has varied with the epochs. The Popes, even the ones most severe in their legislation, never knew this hatred. They knew how to read St. Paul without making him say the contrary of what he wrote.

I have just alluded to legislation. The jurists felt themselves all the more at ease in order to unfold their rigors since between the formulation of the latter and their passage into acts they knew well that the margin was great. Under Innocent III (1198-1216), later under Paul IV (1555-1559), Pius V (1566-1572), Clement VIII (1592-1605), the legal prescriptions destined to preserve the Christians from Jewish contamination became as vexatious as they were meticulous. One rubs one's eyes when one reads today an edict of the Congregation of the Inquisition on this subject[49] bearing the date of the 15th of September, 1751,—thirty eight years before the Declaration of the Rights of Man (finally! but it

was the goddess Reason which the latter invoked, although the
distant sources of it were evangelical).[50] The rigors of which I
speak had however nothing to do with the hatred of the Jews;
they depended on the principle (which one did not use only
against the Jews, and with which we shall concern ourselves later)
that legal constraint must be employed in order to protect the
faith.

Let us leave now the jurists, and let us turn toward existential
reality and toward the testimonies brought by life. In point of
fact, it was in the papal States that the Jews were the least
unhappy (one knows enough the case of the "Jews of Avignon"),
and this is true even of the epochs in which they were pestered in
them by legal vexations, from many of which they had enough
ingenuity to escape (it was necessary for them all the same, in the
papal States, to attend series of imposed sermons). During the
whole of the Middle Ages and the darkest periods of the latter, [51]
it was the Popes who were their great protectors and defenders.
While trying to shackle their proselytism, Gregory the Great (590-
604) condemned the violences against them, prescribed respect for
their worship and for the liberty of their consciences, requested
for them equity and kindness. Were they not the living witnesses
of the history of salvation, and of the purposes of God concerning
humanity? The Bull of Calixtus II (1120) condemning the violences against the Jews and their Baptism under constraint was
confirmed at least twenty-two times up to the middle of the
eighteenth century. The severe Innocent III (1198-1216) defended
them against iniquitous tormentings; at the time of the Black
Plague Clement VI (1342-1352) exerted (in vain) the greatest
efforts in order to protect them, and offered shelter in pontifical
territory to those who were able to escape the general massacre.
Before the rigors of the time of the Counter-Reformation Jules II
(1503-1513) and Leo X (1513-1521) showed them confidence and
benevolence, Clement VII (1523-1534) and Paul III (1534-1549)
overwhelmed them with favors.

Many bishops also were their friends; at their obsequies the
Jews lamented. If others had without doubt the same sentiments
as Bossuet, the episcopal body as a whole kept itself free from
religious hatred of the Jewish people. This hatred was intense in
Luther. The Renaissance marked the beginning of its disappearance. But Voltaire showed that the anti-Judaic rage can very well
not be of the religious order and that it is easy to secularize hate.
On the side of the Church, it was toward the recognition by

Christians of the dignity of Israel and of the bonds of friendship which must be established between them and it that the wind began to blow. Before the interruption of the first Council of the Vatican almost all the Fathers of the Council had signed the *Postulatum pro Hebraeis* presented by the two Lémann brothers, and one knows the remark of Pius IX to these latter: *Vos estis filii Abrahae, et ego.*

Finally the Second Council of the Vatican

Today we are at last completely delivered from the idea of the 'deicide-people' and from the "Christian" hatred of the Jewish people. The religious anti-Semitism which long soiled Christendom has decidedly disappeared. And this is, as also for the idea of the holy war, one of the benefits of the second Council of the Vatican. The person of the Church, one, holy, catholic, and apostolic, has solemnly made her voice heard, too long suffocated by the misfortunes and the crimes of history.

"The Church of Christ acknowledges that, according to the mystery of God's saving design, the beginnings of her faith and her election are already found among the patriarchs, Moses, and the prophets. She professes that all who believe in Christ, Abraham's sons according to faith (cf. Gal. 3:7), are included in the same patriarch's call . . . The Church believes that by His cross Christ, our Peace, reconciled Jew and Gentile, making them both one in Himself (cf. Eph. 2:14-16). . . . The Church ever keeps in mind the words of the Apostle about his kinsmen, 'who have the adoption as sons, and the glory and the covenant and the legislation and the worship and the promises; who have the fathers, and from whom is Christ according to the flesh' (Rom. 9:4-5), the son of the Virgin Mary. . . . As Holy Scripture testifies, Jerusalem did not recognize the time of her visitation (cf. Lk. 19:44), nor did the Jews in large number accept the Gospel; indeed, not a few opposed the spreading of it (cf. Rom. 11:28). Nevertheless, according to the Apostle, the Jews still remain most dear to God because of their fathers, for He does not repent of the gifts He makes nor of the calls He issues (cf. Rom. 11:28-29). . . . True, authorities of the Jews and those who followed their lead pressed for the death of Christ (cf. Jn. 19:6); still, what happened in His passion cannot be blamed upon all the Jews then living, without distinction, nor upon the Jews of today. Although the Church is the new people of

God, the Jews should not be presented as repudiated or cursed by God, as if such views followed from the holy Scriptures. . . . The Church repudiates all persecutions against any man. Moreover, mindful of her common patrimony with the Jews, and motivated by the Gospel's spiritual love and by no political considerations, she deplores the hatred, persecutions, and displays of anti-Semitism directed against the Jews at any time and from any source. . . . The Church rejects, as foreign to the mind of Christ, any discrimination against men or harassment of them because of their race, color, condition of life, or religion."[52]

Digression on the State of Israel

9. As to not religious, but racial, anti-Semitism, it is far from having disappeared. It had however, about twenty years before the Council, showed its full capacity with the Hitlerian death-camps. There was needed this monstrous tragedy, and the liquidation of six million Jews, for history to accord finally a chance to the dream of that return into the Promised Land which during long centuries nourished the hope of generations of humiliated ones and of oppressed ones dispersed among the nations. The blood of the Jewish people paid the price of it, let one never forget this.

As I wrote in *Le Mystère d'Israël*,[53] it is a strange paradox to see disputed with the Israelians "the sole territory to which, considering the entire spectacle of human history, it is absolutely, *divinely* certain that a people has incontestably a right: for the people of Israel is the sole people in the world to whom a land, the land of Canaan, was given by the true God, the unique and transcendent God, creator of the universe and of the human race. And what God has given once is given for ever."

In speaking thus I was not making of the State of Israel a State by divine right, as certain ones have claimed.[54] The State of Israel, insofar as State, is only a State like the others. But the return of a portion of the Jewish people and its regroupment in the Holy Land (of which the existence of this State is the sign and the guarantee),—this is the reaccomplishment, under our eyes, of the divine promise which is without repentance. In short, I remembered what was said to Abraham,[55] to Jacob[56] and to Moses, [57] and what Ezechiel announced:[58] not that I regarded the founding of the State of Israel as a kind of preface to the realization of this prophecy (about this I know absolutely nothing, though it is possible); but in order to keep in my mind respect for the ways of God. And I do not doubt that the event, however enigmatic it may be for the Jews as for the Christians, carries in it the mark of the faithful love and of the pity of God toward the people which is ever his. It appears to me, consequently, that once the Jewish people has put its feet again upon the land which God gave to it, no one will be able anymore to wrest it from it; and that to wish the disappearance of the State of Israel is to wish to reject into nothingness this return which finally was accorded to the Jewish people, and which permits it to have a shelter of its own in the world; in other words, it is,—in another manner, but as grave, than that of ordinary anti-Semitism,—to wish that misfortune hound again this people, and that once more it be the victim of an iniquitous agression. "Anti-Israelism"[59] is no better than anti-Semitism.

On the other hand, racial anti-Semitism, I noted above, continues to blind many hearts, even, and above all perhaps, behind the Iron Curtain,—doubtless because of the mysterious (therefore disquieting) past which the Jew carries in him, and also because he is in general more intelligent than the *goyim,* therefore more formidable for people who see in the intelligence only an instrument of power and of domination.

And with the racial anti-Semitism thus subsisting one can fear, as I have just indicated, lest there mingle itself henceforth (or substitute itself for it, even in Christians who do not believe themselves anti-Semites) a well-conditioned political anti-Israelism. The Jewish people has not finished suffering.

The Ancient and the New People of God

1. This would be the moment to turn our eyes toward the most troubling enigma of history, I mean the relation between the ancient people of God pursuing its life in its descendants and the new people of God which is the Church.

The first point to be brought to light is that God is faithful; His gifts and His love are without repentance. He Who loves all men, He loves the Church with a love of predilection. He has not ceased for all that to love the Jewish people with a love of predilection.

Is it that His love for the Church and His love for the Jewish people are two different loves? No, it is the same and unique love, because in the eternal, divine vision Israel and the Church are but a same and unique people of God, as it will appear in the last moments of human history, the day,—not less resplendent than "a resurrection from the dead,"[60] —when the branches of Israel, "the natural branches," will be again grafted onto "their own olive tree." It is onto this old olive tree, of which the "root is holy," that we others, branches of the wild olive tree, have been grafted. The root is holy, and it is Jewish. It is it which supports the new people of God, together with all the Gentiles who compose it. And have not the marvellously divine beginnings of the unity which will be finally consummated between Israel and the new people of God already illuminated the earth and Heaven? Is not He Whom we adore, the sole Holy One, the sole Lord, the sole Almighty, is not Jesus Christ a Jew "par excellence by nature," as Léon Bloy said? Is not the blessed one amongst all women, the Immaculate One, the Queen of Heaven, a Jew? Were not all the apostles and the majority of the first martyrs Jews? Is it not a Jewish flesh and a Jewish blood which we eat and drink each time that we receive Holy Communion? "Spiritually, we are Semites," Pius XI said.

It is not however that I am forgetting the second point: this same and unique love of God for His new people and for His ancient people in its descendants of today manifests itself under very different forms, because the response which is made to it on the earth is itself very different, and because on the one side it is a love filled to overflowing, on the other a wounded love. God is patient, He does not charge the Jewish people with a crime for that which the Christians call its obstinacy, and which the Jews call their fidelity,—it is not their fault that the bandage was formerly put over their eyes by their high priests, and reinforced again by all the persecutions which they have suffered from Christians. But God has ever before His eyes that which is at the origin of their obstinate waiting for the Messiah already come: His love betrayed and insulted by the house of Israel, when He sent His Son and when Jerusalem did not know the time of her visitation. Who would venture to say that in Him love gave way to the thirst for vengeance and for reprobation? This would be blasphemy. *God has not rejected his people.*[61] *They are beloved by him because of the patriarchs.*[62] But it is not to the house of Israel, it is to the Church, that He gives for soul the pleroma of all graces. And all the faithful of the Synagogue who are individually saved,—it is insofar as they are invisibly a part of the Church,

whatever help their hearts may have been able to receive from
their own religious family.

And wounded love has formidable ways of not making itself
importunate. It is enough for it for this to not intervene, and to
wait—it too. To be loved by God can mean to have to sweat blood.
It is the love of God for the Jewish people which abandoned it
during centuries to the abominable treatments of the Gentiles,—we
are the blindest of the blind if we do not understand this. And this
love is always there, the Jews can count upon it. He watches
always over His people, He weeps for it and with it, He will pull it
always from the worst steps. He will strengthen it always. To tell
the truth this people carries in its own manner the Cross of Jesus,
by enduring in its unconquered soul all the affliction of the world
and bending its shoulders under all the burdens, *in order to
survive;* just as the Church carries it in her own manner, in the
light and the tears of the communion of saints, *in order to redeem
the world* with Jesus and through His blood.

2. And if in spite of the different forms under which it
manifests itself the love of God for His new people and for the
ancient one in its descendants of today is, as I have said, a single
and unique love because in the eternal divine vision the two
constitute but a single and same people of God, the fact remains
that fallen into human history the things which constitute but one
in the divine vision and in the divine love are delivered over to the
dialectic from below, with the bloody oppositions which are
proper to it and its miserable limping progress.

The God of Abraham, of Moses and of David was the God of
all the earth, and it was little by little that the new-born Church
detached herself from the Temple and from the obligations which
it imposed. It was necessary indeed however that the Gentiles be
able to enter freely, without being subject to the specifically
Jewish practices. St. Paul, with the help of Peter, played a decisive
role in this immense adventure. Thus the conflict between the
ancient and the new people of God, opened by the condemnation
of Jesus, very quickly expanded. The Synagogue severely persecuted the first Christians. In the patristic age, we have noted
above, it pursues, not having renounced the universalist idea, an
ardent prosyletism; one is in full controversial battle: the Synagogue against the Fathers, the Fathers against the Synagogue. But
this was still only controversy. As we have also noted, it was much
later, in the second half of the Middle Ages, and by reason above

all of the degrading social status imposed upon the Jews, that
Christian hatred and *Christian* contempt toward the Jewish people
blazed up. Then came racial anti-Semitism. The nineteenth century saw the dialectical conflict which occupies us here assume its
sharpest form. On the one hand, as if history offered then in the
order of the spirit a revenge to the oppressed, the Jewish intelligence,—what great names one could cite!,—shone in an extraordinary manner upon a civilization formerly Christian which from
disavowal to disavowal was entering into full decomposition. On
the other hand history was preparing the Naxi extermination
camps.

3. And then the hour arrived when the blind dialectical oppositions finally relaxed a little, in order to let pass a ray of light. It
seems to me very significant that these two events of such great
bearing,—on the Jewish side the return of a portion of the people
to the Promised Land, on the Christian side the second Council of
the Vatican,—took place almost at the same time, the first in
1948, the second in 1962-1965. They mark, each in its own
manner, a reorientation of history. What is more important, from
this point of view, than the insistence of the Council upon the
friendship to be developed and to be consolidated between Jews
and Christians?

I am not a charismatic author; I can just say what my poor
philosopher eyes believe they perceive in the entanglements of
history. It seems to me that in order to be authentic the friendship
in question prerequires of the two sides a purification of thought:
it is necessary that Christians understand truly that God has not
rejected, but has always continued to love the children of Israel,
and that it is *His love* which has permitted this long passion; and it
is necessary that the Jews understand truly that it is not the will
for power, but the *charity of Christ,* which animates the effort of
the Church toward men. It seems to me also that if this friendship
becomes stronger, it will be the presage of great things, and first of
a common action in order to bring help to a world which is in
jeopardy but in all the corners of which there are souls who are
dying of thirst. The *cross of survival* carried by the Jewish people
and the *cross of redemption* carried by the Church are very far still
from being ready to join each other. But later, much later without
doubt, when there will come the historical catastrophe from which
will arise for a time a renewed human universe, that day, which
will be as a prelude to the resurrection of the dead, the cross of

survival (for it will be the old olive tree of Israel which will flower again in its entirety, πᾶς Ἰσραὴλ σωθήσεται) and the cross of redemption (for it is the new people of God which will assume everything in the light of Christ) will recognize themselves finally and will constitute but a single cross, in order to offer salvation to the men of all the earth,—and perhaps in order that, before the end of time, the earth itself may pass through a moment in which it will be given to it to know the peace which the Lamb of God gives. The dialectics of history would have then reconciled all its oppositions, and opened onto the unity which the Father Who is in Heaven had in view from all eternity.

XIII

A Look at History

(Continuation)

III

WHAT TO THINK OF THE INQUISITION?

The Medieval Inquisition

1. Let us remark from the outset that the establishment of the Inquisition depends on the complex conjunction between spiritual and temporal characteristic of the sacral regime[1] of the Christian Middle Ages. At its first origin there was, in actual fact, the royal power more than the Papacy. It arose as a phenomenon of Christendom as much as a phenomenon of Church. And it is only at the end of the curve that it reabsorbed itself into the sphere of the ministerial "services" or ministerial organs brought into play by the spiritual power for its sole proper ends.

In short, in the drama of the Inquisition one has to deal with four personages: the Faith of the Church (which was not only faith of the Church, but also the most intimate and most exalted principle of the unity of the temporal city); Heresy (which was not only error against the faith, but also profound principle of dissociation from the temporal city); the personnel of the Church, above all the Papacy; and the personnel of the temporal City,

176

above all the Kings or the Emperor, with their political solicitudes, their covetousnesses and their ambitions. And in the drama in question it was the Kings who at the outset held the first role; Robert the Pious is the first to have lit in France the funeral-pile against the heretics.

It was the kings of France who, from this eleventh century in which the idea of the holy war came to the front, took the initiative of the struggle against the Catharians. To tell the truth, they pursued a double end: to protect the sacral body politic against a heresy of Manichaean inspiration particularly dangerous for it; and at the same stroke to settle their account with the velleities of independence of the people of dialects spoken south of the Loire, whose culture rivalled that of the North,—they perfectly succeeded moreover in annihilating this delicate and refined culture.

Let us not forget that in the sacral regime the leaders of the temporal were masters in their own house for the affairs of the earth, but, to the extent that the latter were also the affairs of Christianity, subordinated to the supreme leader of the spiritual, and, on occasion, his instruments; whereas, on the other hand, the spiritual power was the supreme guarantor of the temporal power and of the temporal city ruled by it, so that it had itself a duty of high protection with regard to the temporal, without hesitating to "get its feet wet," if I may say, to this end. There were there the elements of an internal dialectics pregnant with conflicts, sometimes latent, sometimes clamorous, between the two powers. The very Christian kings of France did not fail, in the affair with the Catharians, to recall to the spiritual power its duties toward the body politic such as they understood them themselves, and in a manner which implied, at bottom, a kind of blackmail: either the Pope would assume the head of a pursuit of the heresy which was ravaging the South of France (not without spreading also into the North and even into Flanders), or it was the bishops of the kingdom and the royal magistrates who would undertake to defend the Catholic faith in spite of the Pope, and to lead the holy war against the enemy of the interior. The Popes at first tried to resist, feeling indeed that the mission of the Church is to convert souls rather than to burn bodies. Then they quickly yielded to the blackmail, and quickly judged themselves that the strong method was the good one, their great care becoming then to keep between their hands the chief direction of the enterprise. It was thus that the mediaeval Inquisition came into being.

2. It was a misfortune for the Church. At the same time, while serving the interests of the Crown in France, it protected Christendom from the menaces of a highly seductive and all the more pernicious heresy. But at what a price (and with what consequences for the future) the operation was conducted!

In the eleventh century and in the first half of the twelfth, those had not been lacking, among the saints and among the high ecclesiastical authorities, in whose eyes it was solely by preaching and by sanctions of the spiritual order that the struggle against heresy was to be conducted. *Capiantur non armis, sed argumentis,* St. Bernard said.[2] And even after the second Council of Lateran (1139), Alexander III declared still in 1162: "It is better to absolve guilty persons than to attack by an excessive severity the life of innocents.... Indulgence suits Churchmen better than harshness."[3]

The same Pope, however, assailed by difficulties, and yielding to the pressures of Louis VII the Younger, already the following year appealed to the means of force by prescribing the princes to condemn the Catharians to prison and to confiscation. It was the first step.

Some twenty years later, in 1184, the Council of Verona, presided over by Pope Lucius III, and which the Emperor Frederick Barbarossa attended, was to mark the real beginnings of the Inquisition, whose status was decidedly established in France, in 1232-1235, by the Bulls of Gregory IX.[4] Alexander III had opened the door to the use of temporal punishments. This was now becoming institutional. And once the juridical machine was established, certain ones, perhaps a great many of those who, aside from madmen like a Robert le Bougre or a Conrad of Marbourg, would be assigned to make it function, were going to be men attached in their inner life to the evangelical precepts, who would serve it in all innocent candor. The machine itself was not evangelical.

3. I am well aware that there is associated with the word Inquisition a whole popular imagery in which (with regard especially to the juridical precautions,[5] protecting somewhat[6] the accused, to be observed in the trials) historical exactitude is neglected for the benefit of horror, and in which the old anticlerical zeal has full sway. This does not prevent however things from being that which they are.

The proper domain of the Church is the interiority of souls in their relationship with God,—in which what counts essentially is that they open themselves freely to divine truth and to the divine gifts. It is here that the common good of the Church resides. If there is needed surgical measures cutting off from the Church those of her members whose errors threaten this common good, there is excommunication. But the means which in themselves are proper to Caesar, the means of material force and of physical constraint, are means foreign, unadapted, disproportionate in themselves to the *primary* end to be pursued with regard to those stray ones who are members of the Church: namely, their cure. With regard to such an end they have in themselves no efficacy, except through the intervention of a grace of exception.

From the moment that an institution created by the personnel of the Church caused the cudgel, the dungeon, the rack and the funeral-pile to pass into the service of the spiritual, one was caught in a fatal mesh, in which violence increased endlessly: one seized heretics in order to chastise them in their bodies or in their earthly goods; then they feigned orthodoxy; then one *sought* them, using all means in order to scrutinize their conscience and to unmask their thought; then obstinacy hardened in their hearts, together with hatred of all that which those who pursued them represented; then one pursued them and one struck them still more harshly; then they became for those of their sect martyrs whose example radiated. . . .

Short of going as far as extermination (that which happened with the Catharians and the Albigenses), the Inquisition did not succeed in really stopping any heresy; because the mind, even when it strays most gravely, is always stronger than force.

4. I have said that the Inquisition was a misfortune for the Church. I did not say that it was evil in its primary intention and in its end. The primary intention (to defend the faith) was good; and the end (to extirpate heresy) was good. It is necessary indeed however that in establishing the Inquisition a certain mistake, a certain error of practical judgment gravely culpable in itself, must have been committed. There is here a point which it is important to elucidate, while trying to be faithful to objective truth without for all that being unjust toward the human subject.

In the famous Bull *Unam Sanctam*, Boniface VIII declares that the Church has "the two swords." What are these two swords possessed by the Church? According to the free interpretation which I permit myself to propose, let us not say that it is the spiritual sword and the temporal sword; let us say that in the Church the first sword is the *teaching* authority, the authority of the Word, which says: "this is a truth revealed by God," consequently my faith adheres to it, and: "God forbids one to do this," consequently I refrain from doing it, or I go to Confession if I do it.[7] And let us say that the second sword is the *constraining* or *coercive* authority,[8] whether it uses spiritual sanctions which belong properly to the kingdom of God (and which can be either purely spiritual—spiritual as to their immediate end and spiritual intrinsically or in themselves—like excommunication, or spiritual as to their immediate end but in themselves and intrinsically temporal),[9] or whether even, as is the case in every sacral regime, it uses also temporal sanctions which belong properly to the terrestrial political body and to the civil power, the spiritual power being then the supreme guarantor and protector of these latter, and being able to require their service in the name of spiritual ends and values, which, in such a regime, are themselves integrated in the common good of the terrestrial city.

Let us turn now toward the Gospel, and let us ask the words of the Lord Himself to guide us.

We read in St. Luke (22, 38): "They said, 'Lord, here are two swords!' *He answered, 'Enough.'*" Yes, therefore: the Church has the two swords.

But it is the second sword, that of constraint, which Simon Peter drew from the sheath, when at the moment of the arrest of Jesus he cut off the right ear of the High Priest's servant.[10] And what does Jesus say to him? *"Put back your sword where it belongs. Those who use the sword are sooner or later destroyed by it."*[11]

The spiritual power possesses the two swords. But when it uses the second,—and above all when, as in the Middle Ages, it uses it while having recourse to the temporal means of force,—it must put it back in the sheath without delay. It is a sword which it is necessary to use only *occasionally*, and as little, and as moderately as possible (to cut off an ear,—it is the least that one can do, is it not, in wielding a sword).

Thus in the primary intention of the Inquisition (to defend the faith) and in the end (to extirpate heresy) there was no mistake. But in drawing the sword *so as not to be able to put it back* there was a mistake, an error,—without doubt entailed almost inevitably by the sacral regime and the mentality of the time,—but in itself injurious to God and terribly grave. The mistake, the ill-omened error of practical judgment committed by the Popes of the twelfth and of the thirteenth centuries,[12] was to erect into permanent ministerial service or organ of the spiritual power, in short into *institution,* constituted in order to last, and of capital importance, the use of force and of the means of force in spiritual matters, and a confidence in these means which forgot of what spirit is the Church and of what spirit are her servants. And, thereby, they put for several centuries the personnel of the Church on a path which was not the right one.

As I indicated above, such an institution placed in the first rank a prophylactic action which, by the very means which it employed, destroyed the normal conditions required in order to attain the primary end pursued by the Church: the cure of heretics, and also the conversion of non-Christians. It was itself incapable of attaining really its own end, except by mass expulsion (which was never sure), or by extermination thanks to some crusade (which could only be rare). And while striving to be just (there were canonists for this), it owed it to itself to be implacable: failing thereby in an absolutely primary exigency which corresponds to the expectation of men and proceeds from the will of Christ with regard to his servants: namely, that in the manner in which the personnel of the Church acts, and in that even in which the judiciary and administrative wheels which it employs function, there appear always that divine charity and that fraternal love which are the very life of the Church. *In itself,* the Inquisition was an evil staining human history and a great insult to God.

That is what, considering things in a purely objective manner, and according to what they are in themselves, I reply to the question: what to think of the Inquisition?

But considering now things from the side of the human subject, and of the concrete conditions in which he finds himself, I think that it would be absurd and pharisaical to regard as morally culpable the Popes of the twelfth and of the thirteenth centuries for having done what they did. I am persuaded that in doing what they did their conscience was pure. The stupid mistake constituted by the institutionalization of the temporal means of force, and the reasons for which it was a mistake, *they did not see them.* First, because in order to see this as we see it today, the historical experience which has instructed us was lacking in the Middle Ages; in other words because they were men of their time. The Popes are of their time, as to the ideas commonly received and in which they have trusted without examining them. In the eyes of the men of the Middle Ages, nothing was more natural than the use of force.

And then because they found themselves in a tragic situation: at one and the same time in struggle with the kings and the Emperors who were besieging the independence of the Church, in struggle against the internal troubles which ensued in the latter, and in struggle against the heresy which threatened Christendom. All that which they saw was that the primary intention of the Inquisition was good, and that its end was good. The rest did not count. The affair was for them an affair of public safety; and one knows that to take measures of public safety entails always a certain blindness, which does not necessarily sully the conscience of the one who takes them.

5. All that which I have just said about the Popes of the twelfth and of the thirteenth centuries, both as to the mistake or error of practical judgment which objectively speaking they committed in instituting the Inquisition, and as to the innocence with which, considering the human subject, they committed this mistake, it is clear that it is necessary to say it also of the diverse Councils which in the course of the same centuries likewise prescribed the institution.

These Councils, even if ecumenical like those of Lateran, did not cause us to hear in this the infallible voice of the Church of the earth and of Heaven, did not give us a teaching—valid for all times—in matter of faith or of morals, as they did in some others of their decrees. It was in contingent and particular matter, as to that which was fitting in a given time and in given circumstances, that they produced the decrees in question, as also, for example, those which concerned the situation of servitude of Jews with regard to Christians, or a crusade to be undertaken.[13] The Fathers of these Councils, and the Popes who ratified their decisions, acted then as proper causes, not as instruments of the person of the Church; they could err.

One was obliged to obey them as one is obliged to obey any legitimate authority, even if it errs (except in the case in which conscience would invincibly object, whatever sanctions one would thus expose oneself to, and which it would be necessary to suffer willingly). But with regard to the decrees to which I have just alluded it was not the person herself of the Church whom one obeyed; it was the men—causing then their own voice to be heard, and acting by their own sole initiative—charged by God to govern the Church of the earth; in other words, it was with the personnel—with the highest personnel—of the Church, acting then as proper cause, that one had to deal and it was they whom one obeyed.

6. A last point remains to be discussed. It concerns the manner in which the tribunals of the Inquisition behaved in practice. There are, in this respect, two things in particular which scandalize us and are inadmissible in themselves. I think first of the procedure followed by the Inquisitors in the case in which the sentence declared by them on the enemy of the faith involved the condemnation of the latter to the death penalty, that is to say, to the stake. They took care to note first that the Church prohibits herself from shedding blood; in consequence of which they abandoned the guilty person to the secular arm, which did not prohibit itself from shedding blood and from sending people to the stake. Thus the trick was played; the enemy of the faith was burned; and the theologians acquitted themselves of their double duty of Inquisitors and of Churchmen.

I think in the next place of the use normally made of torture (the rack, the strappado, the fiery torch; later, in Italy and in Spain, the ordeal of the boots and that of water) as means of extracting confessions upon the validity of which one based oneself in order to decide concerning the conduct to be maintained toward the accused himself or toward those whom he denounced.

Here again it is fitting to distinguish between that which things are in themselves or on the side of objective truth, and that which they are on the side of the human subject.

Considering things according to that which they are in themselves, or on the side of objective truth, there is no need to insist upon the moral value of the two procedures in question: they constituted grave faults.

The use of torture in order to extract confessions,—and confessions held to be valid,—was in itself a grave fault against justice.

The abandonment of the guilty person to the secular arm was, in itself, a hypocrisy.[14] For it was the theologians who were the judges, conducted the inquiry, and declared sentence of formal heresy or of sorcery for example. It was therefore they who had full responsibility for the death penalty involved by the sentence; the secular arm was *in reality* only an instrument. One did not fail, moreover, to ask the latter, in a pious formula, to spare the guilty person from death. And if once in a while it happened nevertheless that a prince took seriously this pious formula, he was himself excommunicated. In itself this procedure was besides a grave fault against the Church. For after having recalled that it is unworthy of her to shed blood, it was upon her that in spite of their legal subterfuge the judges of the Inquisition made fall the responsibility of the blood shed, since the Inquisition was a Church tribunal,[15] and inasmuch as one took an act of this tribunal for an act "of the Church" (which is false, moreover, so that the stain launched against her did not at all attain the face of the person of the Church, of the Bride of Christ; they had however launched it). In delivering over a heretic to the secular arm, in order to send him to death, what they did was in itself a betrayal of the spirit of the Church, who does not shed blood, committed by the personnel who wished to serve her.

7. Is it necessary to say after this that considering things on the side of the human subject, the judges of the Inquisition, in committing, in the two cases of which I speak, what in itself constituted a grave fault, were themselves morally culpable and sinned themselves before God? Let us take care here not to commit ourselves a stupidity. There were saints[16] among the Inquisitors. And even those who were not saints,—to suppose that they were all hypocrites and savages would be to fall into an error analogous to theirs.

What it is important to take into consideration here is the total and invincible naiveté of the men of the Middle Ages (a naiveté of which a trace appeared still in the people of the seventeenth century, when they sent unhesitatingly all non-Catholics to Hell); and it is, in particular, the invincible and total ignorance or indifference in which,—however true may have been in other respects their views on the faculties of the soul philosophically analyzed,—they found themselves with regard to the universe of the subjective as such, or of the things which in the intimacy of the subject escape their objective description and belie the representation which one makes for oneself of them according to this sole description. (It is thus, for example, that they imposed on the Jews or on the Mohammedans living in Christian territory to hear regularly sermons on the Christian truths, without seeing that this itself was fit to enrage them against the latter. These Jews and these Mohammedans were *in error:* the Word of truth had to deliver them from it.)

With regard to the abandonment of the guilty person to the

secular arm, it is necessary for us to take into account both the medieval naiveté and the optics proper to the sacral regime. According to this optics (and the belief of the codes of all times in the legitimacy of capital punishment), it was fitting to the secular order, to the body politic in its proper sphere, to shed the blood of heretics, who threatened its common good. The judges of the Inquisition belonged to another sphere, that of the Church, who prohibits herself from shedding blood. Once they had rendered their judgment, and declared: "Such or such a man is a heretic," they had accomplished their task in their proper sphere. The rest did not concern them (and there we have the naiveté, for in actual fact this concerned them eminently, since they were *the judges*); they closed their eyes on the condemnation to death, they ignored it (whereas in reality they did not ignore it and could not ignore it: but they took an abstract line of demarcation,—between declaring someone a heretic and sending him to the stake,—for a wall of real separation). How could the idea that their procedure was a hypocrisy, and that it wronged the Church, have been able to penetrate their mind?

With regard to torture, there was similar naiveté: if a man who knew the truth concerning something refused obstinately to reveal this truth to judges exercising their full rights of investigation, it was because there were in him powerful obstacles: fear of chastisement, or perverse will, attachment to his sect and fear of harming it, to say nothing of the empire of the devil, which prevented him from confessing the truth in question. To the men of law, therefore, to shatter these obstacles! Torture was a particularly energetic, but necessary, medication in order to untie the tongue of the interrogated man and to bring out the truth from his mouth. In the end, while causing the inquiry to progress, it delivered him himself from an otherwise incurable paralysis. How could men who wear such blinkers have been able to see that in torturing this man they did not give only an example of cold cruelty, but did violence to a sacred domain: the dignity and the personality, the interior universe, requiring in itself absolute respect, of a being made in the image of God, and animated even to the slightest fibrils of its body by a soul which is spirit? and that instead of the truth it was most often words confessing anything and consenting to anything in order to make the torment cease that they caused to emerge from his mouth panic-stricken by the suffering?

Our modern civilization is more enlightened on all of this than the Middle Ages, but in all latitudes it does not deprive itself of practicing torture also.[17] In this four kinds of difference distinguish it however from the Middle Ages: today one tortures with bad conscience and while hiding oneself, through the means, according to the countries, either of the State police or of "parallel" police forces and of secret services; today one has at one's disposal much more perfected techniques,—and moral torture [18] shows itself to be as frightfully effective as physical torture; today one knows that extracted confessions sometimes give exact information under the threat of the worst, but also that one can make the tortured person say all that one wishes,—which is very profitable in order to deceive opinion or to deal low blows; today a man who has confessed under torture is a degraded man, whereas in the Middle Ages he was someone whom one had enabled forcibly to do his duty, and who, if after this he converted to the true faith, could aspire to become himself an Inquisitor. . . .

There is finally a fifth difference, and one of great value this time: today a Churchman no longer plays this game.

Have I succeeded (in spite of repugnances tinged with sentimentalism which I confess in my turn) in showing that the people of the Middle Ages and the judges of the Inquisition, when they practiced torture,[19] and when they delivered over the heretic whose blood they did not shed to the secular arm which reduced him to ashes, could do innocently what in itself was a grave fault, and that thus one explains to himself that there were saints among the Inquisitors? The saints also are men of their time, who *do not see* that which the commonly received opinions of their time, and which no one thinks of submitting to examination,[20] prevent them from seeing. It is not pleasant to have to state this; it is true nevertheless.

8. The mediaeval Inquisition lasted four centuries (twelfth to the fifteenth century), which is not much if one considers that the Church will last until the end of the world, but which constitutes just the same a considerable duration. And after the passage of just a little more time it still weighs heavy upon us, because we are beings endowed with memory. And it has been followed by other inquisitorial periods, about which I shall say later a few words. . . . The fact remains that each of us, whatever repugnance he may think of this terrible mediaeval adventure, feels himself obscurely tormented and troubled by the idea that nevertheless God permitted this.

Why did God permit this? To such a question one can certainly reply only by humble stammerings. Let us stammer therefore one more time, since we are thinking heads.

One can say, it seems to me, that if God permitted the Inquisition,—this evil which in itself offended Him gravely, and which was one of the stains of a Christendom by so many other aspects dear to His heart,—it is because it was necessary that at a given moment of history there enter into human consciousness, and down to the depth of our flesh, the sense of the absolute Transcendence—implacable, too high and too divine for any created mind to be able to form for itself an idea of it—of supernatural Faith in its indivisible unity and in its immaculate rigor. It is not here a matter of true propositions merely read in a book; it is the matter of a truth which must burn us to the bones.

Behind the juridical pretences and the tortures of the Inquisition there was a divine mystery infinitely more terrible—and infinitely merciful: that of the exigencies of the Faith which saves in him who has received this gift, exigencies total, unconditioned, absolutely inflexible, of which men had at any cost to acquire the sense, even though God were to let unfold for this a terrible mistake of the personnel of His Church, and a merciless game in which evil and good, fault and innocence shuffled the cards of her ministers as well as of their adversaries. With regard to this mystery of the divine order, the victims of the Inquisition were pale figures and bloodied symbols. I hope that God has received them all in his Heaven. They were sacrificed in order that there be sunk once and for all, with branding iron, into the members of the Church of the earth,—into all those who would come after the apostolic times (they had had the blood of the martyrs) and the high Middle Ages,—a treasure of eternal life: the sense of the absolute Transcendence of theological Faith.

Until the end of time the Church will keep and will cherish this treasure. Let us pity the feebleminded ones who today would like to dissipate it to the four winds.

An epoch in which the flames of the funeral-piles everywhere lit illuminated in the sky the sovereign image of the Faith, founded on the absolute truth and the absolute indivisibility of the Word of God, was certainly greater than that in which in the obscurity of their alcove poor young men who imagine themselves to be Christians pass their flashlight over the Decalogue and the Credo in order to make their choice there, and to declare then, while feeling their pulse: I believe in the Gospel but not in Original

Sin or in Hell, and I doubt very much the resurrection of Jesus, I believe that it is forbidden to me to kill but I do not believe at all that it is forbidden to me to fornicate, etc.

Will such an epoch last a long time? It does not have the naiveté of the Middle Ages, but it has stupidity, which the Middle Ages was far from having. And stupidity is not a good assurance against the accidents of history.

> *Da mihi intellectum . . .*
> *Viam veritatis elegi . . .* [21]
> *Si non credideretis, non permanebitis.* [22]

The Spanish Inquisition

1. It has been said, very justly, that Philip the Fair and Nogaret were in France, in the fourteenth century, the precursors of Torquemada and of Philip II. The Spanish Inquisition began in the following century (in order to last a long time! It was officially and definitively abolished only in 1820, by the Cortes of Cadiz).

In proportion as the fifteenth century advanced, the sacral regime in dissolution made way in Spain for a regime of permanent rivalry between two powers enchained to each other by common interests (and by the holy Christian faith) which struggled unceasingly against each other for supremacy: a royal power more and more intoxicated with absolutism, and a pontifical power whose spiritual arms still caused fear but were despised at the bottom of one's heart and easily reduced to inefficacy by the Catholic Kings. These latter thought only of taking possession of the Inquisition—and they nearly succeeded in doing so—in order to put it at the service of their regalian politics and of their grand design to create a perfect national unity established on a perfect unity of religious faith.

If the eye cannot easily endure the historical picture of the Spanish Inquisition, it is not only because of its cruelty, it is also because of the constant mixture of the political and of the religious of which it offers the spectacle: political ambitions, political trickeries, and political ferocity inextricably mingled with the somber religious ardor which served them as instrument. The great trials of this Inquisition were political trials magnified into trials for the defense of the faith. The Jews, who had long lived in Spain in complete security, passed now in the eyes of the monarchy for a national danger: in 1492, after the capture of Grenada

and their definitive victory over the Mohammedans, the sovereigns
decreed the general expulsion of all Jews from Spain, within four
months: after this time, they would be prosecuted by the Inquisition. . . .

The Popes "advised moderation" (that which was not lacking
in a kind of pious humor: to advise moderation to men such as
Torquemada or Ximenes, and wholly draped with virtues!). And
they did all they could in order to prevent excesses, cruelties and
an inexorable unfolding of violence which dishonored Christianity,
as also in order to keep or retake in hands the inquisitorial
institution. They succeeded in this very poorly, and their interventions, however numerous they were, ended in general in compromises saving only the appearances. The Holy See obtained to
name itself the first general Inquisitor in Spain (he was Torquemada, requested by Isabella and by Ferdinand); but Sixtus IV
accepted at the same time that all the successors of this first
general Inquisitor be named by the civil power. It was also the civil
power which designated the members of the Royal Council of the
Inquisition created by the sovereigns of Castille and of Aragon,
and charged with assisting the general Inquisitor,—by making him
feel the vigor of the royal hand.

We know indeed that the Papacy was then confronted with a
multitude of perils which put its anxious prudence to a rude test.
The fact remains that in general the weakness of the Popes of that
time is painful to see. The only one who showed the necessary
energy was, in the sixteenth century, Pius V when, apropos of the
lawsuit brought by the Inquisition against the primate of Spain,
Carranza, he threatened Philip II with excommunication and with
a sentence of interdict upon the whole of Spain. But he died a
little afterwards, before having obtained satisfaction.[23]

2. In order to conclude these remarks on the Spanish Inquisition, it seems to me important to note that everyone,—I do not
say only the persecuted, the tortured, the expelled, the imprisoned, the burned alive; I say also the persecutors themselves, the
Inquisitors feeling themselves impelled by the zeal of God, and the
sovereigns persuaded that they were fulfilling a duty of their office
and were performing their function of kings,—everyone was in it a
victim of two vampire-ideas, which had then their historical
chance and manifested themselves in full light.

The first is the idea that the unity of the nation or of the
temporal city must be, with regard to the relations of each man

with God as also his fidelity to the political order, an absolute unity, all the members of the body politic comprising from this point of view but a single man, loyal subject of the sovereign; and that consequently this unity in the temporal domain presupposes and requires unity of religious faith.

Consequently, to be a Spaniard was necessarily, and as if by definition, to be a Catholic. And the duty of the kings of Spain was to impose by all means the Catholic faith on their subjects.

Such an idea was in itself a false idea: for the unity of a nation is essentially unity in diversity, and what it requires and presupposes is common devotion to the temporal city, not at all the same and unique religious faith in all. Moreover, for whoever turns toward the first Cause, it appears clearly that in the entire world the diversity, among the people of the earth, of the conceptions of life and of religious beliefs is in actual fact a thing which God permits (which He "wills-permits," in His respect for human liberty, whereas He missions His Church to spread everywhere the preaching of divine Truth). And for each country it is the same as for the world. God gave the earth to all men; and each man, without distinction of race or of religion, has a fundamental right to existence in any point of the earth, as citizen of any country by birth or by naturalization (or also, but this is another question, as stranger respecting the laws of this country). In each country of the earth the service of human life in each of the citizens, whatever be the religion of the latter, is the common good of the country. The kings of Spain thought the contrary; they knew better than God what was necessary for Spain. . . .

And the false idea of which I speak had for inevitable effect that the Catholic faith became, in practice, a means for the temporal end to be attained (the absolute unity of the nation). What one proposed to oneself was, in reality, a temporalization of the spiritual which ignored practically the transcendence of faith as also the supreme dignity and the supreme independence of the Church. It was in order to be truly a Spaniard that it was necessary to be truly a Catholic.

Let us add that today an analogous phenomenon (of a reversed analogy) is observable with Marxism, which is a kind of purely temporal religion.[24] Being itself of the terrestrial and temporal order, not of the sacred order, it is conformable to its nature to be ordered to the temporal. But being a religion, it is not only in a nation or in a country that it asks to spread; it tends in itself to universality. And wherever it has gained power, it is necessary for it, in order to unify minds under its *Weltanschauung,* to make use, along with modern improvements, of means renewed by those of the Spanish Inquisition.

3. The other vampire-idea—long since reigning and held as incontestable in the system of commonly received opinions—was the idea that in the service of the spiritual the temporal means of force, of physical constraint, of threat and of intimidation are normally to be employed and are necessary in themselves. I have already spoken about this. The sword which Jesus commanded Peter to put back in the sheath,—it is it which flashed in the hands of the royal Inquisitors, and which, in actual fact, had the first role in the defense of the faith.

Hence the Baptism by aspersion of thousands of Jews and of Moors,—and at the same stroke the doubtful and subject-to-suspicion character of the faith professed by mouth by these thousands of baptized ones. Twenty to thirty thousand Marranos were judged false Christians and sent to the stake by the Spanish Inquisition. The fact that the latter, not content with converting by force, threw the weight of its sword above all upon the Marranos ("the violated," this is the name which one gives to them in Hebrew) and the Moriscos was sufficient proof that considered in itself, and speaking objectively, the idea in question is false and pernicious.

The men of the fifteenth century were (except the Popes in a certain measure) scarcely accessible to this proof. The commonly received opinions held everybody under their sway. One cannot be astonished that the greatest number in the personnel of the Church, and above all the Inquisitors of Spain, succumbed in good faith to the vampire-idea of which we are speaking, and did—innocently for the majority (when politics did not spoil everything)—what it presented to them as necessary in itself, and which objectively speaking was not good. Certain ones perhaps did it reluctantly (such as, for example, Manrique, the friend of Erasmus), but they felt themselves obliged to it because history had so embroiled things that the mechanism of repression by violence, once put together and established, demanded to function under pain of seeing furious reactions—against the faith itself—explode in minds.

The use of force in religious matters knew again a glittering fortune in the second half of the sixteenth century, at Rome this time. The idea which caused it to be believed normal and necessary in itself, and first required, was always there. It was later that the use of material force gave way to that of purely spiritual sanctions. But at the time in question the idea of which I am speaking (and which in other circumstances would have perhaps begun to grow weak) found itself reinforced by the simple and brutal summons due to the historical conjuncture.

The Roman Inquisition

1. It was at the epoch when the Protestant Reformation was making enormous progress, even among the members of the high clergy, that, under the impetus of Pierre Caraffa, Nuncio at Venice (then Cardinal, then Pope under the name of Paul IV), Paul III instituted in 1542 a supreme Congregation of the Inquisition (the Holy Office) of which the Pope reserved to himself the presidency and which had jurisdiction over the entire world. At the same time there were revived, in the diverse kingdoms of Italy, the local Inquisitions that had more or less fallen into lethargy. Soon, under Paul IV, in 1557-1558, there was also established, following the example of what had been done in Spain, an Index of Forbidden Books. The Inquisition was charged with prosecuting above all heretics, but also blasphemers, Sodomites, Simoniacs, men who lived off the prostitution of their daughters or of their sisters. On the 11th of January, 1566, it was the grand Inquisitor Ghislieri who was elevated to the Papacy, and took the name of Pius V. And under his direction the Inquisition redoubled in energy.

The punishments inflicted were above all imprisonment or the galleys. Capital punishment seems to have been more rarely inflicted, and in general the ones condemned to death were burned at the stake only after decapitation.[25] One prosecuted and condemned also the authors of slanderous denunciations against the accused who were recognized to be innocent.

The Council of Trent (1545-1563) had approved the measures taken by Paul III and Paul IV. The mentality of the epoch considered still as entirely normal the use of the means of force, of torture, of the galleys, of the putting to death for the defense of religion (The Protestants thought likewise: Calvin, in his *Ordonnances* of 1541, organized the pursuit of the heretics of the new faith, with denunciations, spying, torture, and condemnations to death. Michel Servet was burned alive at Geneva in 1553.). As a matter of fact, in the sixteenth century the Catholic clergy, to say nothing of many laymen, was gravely tainted by the Protestant influences; and for Pius V as for the Popes of the twelfth and of the thirteenth centuries, it was a question of an affair of public safety, in which it was necessary to proceed quickly and forcibly. Moreover it is important to take into account, here again, the common mentality in which the saints themselves participate, [26] and above all the fact that, sanctioned by four centuries and a half of historical functioning, the Holy Inquisition had long since established itself as the sole and sovereign resource of the spiritual power in time of crisis. In my opinion, this does not at all excuse the means, considered in themselves, employed by the latter, but this excuses entirely the Grand Inquisitor who had become Pope. He was a great saint whom I venerate (less however than St. Philip Neri). He had enormous love of God; and his rigors, even if excessive (cf. the last lines of note 6), issued only from a fiercely pure fidelity to serve the supreme norms of justice of the kingdom which is not of this world.

2. The wars of religion bloodied France during more than thirty years (1562 to 1598). The Massacre of St. Bartholomew took place on the 24th of August, 1572. After the Edict of Nantes (1598) minds calmed down; it was necessary indeed that Catholics and Protestants accept the historical fact that each other *existed*. This was not yet religious tolerance, and still less that search for a real fraternal friendship in the clear consciousness of dogmatic differences which manifested itself under more or less pure forms after the second Council of the Vatican, and which is in itself an immense progress. But the idea of sending the heretic to the stake had lost its attraction; one contented oneself with the eternal flames to which one judged him deputed. Louis XIV revoked the Edict of Nantes in 1685, many Protestants expatriated themselves then, but those who remained were not massacred, nor were their goods confiscated. The Age of the Enlightenment was near, with the candle-ends which reason would carry about while one still believed in it (not for long), and which, in actual fact, were going to do better than faith in the Gospel and in the true Light of the world could do for the growth-in-awareness of the liberties to which man has a right in the natural order,—they also announced by the Gospel message together with supreme and deiform liberty.

With regard to the Roman Inquisition, things changed also. The combat for the defense of the faith still kept its urgency. The struggle against Jansenism was very difficult, and it was to be followed by the struggle against the multitude of incessantly renewed errors which were going to confirm the personnel of the Church in its defensive position, as in a besieged city. But two new facts seem to me to have here to retain our attention. On the one hand there had ended the melange of temporal interests pursued by the civil power and of religious interests pursued by the Papacy which one notes at the time of the medieval Inquisition and indeed more still at the time of the Spanish Inquisition. And the Roman Inquisition had also relieved itself of the care of dealing severely with certain misdemeanors of common law over which it had jurisdiction in the sixteenth century. Its end henceforth was purely and exclusively the defense of the faith.

On the other hand it did not take long until there ended likewise the recourse to the secular arm as also the use of the means of physical constraint and of material force. The sanctions and the means of constraint to which the Holy Office had recourse were henceforth only the means and the sanctions of the spiritual order proper to the Church.

Does this mean however that the old idea that the use of force in religious matters is normal and necessary had completely disappeared? It had faded from the scene, it no longer played any visible role in the universe of consciousness. But I think that it continued all along the centuries to make its way underground in the unconscious, under rampant forms. I wrote above that the medieval Inquisition and its confidence in the means of force put for some centuries the personnel of the Church on a path which was not the right one. What I mean by this is that under the unconscious pressure of the still active vestiges of this old idea, it happened that the high personnel of the Church, in particular the Holy Office, trusted too much for too long a time in the purely spiritual sanctions and in the purely spiritual means of constraint proper to the Church, in other words in the second sword when it is normally applied (but then its use can only be occasional, and as little frequent as possible, and as moderate as possible). It is not good to rely principally upon this sword. It is not good to install oneself in exclusively defensive positions. It is not good to have recourse in a regular and permanent manner, in the name of an institution which in the juridical structure holds the altogether first place, to harsh means because they are the easiest and the most expeditious, and to measures of coercion (which are those which lend themselves best to routine, as also to the neglect of the healthy concerns of the intellect): putting books on the Index, condemnations or threats of condemnation affecting books or compelling authors to silence, and which irritate without enlightening. It is not good that a habitual climate of suspicion weigh upon people,—especially upon people who rightly or wrongly devote themselves to the works of the intelligence, and of whom a great many are upright minds and admirably disinterested seekers, wholly dedicated in spirit of faith to the service of truth, but of whom a great many also are minds intoxicated with themselves, and endowed with the most susceptible vanity.

It seems to me that a particularly dangerous situation was to develop thus in the course of the nineteenth century and in the first half of the twentieth. Without a vast accumulation of long repressed silent resentments one would not understand that so many theologians and exegetes,—among those who would have the most need of being put back again in the paths of truth, greedy as they are to show themselves of their time and to espouse its errors,—as also so many poor ecclesiastics who do not know much but follow the current of the day all the more passionately, saw in the second Council of the Vatican only an occasion to liberate a kind of morbid rage against Roman authority.

3. The fact remains that the Church has an imprescriptible duty to defend the faith against error;—and that error abounds today.

The fact remains also that she has received from God the two swords, that of the teaching authority, which she must constantly bring into play, and that of the constraining authority, however quickly it is required of her to put back this second sword in the sheath when it has been necessary for her to employ it; the fact remains finally that an authority which does not act runs the risk of becoming forgotten or scorned.

There is no longer today any Sacred Congregation of the Inquisition or any Holy Office. What bore this name is now the Congregation for the defense of the doctrine of the faith. We must pity the Churchmen who in the present conjuncture are in charge of the latter, their job is not easy. It seems that a great effort of imagination is above all required of them, in order to find new ways of action. It is the affair of the Holy Spirit to aid them in this.

It is perhaps permitted however to a mere layman to meddle in what does not concern him, by saying humbly what he thinks on this matter.

On the one hand is it not desirable that at the summit of the ecclesiastical administration there be not a single one, but *two* supreme Congregations, the first (therefore purely and simply supreme) charged with all that which concerns the evangelization of the earth, the teaching of the faith and the radiance of divine truth in the world, as also with that which concerns research to be aided and to be enlightened; the second one charged, like the Congregation which replaced the Holy Office, with defending the faith against error? For in principle the positions of conquest and of progression are more important still than positions of defense.

On the other hand, and in that which concerns this second Congregation, can one not dream that it unfold its activity on two different planes, the first one relating also to the teaching authority? On the occasion of the errors launched through the world by such or such author of renown, capable of exerting upon minds a real influence, eminent theologians would be then charged with setting forth in a wholly objective manner, and with the sole care to enlighten, not to condemn, the truths ignored by the author in question. And these doctrinal expositions, aiming only at truth, would be distributed officially to seminaries and to Catholic universities by courtesy of the Congregation, before being published in book form if need be.

The second plane would be that of the constraining authority, in the cases in which it would become necessary to exercise it, while having every sanction preceded by personal contacts and talks with the person concerned, so that even there the mode of approach remains above all fraternal. I understand well that in fraternal dialogue there are two parties involved, and that on the side of certain interlocutors, above all when they are haunted by the care of publicity, the fraternal charity of the Roman Congregation renewed in its spirit as well as in its name would run the risk of encountering wholly different sentiments. Then, so much the worse, it has the second sword in hand; and however rarely, however moderately this be, it would be necessary indeed for it to use it. As Karl Rahner says,[27] "the Church would betray the Gospel, and the magisterium its mission, if she had not, in certain circumstances, the courage to say a categorical 'No' to a doctrine which surges up in the Church and wishes to acquire in her freedom of the city."

The Great Renewal

1. Laymen also are to be pitied in the present circumstances. There are many more of them than one thinks who, profoundly disconcerted in that which is most dear to them by the behavior and the verbal deluge of "in-the-know" clerics,—and on the other hand accepting willingly the liturgical reform as well as the other reforms, and the use of the vernacular, but disgusted by the unworthy translations which one obliges them to listen to at Mass,[28] —hold in like aversion the bitter zeal of an integrism in the eyes of which "everything has been said" and the outrageous fatuity of a neomodernism in the eyes of which "everything is to be redone" and which no longer wants the supernatural and the sacred. They ask themselves with anguish where "the Church" is leading them (not *the Church*, indeed, but a personnel of the Church a little drugged for the moment).

These laymen scarcely find any comfort in the optimism officially professed by many of their pastors, or in the diverse "organizations" in which one would like to enrol them. They have however the Pope, who prays, who teaches, who suffers, who has solicitude for all and for everything, and who has given to them a profession of faith recalling to them clearly that which they must believe, and which they can repeat after him and with him. And they have the Holy Spirit, Who does not cease to assist the people of God, and they have the angels (those angels of whom St. Ambrose speaks to us in the Matins of Christmas)[29] and the saints of Heaven along with their queen,—the Church of Heaven who is but a single Church with that of the earth, and who asks only to aid them. And if they desire him with enough perseverance, they are sure to find a priest worthy of the name in order to counsel them. The Lord Jesus during his earthly life led a little flock whom He told to have no fear: *nolite timere, pusillus grex.*[30] It is little flocks living in prayer and in the love of the Cross who have today to assume the relief. (There are some admirable ones behind the Iron Curtain, who are abandoned by all and are at each instant exposed to persecution, they make one think of the Church of the catacombs, they attest on earth the graces of the Holy Spirit.)

2. The great renewal to which the second Council of the Vatican has called the Christian people,—it seems to me that in the perspective in which the present chapter places us we understand better the amplitude of its dimensions. The Council made itself

heard at the term of a long process which led to a complete reorientation, to a revolution with regard to ten centuries of history. To tell the truth, what is called for there is simply to return in an explicit *prise de conscience* to that which in the real life itself and the profoundly lived experience of the Church has always held the first place: has she not for soul grace with its free gifts, for life the love of charity? But the profound life of a human being and the consciousness which he has of the rules which he uses is one thing; a quite different thing is the profound life of a city and that which holds the first rank in its juridical structures and in the concerns of those who govern it. It is the major concern with which since the eleventh century the personnel of the Church has been occupied in the government of the latter, and it is the scale of values which, consequently, it used in juridical practice, which have henceforth changed.

The defense against heresy, which remains always for the Church a supreme duty, has ceased to be the purely and simply supreme and absolutely first concern. That which, according to the teaching of the Council, must henceforth be for the personnel of the Church the absolutely first concern is the love of Christ (His love for us, and our love for Him) to be manifested to men, and the truth of Christ to be communicated to them.

It is not surprising, taking into account human fragility, and the turbid desires and the resentments which torment our nature, that the immediate result of a change of such great bearing is in thinking heads less anxious about truth than about the fashions of the day, and in a number of young clerics ill-prepared for the event, a vast doctrinal and moral confusion, and a rush toward a so-called Christianity which knows nothing but the earth. We must believe that such a phenomenon is in itself short-lived. The generations which will come, perhaps sooner than one thinks, will have doubtless other needs, and ones more worthy of the vocation of beings created in the image of God; the problem will be then to be ready to give to them that which they ask.

Meanwhile, it remains nevertheless singularly desirable that when they touch upon things where nothing has sense except through the love of Christ,—which caused Him to die on the Cross,—and through the truth of Christ,—that truth in order to bear testimony to which He came into the world,—men, and especially Churchmen, know a little of what they are speaking. The great renewal called for by the Council is first and above all, and in an absolutely necessary manner, an interior renewal, in living faith. In its absence there is nothing to be hoped. Such is the terrible sign which the Council has inscribed upon the wall.

It is by the soul, in which God dwells secretly, that it is necessary to begin, and for this it is necessary first to believe in the soul. It is to the plenitude of supernatural charity that it is necessary to aspire, and for this it is necessary first to believe in the supernatural order and in grace. It is to the truth hidden in the transcendent God, and revealed by Christ to His Church, that it is necessary to adhere with all one's heart, and for this it is necessary first to believe in the transcendence of God and in the Church of Christ. It is to prayer and to the life of prayer that it is necessary above all to give oneself, and for this it is necessary first to believe truly in prayer. It is the Cross of Jesus that it is necessary to embrace, and for this it is necessary first to believe truly in the Incarnation of the uncreated Word, and in redemption through the Cross.

XIV

A Look at History

(Conclusion)

IV

THE CONDEMNATION OF GALILEO

Brief Historical Account

1. Galileo was born in 1564. It is in 1610 that he publishes *Sidereus Nuntius* and that he begins to manifest his interest for the system of Copernicus and heliocentrism (an old revived Pythagorean idea). He is residing then in Florence, he is 46 years old, and is in full celebrity. Everybody admires him, especially Pope Paul V. But a few theologians are not slow to attack him, in the name of Holy Scripture (forgetting the principles laid down by St. Augustine: the Holy Spirit wished to teach men not the inmost constitution of the things of nature, but that which is useful for salvation, —and by St. Thomas: the Bible speaks of nature according to sensible appearances).

Very naturally he becomes anxious, then reacts. "While the Bible," he writes to Castelli (December 21, 1613), "adapting itself to the intelligence of the common run of men, speaks, in many cases and rightly, according to appearances, and employs terms which are not destined to express absolute truth, nature conforms itself rigorously and invariably to the laws which have been given to it. . . ." Was not Baronius accustomed to say "that God had not wished to teach us how the heavens go, but how one goes to Heaven?" Father Caccini replies that the theory of Copernicus is "contrary to the common sentiment of all the theologians and of all the holy Fathers." Bellarmine advises Galileo not to engage himself in theological quarrels; all is well since Copernicus did not intend to prove that the earth turns about the sun, and gave his theory only as a mere mathematical hypothesis.[1] And Bishop Dini whispers in his ear (letter of May 2, 1615): "One can write as a mathematician, and under the form of hypothesis, as, it is said, Copernicus did; one can write freely, provided that one does not enter into the sacristy."

In February of 1616, on the order of Paul V, the theologians of the Holy Office are consulted on the two following propositions: "1) the sun is the center of the world and, consequently, motionless with local movement; 2) the earth is not the center of the world, nor motionless, but moves respecting itself completely by a diurnal movement." They reveal their answer on the 24th of February: "The first proposition is senseless and absurd in philosophy, and formally heretical, insofar as it contradicts expressly numerous passages of Holy Scripture, according to the propriety of words, and according to the common interpretation and the sense of the holy Fathers and of the theologian doctors." As to the second proposition, "it merits the same censure in philosophy; and, with regard to theological truth, it is at least erroneous in faith."

Two days later, in the presence of Bellarmine, the commissary of the Holy Office notifies Galileo of the censure thus brought against the opinion which claims that the sun is the center of the world and motionless and that the earth moves. This opinion must be neither maintained nor defended, and Galileo is informed that if he refuses to obey he exposes himself to being judged and imprisoned.

Galileo was a man possessed at the same time by a profound virtue of faith and by an eminent virtue of science,—this was his drama, in the presence of men constituted in authority who knew neither what science is nor what its relation with faith is. The precautions which he took against formidable sanctions did not at all exclude his respect toward an authority to which, even in fallible matter, submission was due in conscience. Did he not write, in a letter of the 16th of February, 1615, to Bishop Dini: "I am deeply resolved to tear out my eye in order not to be scandalized, rather than to resist my superiors and to injure my soul by maintaining against them that which at present seems evident to me and which I think I touch with my hand"? Let us add that he doubtless preferred mental reservation (current then) to martyrdom. In the presence of Bellarmine and of the commissary of the Inquisition he assented to what was declared to him and promised to obey.

On the 9th of March, 1616, the Congregation of the Index declared a general condemnation against the Copernican theory and against the works of Copernicus. It is this which one calls the first trial of Galileo, although it was more accurately a grave warning, for he himself was not named in the decree.

2. But the demon of science was in him. How would he have been able not to break more or less his promises? In answer to a book of Father Horace Grassi attacking Copernicus and him, he published in 1623 *Il Saggiatore*, in which his defense of heliocentrism was so well veiled that Cardinal Barberini,—now Pope Urban VIII—with whom he was on excellent terms, accepted the dedication of it; then, in 1632, he published the *Dialogue Concerning The Two Chief World Systems* in which under easy-to-penetrate clevernesses he definitely decides in favor of the theory of Copernicus. Behold the tempest is let loose, and Urban VIII is violently irritated (he thought that Galileo and his friends had tricked him). Galileo, although ill, is obliged to go to Rome, where he is interned, not in one of the cells of the Holy Office, as it was the case for all the other accused, but in the home of his friend Ambassador Niccolini, in the palace of Florence, later in the home of the fiscal of the Inquisition, where they take great care of him and where he receives freely his friends.

The Holy Office subjects him to four interrogatories, in which one reproaches him for having been unfaithful to his promises, and in which above all one inquires, under threat of torture, concerning his inmost personal thought (concerning his *intentio*): did he or did he not adhere willingly to the Copernican doctrine, duly condemned by the Inquisitors? He denies it, assures that he had wished to do only that which was permitted, to show the value of this doctrine as a mathematical hypothesis. The judges accept his denials, and the threat of torture remains in the state of intimidation. (In point of fact, Galileo was never tortured.)

On the 22nd of June, 1633, one reads to him the verdict of

the Holy Office (to which a false official report, added in the dossier to the mention of the interview of the 26th of February, 1616, with the commissary of the Inquisition, and claiming the mere notification received then by Galileo to be a formal *injunction* of the Holy Office, had contributed). Galileo is declared "vehemently suspect of heresy," namely, "for having held and believed the false and contrary-to-the-Holy-Scriptures doctrine that the sun is the center of the world," as also "for having held and believed that a doctrine which has been declared and defined to be contrary to the Holy Scriptures can still be held and defended as provable." The verdict absolves him from the penalties incurred by this, on condition that with a sincere heart "he abjure, condemn and detest the aforesaid errors and heresies." But in order that his earlier disobedience not remain unpunished, one condemns him on the other hand to prison, for a time which the Holy Office will determine at its discretion, and one prescribes him to say three times a week, during three years, the seven penitential psalms.

After which Galileo read and signed the formula of abjuration.

His penalty was commuted by the Pope on the very day of his condemnation. Instead of the prison of the Holy Office he was to reside in the Medici villa; a few days later he was permitted to go to Sienna, as guest of Archbishop Piccolimini, and finally to have his detention place in his own villa of Arcetri, near Florence. Become blind, he was authorized by Urban VIII to reside in Florence, where he died on the 8th of January, 1642, at the age of 77. When he was still at Arcetri, he had received a prohibition to leave his villa (in which he was still considered as detained) on the very day on which he learned that his daughter, a nun in a neighboring monastery, was dying.

The Roman Congregations

1. *By way of preface: a controverted question.*—Before speaking of the Roman Congregations, and in order to be able to do so in a sufficiently clear manner, I am obliged to take a position, I who am not a theologian, on a question vigorously discussed among theologians,—the question of that which, in rather unfortunate terms, one calls "ecclesiastical faith." I shall do so in all modesty, but as clearly as possible. Preliminary remark: this concept is hybrid, because, according as it is employed by such and

such a person, it refers either to *infallible* assertions (then the word "faith" is correct; it is the word "ecclesiastical" which is not), or to *noninfallible* assertions which it is necessary however to hold as certain to some degree (then it is the word "faith" which is incorrect; it is a question of an assent given—in a variable measure—to authorities who merit confidence), or to the two kinds of assertions grouped together.

It is "ecclesiastical faith" considered in the first sense or in the first perspective (according as it has to deal with *infallible* assertions) which concerns us here.

There are things which it is necessary to hold as infallibly true, not *on the word of God*, or because the Church proposes them to us as revealed by God, but *on the word of the Church herself*, because it is she who assures us that they are infallibly true. For example: that which one calls "dogmatic facts"; when Innocent X had condemned five propositions taken from Jansen's *Augustinus*, the Jansenists replied that thus detached these propositions were indeed heretical, but that considered in the context of Jansen they were orthodox; then Alexander VII declared and defined infallibly that these five propositions were condemned in the very sense which they had in Jansen; such is a "dogmatic fact" which we believe on the word of the Pope speaking as voice of the Church, and which is not a part of the formally revealed datum. [2]

Unlike Cardinal Journet, I do not think that in such a case we have to do, with regard to the promulgation of the thing to be believed, with the *declaratory power* of the Church. The latter has for object to bring to our knowledge the truths revealed by God: and what is meant by this, if not the formally revealed truths in their dogmatic tenor itself? In spite of the dialectical ingenuity of great theologians, I do not succeed in seeing how statements such as the fact of the five propositions of Jansen could be held as revealed by God, be it in an implicit manner. It is therefore not with the *declaratory power*, but with the *canonical power* that in my opinion we have to do in the cases in question, with regard to the promulgation of the object to be believed.

But like Cardinal Journet and Father Marin-Sola, I think that with regard to our adhesion to this object, it is by our theological faith itself that we believe the truths in question: I say by our theological faith when, while it adheres to a revealed truth (the mystery of the *Una Sancta*), it applies itself at the same stroke to another object, itself not revealed by God, but which is *in an immediately evident manner* grasped by the intellect as a particular realization of this revealed datum; in other words, we believe in the truths in question by our theological faith in the Church *as immediately applied.*

I believe in the Church, on the word of God. And at the same stroke, *ipso facto,* I believe, on the word of the Church, that which she tells me when it is she herself (the person of the Church) who speaks as principal agent, with her infallibility. I believe in it beforehand, it suffices that she says it: because there is here *absolutely no kind of reasoning,* nor syllogism, nor reasoning with two terms, but *immediate evidence* for the intellect, which sees the point in question (for example that the five propositions exist in Jansen with their heretical sense) as a mere point of application of the infallibility of the Church when it manifests itself to me through the Pope speaking *ex cathedra.* It is my divine faith in the Church which passes then, in an immediate and intuitive manner, to another object than its proper object, and causes me to adhere to the truth in question, infallibly true although not revealed. The object—not revealed—to which it passes thus was, from the moment that I know that the Church holds it as true, *immediately subsumed* by the revealed object—the *Una, sancta, catholica et apostolica*—which is one of the proper and specifying objects of my theological faith.

There is therefore no need of having recourse to a new *habitus,* to a new supernatural intellectual or moral virtue of which neither the Fathers of the Church nor St. Thomas surmised the existence. I rather think that "ecclesiastical faith" was invented in the sixteenth century and baptized in the seventeenth by theologians who had lost the sense of the intuitivity of the intelligence, and who embarked theologians much better than they on a pseudo-problem, concerning which they could, while making a great expenditure of subtlety, only find themselves in disagreement. I have therefore decided to ignore the notion of ecclesiastical faith; and it is without referring, as one has often done, to this notion that I shall try here to clarify our ideas on the question of the assent to be given to religious authority when it expresses itself through organs which are not the ordinary magisterium or the extraordinary magisterium, but which are nevertheless necessary to the government of the Church, such as the Roman Congregations (considered only in themselves, cf. further on, page 207). The point which matters to me is to know when one has or has not to do with the person of the Church using or not using instrumentally her ministers.

2. What one calls *canonical power* (cf. Journet, *L'Église du Verbe Incarné*, I, 2nd ed., pp. 223 *et seq.*) has for its object to assist all through the centuries, in order to assure the concrete execution of it, the absolutely primary mission of the Church (to confer the Sacraments by the *power of order,* and to propose by the *declaratory power* the divinely revealed truths, the doctrine of the faith and of morals) by promulgating decisions required in order to maintain the faith and to govern the life of the people of God (which constitutes a *societas perfecta,* that is to say, perfectly master of itself).

Being given the positions which I have taken, I shall distinguish in the canonical power two different great zones:

on the one hand, the zone in which it prescribes to us to believe, on the word of the Church,—and, if my positions are well founded, through our divine faith in the Church *as immediately applied,* by virtue of an intuitively perceived evidence,—assertions of the speculative order infallibly true without being themselves divinely revealed (whether they concern for example "dogmatic facts," or canonizations, or decrees of the Roman Congregations, in the cases in which they must be held as irreformable); whereas likewise, in the practical order, the decisions of the canonical power participate instrumentally in the superior prudence of the Church;

on the other hand, a zone in which the same canonical power depends on the proper lights of those who exercise it, so that in doctrinal and speculative matters their decisions, while requiring on our part religious obedience, do not imply however infallibility, whereas in disciplinary or practical matters, while requiring also religious obedience, they can likewise escape the superior prudence of the Church.

In the first zone we have to do with the person of the Church acting through the instrumentality of her ministers. In the second zone we have to do with the proper causality of the latter.[3]

It is to this second zone that the decisions of the Roman Congregations belong, unless by virtue of some special guarantee or confirmation issuing from the Pope they depend on something higher.

3. *The Roman Congregations and the Pope.*—It happens in fact that certain decisions of the Congregations must be held as engaging the Church herself and her person,—this not by reason of the Congregation which enacts them but by reason of the Pope

who sanctions them, especially by reason (this is the case which interests me here) of the formula employed by him in order to approve them.

The Roman Congregations are organs created by the Pope and which he uses in order to govern and to teach. But it is in two different manners that the Pope can approve the decision of a Congregation: either, simply, *in forma communi,* in this case this decision emanates directly from the Congregation itself and is issued in its name; or else in a special manner, *in forma specifica,* in this case "the Pope expressly adopts the decree and issues it in his own name, using for example the following formulas: 'By our own authority, of our certain knowledge, in the plenitude of our apostolic power.' "[4]

Well, in the case in which a doctrinal decree elaborated by a Roman Congregation is approved by the Pope *in forma specifica* (to use *his full apostolic authority;* this resembles singularly, does it not, to speak *ex cathedra*), I do not doubt that this doctrinal decree must be held as irreformable. And consequently it finds itself, by virtue of such an approbation, transferred into that which I called just now the first zone of canonical power.

But in all the cases (the most frequent ones) in which a doctrinal decree is approved only *in forma communi,* and is therefore issued only by virtue of the proper authority of the Congregation itself, it belongs to the second zone of canonical power, in other words it remains fallibly issued.

The verdict of the Holy Office which condemned Galileo in 1633 was approved *in forma communi.*

Disciplinary by reason only of the penalties imposed on Galileo, it is very evident that it was in itself a *doctrinal* decree: it based itself upon what had been said by the theologians of the Holy Office in 1616 (let us recall this: to claim that the sun is the center of the world is *"senseless and absurd in philosophy, and formally heretical"*[5]), and declared Galileo *"vehemently suspect of heresy,"* namely for having believed "the *false and contrary-to-the-Holy-Scriptures* doctrine that the sun is the center of the world," and for having believed "that a doctrine which has been *declared and defined to be contrary to the Holy Scriptures* can still be held and defended as provable."[6]

But this decree could not at all claim infallibility, no more than a commission or congregation of experts in theology can hold that which it says on its own authority as the voice of the Church. "It was evident even to all contemporary opinion that this doctrinal condemnation was issued in revocable matter, and by a fallible authority."[7]

The Abjuration of Galileo

1. In the text of the abjuration read on his knees, his hand on the holy Gospels, and signed by Galileo before the Holy Office, he recalled in the first place having been "judged vehemently suspect of heresy, namely for having held and believed that the sun is the center of the world and motionless, and that the earth is not the center, and moves," then he added: "Wishing therefore to cause to disappear from the mind of your Eminences and of every Christian this vehement suspicion which has been justly formed against me, I abjure, I condemn and I detest the aforesaid errors and heresies. . . ."

What are we to think of this abjuration, with regard to Galileo himself? Fear undoubtedly played a role in it, but to think that Galileo signed this text falsely would be a serious mistake. I recalled above the sincerity of his respect for the hierarchy and of his religious obedience ("I am deeply resolved to tear out my eye in order not to be scandalized, rather than to resist my superiors"[8]). His abjuration was a violence done to his conscience, divided between his religious obedience and his scientific conviction ("that which seems evident to me and which I think I touch with my hand"[9]), since one obliged him now by the first to deny and to sacrifice the second, which remained there nevertheless. Contradiction in lived act, which put the mind itself on the rack.

Eppur si muove, the saying is perhaps legendary, it remains absolutely significant. It moves nevertheless. And I swear on the Gospel that it does not move.

2. With regard to the judges of the Holy Office, I do not see another term than that of *abuse of power,* and a singularly grave one, in order to designate that which they did in imposing this abjuration on Galileo by the most violent moral constraint. For (if it is true,—and this is certainly true,—that, as Cardinal Journet writes, all contemporaries held as evident "that this doctrinal condemnation was issued in revocable matter, by a fallible authority"), they were certainly the first to know that they could err. [10] It was their own personal conviction that heliocentrism is a heresy: this conviction was not infallible, nor was the decree by

which it was expressed. They did not have the right to oblige Galileo, *as if* he was constrained to it by a truth of faith, imposing itself on the mind in an infallible manner, to an *absolute* interior denial of heliocentrism and to swear on the Gospel that he *"abjured, condemned and detested"* "the heresy" constituted by this doctrine. In the verdict of condemnation they declared that the opinion of Copernicus had been *defined* "contrary to the Holy Scriptures." Defined by whom? By the Church, by the Pope speaking *ex cathedra?* Not at all. Defined by them alone, fallible men. They could, by virtue of a prudential judgment, make Galileo swear not to propagate this opinion.[11] They could not make him swear that he held it to be heretical and contrary to the Holy Scriptures, and that he condemned and detested it in his heart.

Such an abuse of power shows us that in the seventeenth century the high personnel of the Church continued still to proceed (in another manner, no doubt, but only in another manner) in the path opened by the mediaeval Inquisition: prior use of the means of physical constraint and of violence (become now psychological violence); and confidence principally accorded to these means for the defense of the faith.

These things have a hardy life: a personnel which judges itself invested with the dignity of the person herself of the Church is scarcely ready to recognize openly that it has erred. It was only in 1822 that the Holy Office authorized the printing in Rome of works teaching the movement of the earth around the sun. But in 1734, just a hundred years after the condemnation, it had permitted the Grand Duke of Florence to have the ashes of Galileo transferred to a tomb erected in his honor in the Basilica of Santa-Croce, and of which the inscription praised in him "the great renovator of astronomy," *nulli aetatis suae comparandus.* And in 1744 Benedict XIV had authorized the publication of a revised and corrected (very little corrected) edition of the *Dialogue.* "Juridicism" did not entirely exclude good sense.

The Error of the Holy Office

1. The condemnation of Galileo was an exceptionally grave error of the high personnel of the Church (acting as proper cause): an error which for a long time bespattered the person of the Church, and put in jeopardy many souls who believed this con-

demnation an act *of the Church* herself, of the *Una, sancta, catholica.*

To declare that to think that the earth turns around the sun is *senseless* and *absurd in philosophy,*[12] and *formally heretical,* as the theologians of the Holy Office did in 1616; and to declare, as they did in 1633, that heliocentrism is a theory *false* and *contrary to the Holy Scriptures, an error and a heresy* which, if one wishes to wash himself of the suspicion of having believed in it, it is necessary to *abjure, detest* and *condemn,*—this was to commit a "blunder" of the first magnitude, which was quickly to be recognized as such in the whole universe of culture.

And if the judges of the Holy Office erred so gravely, it was because, through an error of principle still more dangerous because of general bearing, they held the science of phenomena in its own development to be subject to theology, and to a literal interpretation of Scripture against which St. Augustine and St. Thomas had forewarned us. The great mistake, as Cardinal Journet writes, [13] was "to have lacked the courage needed to detach the question of Scripture at once from the dispute over the geocentric issue."

Finally, in order to say things such as they are in actual fact and in the concrete, they erred, no longer in their head and the judgments of their intellect, but in their profound psychology and the reflexes of their unconscious as well as in their practical behavior, by deluding themselves about themselves and about their position (just below the Pope, at the summit of the hierarchy), and by *taking themselves practically for the Church.* Hence the arrogance and the authoritarianism which men whose personal humility could be very profound displayed in their function, and the honorific splendors with which they wished it surrounded. A dream-like error, if I may say, and all the more tenacious, and into which not only the judges of Galileo fell.

If the Holy Office was so slow in recognizing its error, and if it did so furtively,[14] it was because it believed that its decree of condemnation (work of the personnel of the Church acting as proper cause) was an act *of the Church* herself (of the person of the Church).

2. That the condemnation of Galileo took place at the time when it did take place, and that the Holy Office fell then into so remarkable—and so humiliating—an error, did this not have a high historical significance, and the value of a singular warning?

The time had come for the personnel of the Church to take,

for the defense of the faith, another path than that of the means of force opened by the medieval Inquisition. The patience of God is much longer than we think; it has however limits. The error into which the Holy Office fell in condemning Galileo marked the limit of an agelong patience.

But in order to understand the warning it took the personnel of the Church three good centuries still,—until the person of the Church herself makes her voice heard through the second Council of the Vatican.

V
THE FUNERAL-PILE OF ROUEN

On, On, On, Daughter of God, On!

1. The story of Joan of Arc is the most extraordinary story of Christian times: the most dazzling and the most secret. Can one try to form for oneself an idea of it, accurate as far as possible; to understand it, with our poor ratiocinations? It is too exceptional and too lofty. Each one knows it roughly. It is good nevertheless to recall the facts, and to insist afterwards on certain points of particular importance.

At Domremy, the guarding of the common flock devolved upon each family, in rotation; and when the turn of her parents had come, Joan accompanied them no doubt. But it is not at all true that she was a sheperdess, in spite of Catherine of Pisa and the "joli mestier" which she attributed to her in her verses and caused to pass into the legend. "Did you in your youth learn any craft?—Yes, I learned to sew and to spin. In sewing and spinning I fear no woman in Rouen. When I was at home with my father, I saw to the ordinary domestic tasks. I did not go to the fields to look after the sheep and other animals."[1]

She was born on the 6th of January, 1412. It was at the age of thirteen that she began to hear her Voices. The first time she was very frightened. "It was about the hour of noon, in the summer-time, and it was in the garden of my father." There was a light on the side from which "the great Voice" came. It was St. Michael, she knew this[2] only at the time of one of the subsequent apparitions (the third one no doubt), in which she engaged her faith.[3] He announced to her that St. Catherine and St. Margaret[4] would come also in order "to help her to direct herself." At their first visit they told her their names; then they returned unceasingly to instruct her and to guide her. She undoubtedly consulted them before taking the vow of virginity.

"Never did I have need of them that they did not come." It was so as long as Joan lived, and wherever she was.

The three who composed her "counsel,"—she saw them "really and corporeally," they were like us physically in space. St. Michael appeared for the great directives concerning her mission, the two saints each day. She untiringly repeated "that her Voices came from God, that she heard them every day, several times a day, that she saw them with her eyes, heard them with her ears, 'just as I see you, judges, believe me if you will!' " She knelt down before St. Catherine and St. Margaret, "kissed them and embraced them,—taking their knees between her arms; she smelt their good odor; felt their figure, which did not vanish at the touch."[5]

Their voice was "beautiful, gentle and humble": Daughter of God, Daughter of great heart, it was thus that they called Joan. They promised her Paradise.

In the inquiry preliminary to the trial of rehabilitation, Dunois will testify that one day the king, he and the Count of Harcourt asked Joan: "When you say that you have recourse to your counsel, what is it that takes place in you?" She replies: "It is very simple: I withdraw apart, I pray to God, and after having prayed to God, I hear a voice: *Daughter of God, on, on, on, I will help you, on!*" And when she would hear this, she used to wish that it would last forever.

2. At Domremy, the child is instructed by her voices concerning the conduct to be followed by a Christian servant-maid loving God above all. She grows up. And lo then the Archangel, on many occasions and with great insistence, begins to reveal to Joan at first very frightened her astonishing mission: to come, she, poor ignorant peasant girl, to the help of the great pity of the Kingdom of France, to become a leader of war, to cause the Dauphin to be anointed and crowned, to deliver Orleans, to expel the English.

In March of 1429 she is received at Chinon by the Dauphin, whom she recognizes among the lords of his court (he had disguised himself as one of them),—just as she had recognized Baudricourt at Vaucouleurs,—and whom she tells on behalf of God that he is the true heir and son of Charles VI. A commission presided over by Regnault of Chartres, Archbishop of Rheims, examines

Joan. (It is then that to Master Seguin, asking her what tongue her voices speak, she replies: "A better French than yours."—"It was true," he said, "I spoke Limousin.")

She does not wish any other sword than that of which her voices have revealed to her the existence,—buried in the Church of St. Catherine of Fierbois. One makes for her a standard such as her Saints wished, and which she will carry always in the battles. (She herself never shed blood, "I have never killed anyone." Moreover, as she declared several times, there was in her heart no hatred toward the English. She wanted that they return to their own country; and she took care to ask them first to do this willingly. But they scoffed at her letters, and she took up battle against them.)

On the 8th of May, Orleans is delivered.

On the 17th of July, Charles VII is crowned at Rheims.

Joan was then in her seventeenth year.

Once anointed and crowned, the king hastens to turn to diplomatic means, neglecting Joan while, badly supported militarily, she continues the war. She fails before Paris. She goes to the defense of Compiègne; on the 24th of May, 1430, she is captured there by the Burgundians. Prisoner in the Castle of Beaurevoir, she tries to escape, "makes the leap" from the top of the tower in which she is confined, falls down in a faint on the ground; they lock her up again.

The King of England and the Duke of Bedford form their plan: it is necessary to have her condemned by an ecclesiastical tribunal, so as to dishonor at the same stroke Charles VII and the crown which he holds from a heretic and from a sorceress whom "the Church" has sent to the stake. Their man will be Pierre Cauchon, Bishop of Beauvais, and conservator of the privileges of the University of Paris, which is very devoted to the English. In November, through the agency of Cauchon, Joan is sold to the English by the Burgundians, at the price of ten thousand *tournois* francs, and taken to Rouen, where they refuse her an ecclesiastical prison and lock her up in an iron cage.

The Condemnation

1. The trial of Rouen, which began on the 9th of January, 1431, was completely irregular. It was a "trial of the Ordinary," not of the Inquisition; and Cauchon, who presided over it under the pretext that Joan had been captured on the territory of his

jurisdiction, was by no right the Ordinary of Joan. He had been designated by the King of England, not by the Pope, whom they had not notified and whom they tried to keep in ignorance. He did not hesitate to use falsified or forged documents. The judges were all friends of England and enemies of Joan, who thought only of setting snares for her (but in order to reply she had her marvellous ingenuousness). She had asked that theologians of the French side be added to the assessors,—which was naturally refused. Among the one hundred and thirteen assessors,—jurists, canonists, etc., secular priests or regular priests,—who answered Cauchon's summons, eighty were doctors sent by the University of Paris. At the six public interrogatories of Joan some fifty or some sixty of these assessors were present. She undergoes afterwards nine other interrogatories in prison.

This trial was an ostentatiously staged ecclesiastical trial, gotten up by the King of England and prompted by an implacable political hatred, but, however irregular and fraudulent it may have been, purely ecclesiastical in its whole procedure. All the leaders of accusation were purely religious.

In answer to the twelve articles summing up the accusation, the University of Paris called Joan a tool of the demons, a liar, a blasphemer, an apostate, etc. However, in order that she be condemned to death and burned, the safest course was that she be a relapse. It was important therefore above all to lead her first to an abjuration, after which one expected indeed that she would have a relapse. At the churchyard of Saint-Ouen, on the 24th of May, one made to her all sorts of promises, and one presented to her a memorandum of which she understood nothing. She certainly did not deny her voices and her mission, but, at the end of her physical energies, and *through fear of the fire*, as she will say, "I prefer to sign than to be burned," she consents to give up her men's clothes, disobeying thus her Saints,[6] and signed with a cross the memorandum while declaring that she revoked nothing except on condition that this pleased God. After this pseudoabjuration she was condemned to perpetual imprisonment.

Brought back to her prison, she put on therefore women's clothes; but during her sleep her guards stole them from her, so that obliged to get up from bed by necessity of nature she had to put on again for a moment men's clothes (testimony of Jean Massieu at the trial of rehabilitation). The next day or the day after an English lord tried to rape her. After which she decidedly resumed men's clothes (testimony of Isambart de la Pierre and of

Martin Ladvenu). Lo! she is a relapse. The 29th of May, trial of relapse: condemnation to be burned on the following day.

After having declared that she had fallen into schism, idolatry, the invocation of demons, and many other crimes besides, and that after having abjured these misdeeds she fell again into the same errors, as the dog returns to his vomit, the verdict concluded: "You are a relapse and a heretic: Member of Satan, cut off from the Church, infected with the leprosy of heresy, we judge and decide that in order that you not infect others, you must be abandoned to the secular arm, and we abandon you to it."[7]

In the early hours of the morning of Wednesday, the 30th of May, Brother Martin Ladvenu, the confessor of Joan, came to her prison to announce to her that she was going to be burnt at the stake. She cried out and protested before God, tearing her hair. "My body which is pure, reduced to ashes!"

Then Cauchon arrived with seven assessors. "Bishop, I die because of you," Joan says to him. "If you had put me in a Church prison, this would not have happened; that is why I appeal against you before God."

After his departure, Joan went to Confession twice to Brother Ladvenu, and received the Eucharist.

2. It was not without purpose that Cauchon visited Joan before her execution. Had she not until the end hoped against all hope for the deliverance promised by her Voices?[8] The wretch wanted to triumph over her, tormenting until the end her soul now in agony. "Did not your Voices promise you that you would be delivered? And you are going to die. You see now how they deceived you,"—this is what he came to tell her.[9]

Did her two Saints come at this moment to comfort Joan? I think that if they came they kept silent. Joan knew well that she "would incur damnation if she said that God did not send her." It belonged to her, in full catastrophe, to enter entirely alone into the great night of God. All the assurances which her counsel had given to her,—it was in a marvellous aurora of enthusiasm, of boldness and of exultant confidence that she had seen them accomplished during a full year of prodigious events, of predictions realized to the letter, of difficult victorious combats.[10] And when her Voices, as she declared on the 14th of March, had told her that she would be delivered "by great victory," and to not fret about her martyrdom, and that she would go finally to Paradise, what was this martyrdom? Without doubt "the pain and adversity which she would suffer in prison." Would it be necessary to suffer more? She did not know this and trusted thereupon in Our Lord.[11] And even when (as she says on the 8th of May, in the Great Tower, before the instruments of torture), she had asked her Voices if she would be "burnt," and when the reply had been: "Trust in Our Lord, He will help you," let us not imagine that she understood all that which this reply implied; she believed still that the fire would be spared her, she believed literally in that which she had heard, and that deliverance and "great victory" were for the life of here on earth,—on, daughter of God, I will help you, on,—earthly hope had not left her. Now all is done with; it is necessary to understand the deliverance and the great victory and the supreme favor of God,—it is the pitiless flame, and "her body which is pure, reduced to ashes."

We are here in the presence of an ordinary method of God. His promises have a double meaning, their truth is too lofty, their splendor too sacrificial in order for us to be able to grasp right away the final and decisive meaning. God hides it in the shadows of this life. And He spares His friends while preparing them little by little. . . .

The Virgin Mary herself, on the day of the Visitation, when she said to Elizabeth: "He has upheld Israel his servant, ever mindful of his mercy," was it of Calvary that she was thinking then, and of the Church of her Crucified Son, and of the new people of God? No, but of the old Israel which perpetuated the seed of Abraham. And when the old man Simeon announced to her that the sword would pierce her, she kept this utterance in her heart, but it was only at the foot of the Cross that she understood it in all truth.

There is here a law which in one manner or another applies itself one day in the life of every Christian.

3. This morning of the 30th of May, before nine o'clock, Joan takes her seat with Brother Martin Ladvenu in the cart which takes her to the Vieux-Marché. The mitre which she has on her head bears the inscription: heretic, relapse, apostate, idolatress. Another sermon to be heard, delivered by Nicolas Midi, and during which she invokes her Voices. Then she ascends the stake, accompanied by Brother Ladvenu, to whom, when she sees the flame, she says: "Brother Martin, go down! The fire!" She had asked that one raise the Cross bearing the image of Jesus Crucified, in order that she could see it "until the threshold of death." Brother Isambart holds

the Cross before her; she cries out "Jesus, Jesus, Jesus," invokes the Saints; she dies crying: "Jesus!"

She was nineteen years old.

4. "My body which is pure, reduced to ashes. . . ."

At the inquiry preliminary to the trial of rehabilitation, Brother Isambart will testify that after the execution the executioner came to him and to his companion Brother Martin Ladvenu, "struck and moved to a marvellous repentance and terrible contrition, all in despair, fearing never to obtain pardon and indulgence from God for what he had done to that saintly woman; and said and affirmed this executioner that despite the oil, the sulphur and the charcoal which he had applied against Joan's entrails and heart, nevertheless he had not by any means been able to consume nor reduce to ashes the entrails nor the heart, at which was he as greatly astonished as by a manifest miracle."[12]

The Rehabilitation

1. It was in 1451 that Cardinal Guillaume d'Estouteville, Legate of Pope Nicholas V to Charles VII, opened,—doubtless at the request of the king, anxious to cleanse his crown of the dishonor which reflected upon it on account of the shame cast upon Joan,—a canonical inquiry concerning the trial of condemnation. He was assisted by the Dominican Jean Bréhal, general Inquisitor of France, great and noble figure who was to be the soul of the trial of rehabilitation. The Pope hesitated however to intervene, and to take sides in a debate between England and France, two great Catholic powers. In order to help him out of his difficulty, Bréhal suggested having the opening of the new trial requested by the mother and the two brothers of Joan, who sent to the Holy See a petition to that end. Nicholas V died meanwhile, and it was his successor Calixtus III who, in a rescript of the 11th of June, 1455, had the new trial opened.[13]

This trial,—the trial of rehabilitation,—was a perfectly regular ecclesiastical trial, in which in multiple inquiries all the surviving witnesses testified, and to which we owe precious information concerning Joan, as also remarkable doctrinal elucidations. It was conducted by men no doubt fallible but honest, and who had certainly their political attachments,—to France this time (now completely delivered as Joan had predicted),—but first and above

all the passion for justice and for truth, and the sense of their
duties before God and before the Church.

The verdict was rendered on the 7th of July, 1456, in the
Archiepiscopal Palace of Rouen. The decisions and the verdicts of
the judges of 1431 were declared in it "tainted with deceit, with
calumny, with iniquity, with contradiction, with manifest error in
fact and in law," and therefore "null, without value, without
effect, and dismissed."[14] This verdict of rehabilitation was prom-
ulgated the same day on the Square of Saint-Ouen, and on the
morrow on the Square of Vieux-Marché, with a solemn sermon
and the planting of an expiatory Cross.

2. The memory of Joan of Arc was thus avenged, and historical truth reestablished before men. Was this enough for Him
Whom Joan had loved until death, and Whose name she cried out
upon the stake?

Five centuries passed.

Leo XIII introduced the cause of beatification of Joan on the
29th of February, 1894.

She was beatified by Pius X on the 18th of April, 1909.

Joan was canonized by Benedict XV on the 16th of May,
1920. Here we have the term of the curve, the final point toward
which the rehabilitation tended, the inscription on the standards
of Heaven of the full accomplishment of the destiny of Joan and
of the purposes of God concerning her.

Canonization is an infallible act of the Pope. The "heretic,
relapse, apostate, idolatress" condemned to the fire by Cauchon
and the judges of Rouen was, with infallible certitude, a saint,
beloved by God, and whom the whole people of God invokes now.
Her Voices had rightly told her that she would go straight to
Paradise.

3. The condemnation of Galileo was the greatest error committed by the personnel of the Church acting *regularly*, but as
proper cause, and therefore fallible.

The condemnation of Joan of Arc was the worst iniquity
committed by a personnel of the Church acting *irregularly and
fraudulently*, and as *proper cause, and therefore fallible*.

The canonization of Joan, her rehabilitation consummated in
the glory of the saints,—it is the universal Church herself, the *Una,
sancta, catholica, apostolica*, the mystical Body of Christ and His
Bride, it is the person herself of the Church and her infallibility

who make themselves heard there, through the Pope acting *instrumentally, and infallibly,* as *the voice* of the *person* of the Church of the earth and of Heaven considered in her integrality.

On Private Revelations

1. When they treat of revelation in the most general sense of this word, theologians make two distinctions: they divide revelation into *theological* and *nontheological* according as the object which it makes known is or is not ordered *ad fidem deitatis,* to the truth of God itself as first object of belief; and they divide it into *Catholic* (or *public*) and *private* according as the organ which transmits it or "proposes" it to men is the public magisterium of the Church or only the private person who has received it.

St. Thomas teaches that since the coming of the only begotten Son no revelation henceforth can be *theological,* that is to say teach us anything new, anything which would not be contained in the deposit of Faith, concerning God or with reference to the truth of God as first object of faith.

Revelations newly produced in the Church relate not to what God is, but to what God wishes of us, they are of the practical order and for the direction of human acts, *ad directionem actuum humanorum.*

2. This is what the theologians tell us: private revelations concern the direction of human conduct. However do not the spiritual masters tell us the exact opposite? They warn their disciples that it is never necessary to act according to the private revelations which they themselves have been able to receive or which, received by others, have been able to come to their knowledge. St. Theresa and St. John of the Cross do not tire of insisting on this, with all the more vigor, it seems, as they themselves were not without being in many cases enlightened by such private revelations, which proved very useful in their practical behavior. But does one ever know with the saints? And with that measure of theirs which is not like our measures, and which serves them as a secret radar? St. Philip Neri was overwhelmed with extraordinary graces, and it sufficed that a soul be visited by such graces for him to display concerning it the most marked suspicion and the most marked severity.

As a matter of fact the apparent contradiction clears up easily.

In general one would expose oneself to error and to illusion if one took a private revelation for an immediate *rule of action.* The rule of human acts is reason, superelevated by faith (and by the gifts of the Holy Spirit), and it is to this rule, not to visions and revelations, that we must submit our acts. But private revelations are as it were lights in the sky or flares which *attract our attention* and project a glimmer of light on such or such an aspect of the situation which would have been able to escape the weak and distracted human reason. Then, thus alerted, behold man is able to use his prudential judgment, work of reason and of faith, as a rule of action of a rare and surprising accuracy, in particularly difficult occasions. It is indeed in this manner that the great spiritual masters, in their own conduct, put into practice the doctrine of the theologians concerning private revelations, given *ad directionem actuum humanorum.*

3. There are however exceptional cases, of which the case of Joan of Arc is an eminent example. These exceptional cases are distinguishable by two particular characteristics: in the first place the private revelation of which it is a question then is *"perfect"* or interiorly *"evident"* revelation, and the soul thus instructed knows therefore with a complete certitude that it is indeed God Who instructs it; in the second place this revelation, while being in itself a private revelation, concerns (according to a distinction indicated by Cajetan and by Benedict XIV) not the private good of an individual but the *common good* of the social body, and above all of the Church or of Christendom.[15]

Private revelations which concern thus the common good of the social body, and above all of the Church or of Christendom, confer by themselves a *mission,* and a public mission. They constitute the one who receives them in a determined function which has its own exigencies; they make of him an ambassador of God, a messenger, an *"angel."* Consequently the latter finds himself, from the point of view of the subjective conditions in which he is placed, in a case similar to that of the prophets of the Old Law: the received revelation links him to a divine mandate. At the same stroke it becomes *imperative rule,*—which certainly does not abolish the liberty of the practical judgment (Joan kept always this liberty of judgment, to the point even of disobeying twice her saints), but which the practical judgment has the duty to carry into effect.

4. Furthermore, the soul would lose faith if it refused or ceased to believe in the received revelation. This is a consequence of the other exceptional characteristic which we have noted in the private revelations in question: they are express or "perfect" revelations, accompanied by the certitude that it is God who instructs, in other words given with *evidence,*—an evidence which bears upon *the one who reveals (evidentia in attestante)* and upon the very fact of the received revelation.

Consequently, and I believe that on this point all the theologians are in agreement, the things about which God instructs the soul in such a revelation give rise, for the one himself who receives it, to an act of faith not human but divine.

This act of faith, according to the teaching of the Thomists, does not proceed from the virtue of theological faith, because that alone which God reveals with respect to the mysteries of the Deity itself as first object of credence is the object of the theological faith; but private revelations under the New Law do not have for their object the truth of the things hidden in God, but the direction of human acts. The act of faith which bears upon a private revelation when the one who receives it knows, through an evident supernatural light, that it comes from God, proceeds therefore from another kind of faith than theological faith; it proceeds, the theologians of Salamanca tell us, from that "faith" which is counted by St. Paul among the *gratis datae* charisms or graces.

But, and this is the important point, the same theologians teach that if the soul which receives an evidently divine revelation refused or ceased to believe what God told it, it would lose not only the faith of the charismatic order which it received as to this private revelation, but also all supernatural faith, and therefore theological faith also. For the fact is that the genus being destroyed, all the species contained in this genus are also destroyed. But what constitutes the genus *supernatural faith* (whatever *the object revealed* may be) is the formal *motive* for which one believes, that is to say the veracity of God revealing, and this formal motive is absolutely indivisible. To refuse its adhesion to a private revelation which it knows to be divine would be therefore, for the soul which has received such a revelation, to call in question the infallible authority of God revealing, to destroy the formal motive of supernatural faith, and by this to lose also that kind of supernatural faith which is theological faith, the faith which saves.

This is why Joan knew that if she denied her Voices "she would incur damnation." "If I said that God did not send me, I would incur damnation. True it is that God has sent me."

"For that which is to be believed in my revelations, I do not consult bishop, priest or anyone else."

"She believes as firmly the sayings and the deeds of St. Michael, who appeared to her, as she believes that Our Lord Jesus Christ suffered death and agony for us."

God First Served

1. Joan, do you submit to the Church? It is with this question that the judges of Rouen most harassed her.

As I have just noted, she had evidence that her revelations came from God: *evidentia in attestante,* evidence so strong that Joan went as far as to declare that what she heard was from God *without other means (sine alio modo),*—without intermediary. [16] Her Voices did not transmit to her a word which God had told *them* for her; it is the very word of God told *to her* directly that she heard in hearing them; her Voices were not intermediaries, *media;* they were the vibration in her ears, the expression in human language of the very word of God.

This is the principal motive of the clause which she does not fail to add to her replies: I am ready to obey the Church, *God first served,* [17] or *if one does not command me anything impossible.* [18]

2. If it is a question of the revealed deposit transmitted by the Church, and of the disciplinary authority of the hierarchy, here there is no problem: "If there are in her replies anything which is opposed to the Christian faith commanded by Our Lord, she would not wish to maintain it and she would be right eager to come to the contrary opinion."

"She believes that Our Holy Father the Pope of Rome, the Bishops and the other Churchmen have the duty to guard the Christian faith and to punish those who falter. . . ."

But if it is a question of her "sayings and deeds," as it was actually the case, in other words of the revelations received by her,—here "she will not revoke for anything in the world, nor for man who lives, what she has said and done on behalf of God." No one in the world can make her deny that which she knows that God has told her.

No one in the world, not even the Pope? She herself, on the 24th of May, 1431, asked: "of all the works I have accomplished, let them be sent to Rome to Our Holy Father the Sovereign Pontiff, in whom, and in God first, I trust."

Here still one notes however a certain reserve (indicated by the words *in God first*). What she wishes is to see herself the Pope and to be able to reply to him. "Asked if she wishes to submit herself to Our Holy Father the Pope, she replies: 'Take me to him and I shall reply to him.' " "I request to be taken to him, and then I shall answer before him all that which I shall have to answer." The fact is that Joan certainly did not fear that the Pope would judge her to be insane, or that he would order her *not to believe* in her revelations.[19] But who knows if he would not prefer that by reason of such or such circumstances she *act* differently? Better to be taken before him, to listen to him and to be able to reply to him (her Voices would have counselled her).

3. At the churchyard of Saint-Ouen she therefore appealed to the Pope. But one replied to her that the Pope was too far away; it is to the bishops who have charge of her that she must submit (to the Bishop of Beauvais, for example, to whom she had said: "As for you, I do not at all wish to submit to you, because you are my mortal enemy"?).[20] "It was said to her that to go such a long distance to fetch the Pope could not be done, that the Ordinaries were judges, each in his own diocese, and that it was necessary that she throw herself upon the Holy Church and that she abide by what the clerks and other learned men said and had determined on her sayings and deeds."[21]

In the sentence of death of the 30th of May, the clerks and other learned men will be called *scientifici doctores* to whom this obstinate, wretched girl refused to submit. "Licet debite et sufficienter tam per nos quam, pro parte nostra, per nonnullos scientificos et expertos doctores ac magistros salutem animae tuae zelantes saepe et saepius admonita fueris. . . ."[22]

The judges of Joan had themselves a confused idea of the Church. And they rendered this confusion willingly worse still, absolutely insurmountable, by profiting from the *humanly* total ignorance of the girl of great heart in order to astound her with learned words which she did not understand, in their questions and so-called explanations concerning the Church militant and the Church triumphant. Joan felt that they were doing everything in order to confuse her. The irremediable ambiguity of the word

'Church' such as they employed it, in order to make of it a fief of
experts and of scientific doctors who demanded obedience in
judging and "determining" concerning the secret of hearts and
concerning words received from God,—this is the second motive of
the clause *God first served* which Joan never failed to use.

4. As Bréhal says in his *Recollectio*,[23] apropos of the judges
of Rouen, *clarum est quid per Ecclesiam isti intenderunt, non
quidem Ecclesiam romanam aut universalem, sed potius semetip-
sos.* What they understood by "the Church" was *themselves.*

Consequently it is with full right, and with a perfectly pure
orthodoxy, that Joan (concerning the simplicity of whom Bréhal
and his friends, doctors like him, insist a little heavily,— she understood nothing of the jargon of the experts of Rouen, but she was,
in her own way, much better informed than they concerning the
Church) did not hesitate to reply: "I do believe that the Church
militant cannot be at fault or fail, but as for my sayings and deeds,
I place them and refer them in all to God Who has made me do all
that I have done."[24] "Replies that she believes indeed that Our
Holy Father the Pope of Rome and the bishops and the other
Churchmen have the duty to guard the Christian faith and to
punish those who falter; but as for her, concerning her deeds, she
will submit only to the Church of Heaven, that is to say to God, to
the Virgin Mary, and to the saints of Paradise."[25]

It is surprising that on this subject an enormous misconception
has been committed by many historians and critics, and still makes
its way in the best minds.[26] One has thought that she made of the
Church of Heaven another Church, a Church *separate* from that of
the earth, and to whom she appealed *against* the Church of the
earth, whereas in reality it was for her a single and same Church,
but who there above saw God and here on earth did not see Him;
so that she believed in the Church of the earth as well as in the
Church of Heaven, and did not at all appeal to the Church of
Heaven against the Church of the earth, but only with reference to
a matter (her revelations) which, concerning exclusively what she
herself had to do by order of God, and no point of doctrine, *was
not within the province* of the Church of the earth or of anyone
here on earth (except the Pope, *and God first*[27]).

She said everything on this point in a reply of inexhaustible
meaning: "She replies: 'I abide by God who sent me by the Holy
Virgin and all the saints in paradise. And I am of opinion that *it is
all one and the same thing, Our Lord and the Church* [in other

recensions: *it is all one and the same thing, God and the Church*],
and that of that one should make no difficulty. Why do you make
difficulty over that?' "[28]

God and the Church,
It Is All One and the Same Thing

1. In this dazzling reply and a flash of intuitivity, Joan, who
could not explain herself with the words of the theologians, said
all that which these words can and will ever be able to say that is
most true concerning the mystery of the Church.

In saying: God and the Church—it is all one and the same
thing, Joan was saying that the Church is not God because she is
created, but that she is the universe of created spirits living by the
very life of God through grace (grace *in via* here on earth, consummated grace in Heaven). She was saying that the Church is composed of angels as well as of men. She was saying, after St. Paul,
that the Church is the Body of Christ and the Bride of Christ and
the plenitude of Christ. She was saying that the Church of Heaven
and that of the earth are not two different Churches, but essentially the single and same and unique Church of Christ under two
different states.[29] She was saying,—I dare to think it, that which a
poor idiot philosopher tries to show in the present book,—that this
single and same and unique Church who is at one and the same
time in Heaven and on earth, and who is but one with Christ as the
Bride with the Bridegroom, is a created person as He is an
uncreated person, and that her personality unique in its kind is a
personality which embraces in its supernatural unity and supernatural individuality the numberless multitude of all the members
of Christ, whether they see the divine essence or whether they
tread their way in faith.

2. And in saying that God and the Church—it is all one and
the same thing, she was saying that in relying for her deeds and
sayings upon the saints of Paradise she was not failing in anything
in that which she owed to the Church of the earth. She was saying
that the persons of the Church of Heaven knew in the light of
Vision, as she herself knew with divine evidence, that the revelations received by her came from God, whereas the persons of the
Church of the earth, who live by faith, could judge only of that
which is consonant with or contrary to the faith common to all

Christians, which she herself professed integrally with her whole heart. And that in relying for her deeds and sayings upon the Saints of Paradise, while relying upon the Church of the earth as to the truths revealed by Christ to all men, it was still and always upon the same person of the Church that she relied, and not without showing respect to the Church of the earth, since she was ready, and she asked, to submit—God first served—her deeds and sayings to the leader of the Church of the earth, and even to the Council, the sole ones, in such an unusual case, able to represent the Church in her universality, and to decide and to judge in her name.

Two Aberrations Concerning the Mission of Joan

1. The first has been a "pious" aberration. In the last century, Frenchmen, and above all so-called French Catholics "of the right," venerated in Joan of Arc a saint sent by God in order to attest that France is the chosen nation among nations. Joan, idol of national vanity: one could not better disfigure her memory. As if the sole chosen people was not the people of Israel,[30] and as if God did not take care in like manner of all the nations of the world! The young Frenchmen of today no longer reduce the mission of Joan to the glorification of their native country, but this is because, even if they are Christians, they no longer wish to hear about saints and about angels, and because on the other hand they do not feel very proud of their country.

It is indeed true however that the immediate visible mission of Joan was,—and in what a miraculous manner!,—to liberate France and to cause her to recover her political independence. But this was not at all with a view to showing that France is the first of the nations; it was only because, at that given moment of history, France, whose titles in medieval Christendom were so firmly established, suffered cruelly injustice, and because this injustice had to cease. "And the Angel told her the pity which was in the kingdom of France." It was a question there only of justice, and of compassion for the oppressed,—"I have been sent to the poor and to the destitute,"—and of reestablishing a country in its rights and in its liberty.

2. The other aberration has been a "scholarly" aberration. One has seen some serious authors ask themselves what disastrous

results would have occurred inevitably in the history of the world if Joan had not succeeded in driving out the English. They doubtless imagined God as an earthly leader of government drawing up plans for the future, and forgot that He holds all second causes in His hand, and causes them to vary as He pleases.

In itself, the canonization of Joan put an end to these two aberrations, by showing that the true mission of Joan, her great invisible mission, was a universal mission.

The True Mission of Joan

1. However rash this may be, it is necessary indeed to try to form, as best one can, an idea of the true mission of Joan, a mission which rises in tiers upon several different planes, and which one conjectures to be as vast as it is mysterious.

In the first place, it seems to me that, first and above all, Joan (it was in the fifteenth century that she lived, and underwent her martyrdom) was sent as a marvellous *adieu* of the Lord God to medieval Christendom on the point of ending.

In spite of the vestiges of barbarism which it still carried, this Christendom was the highest summit of Christian civilization in human history. Let one think of the admirable faith of the whole Christian common people of that time, and even of the great of this world (although they may have lost everything through the ambition and the moral weakness of the majority of them). Let one think of the immense work of reason,—in the highest spheres of thought, and under the light of faith,—accomplished by this time; of the intellectual and moral heritage which we owe to it, of its mystics, of its saints, of the builders of its cathedrals, of the idea of honor, of human dignity, of the service of the poor, which, however betrayed it may have been able to be in practice, it nevertheless bequeathed to us. Let one imagine to oneself St. Louis and St. Thomas Aquinas eating at the same table . . .

God loved this medieval Christendom, and rejoiced at all the goodness and holiness there was in it. In the moment when it was about to perish, He made to it in the person of Joan an altogether extraordinary gift,—not as recompense (to whom would it have been directed?) but as *sign*, sign of love and of gratitude. It was as if Heaven had made a gift to the earth of an incomparable icon of blue and of gold, in a screen studded with flowers of Paradise moistened by the Precious Blood and by the tears of the Blessed Virgin.

But this blessed icon was that of an executed girl criminal,—executed by priests of Christ: and the gift of Heaven brought also to earth a sign of the divine severity toward the blunders and the violences which so stained with blood medieval Christendom,—especially toward that Inquisition of which the atrocious caricature exhibited by the trial of Rouen was signed with the wrath of God. *Causae ad invicem sunt causae.* The end of medieval Christendom entailed the end of the medieval Inquisition; and the medieval Inquisition was one of the irreparable historical mistakes by which medieval Christendom was to perish.

The adieu of the King of Heaven to medieval Christendom,—the primordial aspect of the mission of Joan and of her passage upon earth,—was at one and the same time an adieu of sublime gratitude and an adieu of inevitable chastisement.

2. In this mission of Joan, what strikes us first is the immediate visible mission, of which I have said a few words above: the liberation of France, and which fully succeeded (it reached completion very quickly after the death of Joan).

But there was also, still on the same plane of the temporal work to be accomplished, a secret mission, and one of greater bearing, of which, during the lifetime of Joan, something was manifested. I am thinking of the astonishing scene which took place at Chinon in 1429. "One day," the author of the *Breviarium historiale* relates, "the Maid asked the king to make her a present. The request was accepted. She asked then as a gift the kingdom of France itself. The astonished king gave it to her after some hesitation, and the young girl accepted it. She wished even that the deed of it be solemnly drawn up and read by the four secretaries of the king. After the charter had been written out and recited in a loud voice, the king remained a little stupefied, when the young girl pointed to him and said to those present: 'Behold the poorest knight of his kingdom.'

"And after a little time, in the presence of the same notaries, disposing, as mistress, of the kingdom of France, she returned it into the hands of Almighty God. Then, at the end of a few other moments, acting in the name of God, she invested King Charles with the kingdom of France; and of all this she wished that a solemn document be drawn up in writing."[31]

What took place there was for Joan of major importance. She

was sent not only in order to liberate France. She was sent also in order to restore "the holy kingdom" to its true vocation: to serve the King of Heaven. It was according to the ideas of the time, and in the perspective of the sacral regime, and of a monarchy which by the Holy Ampulla was assigned in a quasi-sacramental manner to an essentially Christian temporal task, that Joan conceived the significance of what on that day she had Charles VII do, and the secret mission with which she herself was invested. Under another regime than the sacral regime, it was not impossible for kings truly Christian in heart to act according to the spirit which she requested. In actual fact, seeing the behavior of the kings who succeeded Charles VII (and in general the politics of all our rulers), it is necessary to state that this secret mission of Joan was a total failure. However, if one thinks of the wholly different manner in which the Christian spirit no longer of kings but of the faithful people must more than ever strive to vivify the temporal order, is it to be believed that in Heaven Joan has forgotten a mission which was so dear to her?

3. Let us pass to an altogether different consideration, in which this time it will be a question of the mission of Joan according as it continues in human history on the plane of the spirit (which by its very nature is a universal plane).

I remark in the first place that no Saint has attracted as much as Joan the attention of writers and of poets, outside as well as within the frontiers of our country, and to whatever spiritual family they may belong. Come first Villon and Christine of Pisa. Voltaire detested her; it is doubtless because she irked him exceedingly. Anatole France loved her against his will. Among those who loved her gladly, the most celebrated ones are Schiller and Bernard Shaw.

On the other hand there are those in whom one can discern either a kinship of spirit with her (sometimes unknown to themselves), or a direct influence of her genius: from Pascal for example (who, as far as I know, never spoke of her, but who also was under the sign of "God first served") to Villiers de l'Isle-Adam, Léon Bloy, Charles Péguy, Claudel perhaps, and, perhaps in a sense, André Breton, and, certainly, a great painter like Georges Rouault. . . .

But what matters most here is the plane of spirituality itself. The milieu from which St. Theresa of Lisieux came, and her natural temperament, had nothing in common with those of Joan.

And yet not only did she love her as a sister, and, in the heart of the cloister, live with her spirit, but one can say that in the domain of the pure interior life her mission among us has been stamped with a mark which allies it singularly with that of Joan: extraordinary liberty, extraordinary simplicity, extraordinary courage, and, above all, total gift-of-oneself to give heroically assistance to the pity which is in the kingdom of the earth.[32] The celebrated saying of Theresa: "I shall spend my Heaven doing good on earth," has the resonance of a reply of Joan.[33] And what light it gives us! So many Christians, understanding wrongly the *Requiem aeternam,* have thought for such a long time that the Saints spent their Heaven *resting* and slept there with a blessed sleep! Actually the vision of God exalts unceasingly in them an inconceivable ardor—and one which will last until the end of the world—to come to the assistance of the poor lost sheep here on earth. "Since the time that I have been suffering for you," the Blessed Virgin said to the two little shepherds of La Salette, in her message to all. And again: "If I desire that my Son not abandon you, I am instructed to pray to Him unceasingly. And you, for your part, do not appreciate it. Pray as you may, do as you may, you will not be able to recompense the grief which I have accepted for the sake of you."

4. May a moment's remark—in order to catch my breath—on a much lower plane be permitted me here,—a small digression, parenthetically, in which I would like to return to my old professional concerns as philosopher? My Scholastic masters taught me a doctrine which I cherish. But I have always thought that the so-called "Scholastic" mode of exposition, manner and style have had their day, because they have become an obstacle to the life and to the progress of this great doctrine in human history. What it needs is no longer a doctoral and magistral approach, inscribing in marble a majestic *sed contra* and peremptory responses to numbered objections; it is a free approach, inquiring, humble and proud at one and the same time; it is to advance under the standard of Joan. (There was something of this in the style of Bergson.)

I dream of students in theology and of seminarians who would pray each day with all their heart to St. Thomas Aquinas in order that he may enlighten them and help them to adhere in the truth, and to St. Joan of Arc in order that she may give to that which they will have to say and to do among men the manner and the style which are required today.

5. A third and final consideration, which concerns things of singular importance, but which I shall present in the briefest manner (it would take a whole book in order to develop it suitably).

I think that Joan of Arc—who failed, but not forever, in the secret mission of which it was a question above—is par excellence the saint and the patron of the temporal mission of the Christian; in other words the saint and the patron of the Christian laity: for this temporal mission is the affair of laymen, to be conducted under their initiative and at their risks and perils,[34] —*on condition* that in their collaboration with men of every belief and of every nation for a common temporal work they keep in their hearts a faith as pure, total, and absolute as that of Joan. (This is required not only by loyalty toward God, but also by the loyalty—and for the efficacy—of a true friendship with non-Catholics and non-Christians). Let us note that in the temporal work in question it is not a question of bringing about the happiness of man upon the earth. In a civilization more and more dehumanized by techocracy, it may be that this temporal work, of the necessity of which we have finally become conscious today, occurs quite precisely, in our historical age, to compensate the greater evils and to avoid the greater destructions which threaten the world.

I think also that Joan is par excellence the saint of the last combats of the Church; and that it is by small flocks faithful to God first served that these combats will be conducted; and that from the supreme torments of the world, in the midst of which she herself will be assailed on all sides, the Church will emerge radiant and martyrized. It will be the hour of Joan.

XV

In Search of an Exact Language

An Error of Current Language

1. "Churchmen will never be *the Church.*"[1] One knows it well and they know it well. They happen however sometimes to act or to seem to act *as if* they were the Church. And the manner in which current language employs the word "the Church" invites us to commit the same confusion. There is here, it seems to me, a point which it is important to consider closely.

When it is a question of any human society, let us say for example of a State or of a nation, language attributes readily to the society in question that which is done by its directing personnel. When an Ambassador of France pays a visit to the Minister of Foreign Affairs of the power to which he is accredited, he will say to him for example: "France cannot tolerate such an affront," or "France refuses to participate in such an agreement." France! It is not France; it is the French Freign Office and the French government, and no one is mistaken about it. The language is inexact, but this inexactness—"France" instead of "the directing personnel of France"—is normal and without risk, because it is a question then of a collectivity, the French Nation, which has without doubt psychological traits and moral characteristics, but which has not itself a personality in the ontological or metaphysical sense of the word.

If on the contrary it is a question of a person, let us say of a very busy professor, and of the secretary in charge of his correspondence, it will not be rare that on his own initiative this secretary may reply to someone who requests an appointment: "Professor cannot receive you," and this reply can be erroneous, and be contrary to the wish of the professor himself, in the case for example in which the one who requests the appointment would have some information to provide him that would be useful to his work; whereas when the professor writes a report which his secretary reads to some academy, one is sure of having to do with the thought of the professor himself, and with views which he desires to communicate.

2. With regard now to the Church, who like a nation is a human collectivity, but who, unlike all other human collectivities, has received from God a supernatural personality, it has happened that for centuries one has acquired the habit of saying "a decision of the Church" or "an act of the Church" each time that her directing personnel posited an act or reached a decision.

It was thus because one followed the natural bent of language (as in the case of an ambassador who says "France" apropos of a decision of the French government), and also because this rendered the exercise of authority easier and gave more prestige to those who exercised it. But then the language employed was not only inexact in its formulation; the inexactness which it comprised was in itself dangerous and capable of leading into error. It ran the risk of causing one to forget that unlike all merely natural collectivities or societies the Church, Body of Christ, Bride of Christ, Plenitude of Christ, has her own life and her own personality which transcend the activities of her personnel and express themselves by the latter only when she herself employs them instrumentally, in short the inexactness of the language in question ran the risk of causing the mystery itself of the Church to be disregarded in actual fact.

It suffices to read a history of the Church or a manual of theology in order to see how frequently current usage attributes to "the Church" an act or a decision of her directing personnel, without distinguishing whether the latter has acted as proper cause or as agent instrumentally employed by the Church herself, by the person of the Church. This does not trouble at all the historians of the Church. But it seems to me that for a long time this has troubled quite a lot the theologians: having, at least vaguely and subconsciously, the idea that the acts and decisions of the personnel of the Church, even when the latter acted as proper cause, and therefore fallible, were acts and decisions "of the Church" herself and engaged her responsibility, did they not have a tendency, if not to excuse the mistakes and the errors committed by the personnel of the Church, at least to present them under the least unfavorable light possible, without declaring squarely that they were mistakes and errors rightly characterized, and sometimes very grave ones? It is perhaps for the same reason that of neither the populations which were victims of the violences of the Crusades, nor the elder people, the people of Jesus and of Mary, have those who have the responsibility of authority in the Church ever yet, to my knowledge, asked solemnly pardon for Christians for the evil of which the latter once rendered themselves guilty concerning them.

3. Today the situation has completely reversed itself. But one continues more than ever to make the confusion between the Church herself and her personnel; and, this time, it is in order to say that finally the Church recognizes that she errs, finally she confesses her fallibility, finally one can proclaim that she has not ceased to accumulate mistakes in the diverse epochs of her history; and that if Vatican II declared her indefectibly holy, in actual fact she is however constantly subject to error, even a sinner herself. In the final analysis she is a human society like the others, a merely human society to which the Holy Spirit gives a helping hand from time to time, above all by theologians endowed with prophetic charisma who erect themselves into a magisterium,—a "scientific" magisterium,—with which the sole true magisterium would be doubled.

The inexactness of language which one thus turns to account in order to impute to "the Church" the mistakes and the errors committed by her personnel is not only dangerous and capable of leading into error; it has become decidedly pernicious, because it vitiates thought by blinding it concerning that which the Church *is* in reality.

The Church,—the one, holy, catholic and apostolic,—the universal Church considered in her integrality is, as we have seen, a single and same person under two different states,—peregrinating on earth and blessed in Heaven. And it is only, on the one hand in the whole sacramental order (in which the priest acts under the direct motion of God omnipotent, and at the same time, under another relation, as instrument also of the person of the Church), on the other hand when (owing to the fact that the high personnel of the Church teaches then, under an infallible assistance of the Holy Spirit, as instrumental agent of the person of the Church) the magisterium expresses itself with an absolute authority and in an irrevocable manner,—in other words when the Pope "teaches alone (solemn magisterium not communicable to the Roman Congregations)," or "conjointly with the bishops assembled in General Council (solemn magisterium)," or "conjointly with the bishops dispersed through the world (ordinary magisterium)"[2]—it is only in these diverse lines of activity that it is given to us in a determinately and perfectly manifest manner to see at work and to hear speak the person of the Church, the Church herself. And the latter,—although composed here on earth of sinful members, as also of a personnel which holds from her its authority, but is fallible when it acts only as proper cause,—the latter, I say, the Church herself, has for inamissible properties infallibility as also holiness.

This is what is disregarded today by many authors and orators more than ever sure of themselves, new *scientifici doctores* who, continuing to confuse in their language, like their ancestors, the person and the personnel, and victims, in a manner much more grave still than their ancestors, of this same confusion in their thought, have now passed to the opposite camp, in trying to ruin as much as they can Roman authority,—which, as Jean Bréhal noted, is none other than the authority of the universal Church.

For whoever, today, wishes to keep truly in his mind the sense of the Church, and faith in the Church, I think that it has become a necessity to put decidedly an end, first and above all in his thought, but also in his language, to the confusion between person of the Church and personnel of the Church against which one has for so long a time badly defended oneself.

If it was not the act of Churchmen only, Popes and preachers (acting as proper causes), but the act of *the Church* herself, to have, in the Middle Ages, stirred up in the soul of Christians the zeal of the Holy War, while omitting to condemn the exactions and the plunderings of the Crusades; if at the same period it was not the princes and the Churchmen, but it was *the Church* herself who subjected the Jews to an odiously inhuman regime, if it was *the Church* herself who instituted the medieval Inquisition, and was responsible for the Spanish Inquisition, for all the decisions of the Roman Inquisition and of the Roman Congregations; if it was *the Church* herself who condemned Galileo; if it was *the Church* herself, though the trial was irregular, who sent Joan of Arc to the stake, at the risk of canonizing her afterwards; if it was to *the Church* herself that were imputable the court habits and the apparent solidarity with the powers of this world which masked the true visage of the Papacy at the times when it had itself a temporal sovereignty to be exercised;[3] if it was the *Church* herself who burned Savonarola and Giordano Bruno, and so well "questioned" Campanella that he escaped condemnation only by feigning madness; if it is the *Church* herself who did all this, then, yes, one can take pleasure in regarding her as a haughty and quite cruel old sovereign of past times, routinish also and pestering, enamored of her privileges and haunted by the concern for power or for the appearances of power, who wishes at any cost to be obeyed while making often faulty decisions and while giving often orders sullied with error,—all these proud, futile judgments issuing from an absurd mistake and wronging unworthily her who in reality is the kingdom of God already begun among us.

To Correct Language As Much As Possible, and, in Any Case, Thought

1. What is required in itself is to correct our language in order to render it exact, in other words to employ the words "the Church," "a decision of the Church," "an act of the Church," only when we are speaking of the person of the Church *acting herself* here on earth *through the instrumentality* of her ministers.

I think that in general this is not impossible, and that in the cases in which the personnel of the Church is not instrumental agent of the latter, one could, in order to designate that which it does then, employ other words than the word "the Church": one could say, for example, now "the ecclesiastical authority," now "the priesthood," now "the hierarchy," now "the Popes," or "such and such a Pope" (Pastor wrote a *History of the Popes*), now "the Roman Congregations" or "the Roman Curia," now "the Episcopate of such and such a country," now "the religious leaders," now "the high clergy," and so on, not to mention the word "the curés" dear to Péguy who put into it tenderness at the same time as some peasant mistrust.

The search for the proper word in such or such particular case would doubtless require a great effort of attention, and a permanent struggle against the facilities of language, but it would be worth the trouble of it.

I understand well that sometimes one would not succeed in breaking the old habits and a vocabulary consecrated by usage, and that for example one will say always "the Church and the State." The fact remains that the use of the word "the Church" there where what is involved is not the *One, holy, catholic and apostolic* in her universality,—the Church herself or the person of the Church,—but the personnel of the Church acting as proper cause, and therefore fallible, is an abuse of language likely to mislead the mind, and to which it is of major importance to strive to put an end.[4]

2. However it may be finally with vocabulary, and whatever may be the fate of the suggestion which I am making here as to language, and which I would like to shout from the housetops (but I know well that its justness will not prevent it from remaining futile), it is essentially important to maintain *in thought* the distinction between the Church herself, or the person of the Church, and the personnel of the latter.

The books entitled "History of the Church" speak to us much more of the personnel of the Church than of her person herself. The term "History of the Church" is nevertheless normal and justifiable in itself, since the Church of the earth is in time, and since she is the person of the Church under one of her two states, so that the latter finds herself always in the background of that which the works thus entitled tell us. It belongs to their authors and to their readers to have their minds on the alert, and to never forget in their thought the distinction between the Church herself and her personnel.

How the Person of the Church Is in Time

1. According as she is in the state of glory or of consummated grace the person of the Church is, as to the Beatific Vision, in eternity, and, as to the events which there also supervene, in that duration which one calls *aevum* or eviternity. According as she is in the peregrinal state she is in time,—like us, with us on the earth.

In proportion as time advances, she progresses, through the

new dogmatic definitions which the Councils and the Popes speaking *ex cathedra* promulgate, in the explicitation of the divine truth itself which she has the responsibility of proposing to us. She purifies herself, not as to the degree of her holiness, which found itself at the highest point at the time when the immaculate Virgin had taken John for son, time of the apostles and of the martyrs, but,—while the number of her members succeeding each other from generation to generation grows unceasingly,—as to the progress in them of the illumination by faith of the higher activities of reason, and of the diverse activities of human life,—and also as to the progress and to the deepening, in the best among them (although all sinners in some manner) of the growth-in-awareness of the exigencies of the Gospel, and of the nature of the work to be accomplished here on earth by Christians.

It is true that at the same time the occasions of sinning assume new forms for men. In the Apostolic Age one supposed the Second Coming to be near. Can one not think that the latter is delayed from century to century by the penance which the Church does not cease to have to do for the sins of men?

2. The life of the Church on earth is of an order which transcends that of culture or of civilization, but it is in close contact and in constant exchange with the diverse cultures or civilizations which divide the world; and in passing through the diverse ages of culture it gives much to each and receives from it much.

In the Middle Ages the culture of the epoch made to the Church and to her personnel a precious gift with the critical study of the Greek philosophies and of the Arabian philosophies to be assimilated and transformed by theology. And it made to the Church and to her personnel a very bad gift with the idea, current then, that the means of force, and temporal sanctions, and physical constraint must be employed in the service of religion.

In modern times the culture of the epoch has made to the Church and to her personnel a very beautiful gift with its sense of the respect due to the researches of science and with its proclamation of the liberty of conscience; and it has made to the Church and to her personnel a very bad gift with its aberrant philosophies, and furthermore, these last years, with that infernal enterprise of dehumanization which claims to substitute calculators and electronic machines for the intelligence *in the very domain of thought and of liberty:* in order to compose a symphony for example or an architectural plan, or in order to compose works of religious sociology,—why not manuals of pluralist theology?—even in order to give on a card, to a girl or to a boy, the characteristics of the husband or of the wife to be chosen, even also, in certain convents, in order to make judgment concerning the value of a vocation. . . .

3. The person of the Church is there, before our eyes, manifestly at work, through the magisterium when it teaches infallibly. She is there, before our eyes, manifestly at work—and in what a sublime manner!—through the Sacrifice of the Mass, she is there through the Sacraments, through each Baptism, each absolution received, each communion in the Body and in the Blood of Christ. And she is there also, before our eyes, under an indeterminately and imperfectly manifest mode, through the grace and the charity which God gives invisibly when man does not slip away from it, and which are a participation in the soul and in the life of the Church, and which express themselves in a more or less clearly discernible manner by the acts which they cause to be posited. The person of the Church is there before our eyes, under an indeterminately and imperfectly manifest mode, each time that a good work accomplished, an act of justice or of mercy, a word which enlightens and comforts, emanates from a heart in which God dwells. The person of the Church is there before our eyes under an imperfectly manifest mode, each time that in everyday life, and to the extent that we can judge it, a member of the personnel of the Church,—whether he acts, under a special impulse of the Holy Spirit, as instrument of the Church, or even whether he acts only as proper cause,—performs well his ministry and uses well his authority.

Finally, even when one of the members of her personnel uses badly his juridical authority or his moral authority, the person of the Church is still there in a certain indirect manner, which does not at all render her responsible for that which he does in betraying her spirit (even, as in certain lucubrations of today, her faith itself), she is there in this sense that it is she who, by a Sacrament, invested him with the authority which he holds. Whence it comes that there is for us a duty of conscience to obey (except if it is an act forbidden by God which finds itself then prescribed) the prescriptions which are given to us by the personnel of the Church exercising regularly its juridical authority, even when, acting as proper cause, it happens to err in such or such occasion.

4. The essential point remains to be said, and I feel very unworthy to touch on it. If as Church of the earth the person of the Church is in time, it is above all in order to continue in it all along the ages—she, the Body of Christ and the Bride of Christ—the work of redemption which Christ accomplished once and for all upon the Cross. This is the great mystery of the coredemption. Until the end of time the Passion of the Lord continues here on earth in His martyrs, in His Saints, in His friends, even in the most imperfect of His friends, to the extent that they love Him truly. United by love to His sufferings and to His love, they form but one with Him in order to apply little by little, at each step of human history, the infinite merits of Jesus. Thus their sufferings are His sufferings, and their love is His love.

In Conclusion of This Book:
A Few Remarks Concerning It

1. I have an idea that this book will displease everybody, I mean all those who today have taken position either "on the right" or "on the left." (And this does not displease me, although I certainly did not have this intention in writing it.) It will displease some because of the primordial importance which I attach to the person of the Church, others because of the liberty with which I speak of her personnel.

And, however, of the personality with which God has supernaturally endowed His Church (and on which, in my opinion, the majority of theologians have not sufficiently insisted) one can say, in equivalent terms, what John of St. Thomas[5] said concerning another controverted point: although in the faithful people (let us not speak of the pseudosavants) many take no account of it or take little account of it *speculative et in actu signato,* in their speculative reflection and the manner in which they express themselves, no one however calls it in question *in ipso exercitio et quasi practice,* in the spontaneous movement of his thought and in actually lived practice.

And as to the personnel of the Church, each one notes readily, in passing, that, according to the saying quoted at the head of this chapter, "Churchmen will never be the Church." But when one comes to speculative reflection and to historical statements, one hesitates often to mark in a sufficiently firm manner the real bearing of this distinction, with respect in particular to the gravity of the risks to which, when they act as proper cause, Churchmen are exposed like each one of us; at a time, however, when concern for truth and attention itself to the sacred mystery of the Church should lead one to speak bluntly, in ignoring the veils of modest reverence with which the good traditional customs required that one shelter them, of the mistakes and of the errors which Churchmen, when they act as proper cause, can commit, and which in actual fact they have often committed, and which they commit at present for reasons exactly the opposite of those of long ago,—and which are not mistakes and errors of the Church herself.

2. I have written these pages while working against the clock (at my age one is indeed obliged to do so). On such and such particular points it may be that they contain errors which I ask only to be corrected. But concerning the major themes upon which they are centered,—the notion of the person of the Church, who is a single and same person in Heaven and on earth, and in whom are inherent holiness and infallibility; the distinction between the person of the Church and her personnel; the distinction between the personnel of the Church acting as instrumental cause of the latter (whose voice then it causes to be heard and through which she herself acts then) and the personnel of the Church acting as proper cause (then it is exposed to mistake and to error),—concerning these diverse themes my convictions are absolutely firm: to the point that I venture to hope to have them shared by some, among those—more numerous than one thinks, but of whom the *mass media* scarcely reveal to us the existence— who in the midst of a tempest of widely diffused foolish ideas suffer much in their faith, and desire to have done with the demythization of dogmas and the secularization, or profanization, of a Christianity which our new doctors and spiritual guides would like to entrust into the hands of the sociologists, of the psychoanalysts, of the structuralists, of the Marcusists, of the phenomenologists, and of the pioneers of technocracy.

3. What I have tried to furnish here is the last testimony of an old solitary aided in his weakness by her who has always inspired his work.

As I wrote above, I have an idea that today it will displease many. But who knows? In fifty years one will find perhaps that all of this has been very poorly said, but, that after all, it was not so stupid.

Notes

NOTES TO CHAPTER I

1. Cf. Vatican II, *Dogmatic Constitution on the Church,* Ch. I, Sections 3 and 5: Christ "inaugurated the kingdom of heaven on earth and revealed to us the mystery of the Father. By His obedience He brought about redemption. The Church, or, in other words, the kingdom of Christ now present in mystery, grows visibly in the world through the power of God."

"In Christ's word, in His works, and in His presence this kingdom reveals itself to men. . . . The miracles of Jesus also confirm that the kingdom has already arrived on earth: 'If I cast out devils by the finger of God, then the kingdom of God has come upon you' (Lk. 11:20; cf. Mt. 12:28). . . . The Church consequently, equipped with the gifts of her Founder and faithfully guarding His precepts of charity, humility, and self-sacrifice, receives the mission to proclaim and to establish among all peoples the kingdom of Christ and of God." (Walter M. Abbott, S. J., ed.: *The Documents of Vatican II,* New York: Herder and Herder; Association Press, 1966, pp. 16, 17-18.)

2. "Καὶ ἔδωκεν κεφαλὴν ὑπὲρ πάντα τῇ ἐκκλησίᾳ." The Vulgate translates: "Et ipsum dedit caput supra omnem Ecclesiam." Head over all the Church.

3. Cardinal Journet translates: " . . . l'Église, qui est son Corps, l'achèvement de Celui qui s'achève de toutes manières en toutes choses." And he adds: "En sorte que saint Jean Chrysostome peut écrire que le plérôme (c'est-à-dire l'achèvement, la plénitude) de la Tête est le Corps, et le plérôme du Corps, la Tête." (*L'Église du Verbe Incarné,* Paris, Desclée De Brouwer, 1951, t. II, p. 53.) This difference in translation comes from the fact that one gives to the last word *plérouménou* the sense either of a passive participle or

243

of a middle participle. Cf. A. Feuillet (*Le Christ, Sagesse de Dieu*, pp. 277-292), who opts for the passive and translates: "l'Eglise est la plénitude, la totalité des richesses de Celui qui est rempli de toutes manières [le Christ, rempli par Dieu]."

4. Cf. *Dogmatic Constitution on the Church*, Ch. I, Sect. 7.

5. *Gen.* 2, 24.

6. Cf. *Dogmatic Constitution on the Church*, Ch. I, Sect. 7: "Having become the model of a man loving his wife as his own body, Christ loves the Church as His bride."

7. *Indefectibiliter sancta. Dogmatic Constitution on the Church*, Ch. V, Sect. 39.—Cf. Ch. I, Sect. 6.

8. στῦλος χαὶ ἑδραίωμα. The word ἑδραίωμα signifies "that which renders unshakeably firm." This is why the Vulgate translates it by *firmamentum.*

9. Cf. *Dogmatic Constitution on the Church*, Ch. II, Sect. 9, where this text of St. Peter is cited. See also further on, Ch. IX, pp. 133 et seq.

Summarizing this chapter of the *Dogmatic Constitution on the Church*, Cardinal Journet points out that the Council took up again there "apropos of laymen that which had been affirmed in general of the whole Christian people. 'Laymen,' it is said there, 'are members of the people of God in which there is no inequality in regard to race or to nation, to social condition or to sex, they are brothers of Christ who came in order to serve not to be served. They share in the salvific mission of the Church, in her prophetic mission, in her royal service.' The innovation here—it is evident in the Constitution *De Ecclesia* as well as in the general orientation of the Council—is the no longer secret and painful, but imperious, 'growth-in-awareness,'—not certainly of an inadequateness to the world of her essential and structural catholicity,—but of the immensity of the effort to be accomplished, two thousand years after the coming of Christ, in order to rejoin the ever-increasing mass of humanity.... The Church turns toward her lay children with the concern less to *preserve* them from evil than to *send* them into the midst of the dangers with God in their heart, in order to bear witness to the Gospel." (Charles Journet, "Le Mystère de l'Eglise selon le IIe Concile du Vatican," *Revue Thomiste*, 1965, pp. 34-35.)

NOTES TO CHAPTER II

1. One is no longer a member of the Church if one has not kept the faith. (Cf. Ch. Journet, *L'Eglise du Verbe Incarné*, t. II, pp. 1056-1081.) Whoever has lost grace and charity is a "dead" member, and his faith is "dead" also (as to eternal life). In itself it is however always a gift of the supernatural order, so that such members "receive still from Christ a certain act of life, which is to believe" (*Sum. theol.*, III, q. 8, a. 3, ad 2).

2. "The saint does not place himself in the perspective of an ideal of perfection proposed to his effort, in order to measure afterwards whether he has come near to it or even whether he has accepted it. The misery with which he groans and which is revealed to him in the light in which he perceives—however confusedly this may be—the divine transcendence, is not

that of his virtue, nor even of his intention. More profoundly and more absolutely it is the misery of his *being*, not by way of abstract or metaphysical knowledge, but by way of vital reaction before the Presence of the divine *Being*." (Dom Pierre Doyère, Introduction to *Héraut de l'Amour divin*, t. 2 of *Oeuvres Spirituelles* of St. Gertrude, Paris, éd. du Cerf, 1968, pp. 39-40.)

3. I add however that for the aversion today evident toward the use of the laughably sinister piece of furniture called 'Confessional' there is an altogether different reason. I believe that those who—very justly—held frequent Confession to be a normal custom in the spiritual life felt more and more painfully the discordance between the idea that the sin of the world caused God to die on the Cross and the weekly drawing up of a list of current faults, always identical, to be confessed without forgetting anything, which resembles a little too much a list of provisions to be bought at the market. Would it not be desirable that all these sins always the same become the object of a formula of confession periodically recited by the community, and followed by a public absolution,—private Confession being reserved for the sins which really torment the soul of the penitent?

4. *Dogmatic Constitution on the Church*, Ch. V, Sect. 39.

5. One will note that in the Oriental form of the Apostles' Creed (St. Cyril of Jerusalem) the same preposition εἰς is employed for the Church as for God. (Cf. Denz.-Schön., 41.)

If one does not give to "croire *en*" the eminent sense of manifesting adoration, but the current sense in French of *adhering fully without seeing* (to the truths revealed by God), I think that the Greek use is preferable, and that it is better to say "je crois *en*" all through the Credo. This is moreover what one does now in the missals in French.

In his beautiful book *La Foi Chrétienne* (Paris, Aubier, 1969) Father de Lubac brings strongly to light the difference between "credere *in*" and "credere" followed only by the accusative. But in order to justify the use, in the French language, of "je crois *en* Dieu," one can argue from the remarkable chapter (Ch. VIII) of the same work, where the author shows that the radical novelty of the Christian message has obliged one to do violence to the Latin language, to the point of cramping exceedingly the Ciceronianism of St. Jerome and of St. Augustine. Introduced forcibly by the Christian faith in the three divine Persons, "credere *in*" is a solecism in Latin. But this is in nowise the case for "croire *en*" in our language. We say "je crois *en* la dignité de l'homme" as we say "je crois *en* Dieu." "Croire *en*" is not an unusual grammatical form, introduced forcibly into French in order to connote the idea of adoration. When one expresses oneself in French, there is no reason not to say "je crois *en* l'Église."

6. Cf. above all his great treatise *L'Église du Verbe Incarné* (Paris, Desclée De Brouwer).

7. Cf. I Cor. 3, 16; 6, 19.

8. *Dogmatic Constitution on the Church*, Ch. I, Sect. 4.

9. *Ibid.*, Sect. 7.—Cf. Leo XIII, encycl. *Divinum illud*, and Pius XII, encycl. *Mystici Corporis*.

The Holy Spirit is the Soul of the Church because He is the first principle of her life, dwells in the depth of the hearts of her "living" members, inspires and directs—He, the Spirit of Christ—the behavior of this great Body through human history. But it is in a hyperbolical sense that He is thus the uncreated soul of the Church. It is clear, indeed, that He cannot inform the body of the Church in the manner, however analogical it may be, in which the soul informs the body, or be a part of the ontological structure of anything merely created. (In the hypostatic union, in which the Person of the Word has assumed a human nature, Christ is not *purus homo*. And the Church is not God, as Christ is.)

This is why we must recognize in the Church, as Cardinal Journet does, a *soul* which is *created* as she is, and which informs her body in the manner— analogical—in which the soul of a living being informs the body of the latter. Considered in its nucleus, this created soul of the Church is, Charles Journet tells us (*L'Église du Verbe Incarné*, t. II, p. 613), "the capital grace of Christ unifying in it the triple privilege of His priesthood, of His holiness, of His kingship"; considered in its blossoming forth in the Church, it is (*ibid.*, p. 646) "charity insofar as related to worship, sacramental and orientated."

But desiring (without succeeding always) to employ in this book the least technical language possible, I think it preferable to say simply that the created soul of the Church is *the grace of Christ;* for grace is a divine gift (created) which perfects our soul and invests it with a new nature, and it is from it that charity proceeds, which perfects our will and our action, so that one can regard it as the very life of the Church. These two notions of grace and of charity are so closely related that it is normal to join them by saying that grace and charity are *the soul and the life* of the Church.

10. Cf. Charles Journet, *Théologie de l'Église*, Paris, Desclée De Brouwer, 1958, pp. 193-213.

11. Grace is given by God directly to whoever receives it, in a relation of Person to person. But the grace received by each is one of the constituent parts of that pleroma of all graces which is the soul of the Church, so that whoever lives by the grace of Christ lives, by that very fact, by the soul of the Church. (Cf. further on, Ch. X, pp. 102-103, 104-106 and note 27).

12. *Théologie de l'Église*, p. 244. "It is true," the author continues, "that Apostolic men could complain loudly to the bad Christians that they were staining the Church. We think however that their intention was less at that time to defend the theological thesis of the Church stained by the stains of her members, than to cause Christians to understand that they belong de jure wholly to the Church (which is true), that the world will hold her responsible for their lapses (this also is true but it is an injustice) and that in this sense they stain her in staining themselves."

13. Charles Journet, *Nova et Vetera*, 1963, p. 302 (cf. same review, 1958, p. 30).

14. *Théologie de l'Église*, p. 236.

NOTES TO CHAPTER III

1. "*Id quo,*" in the Aristotelian vocabulary.

2. "*Id quod,*" in the Aristotelian vocabulary.

3. For a technical discussion of the notion of subsistence, cf. *The Degrees of Knowledge*, Appendix IV. It is the second draft of this Appendix

(new translation, pp. 434-444) which expresses on this point my definitive thought, and it is it which I have briefly summarized here.

4. I mean by this an actuation by which a creatable is freed from the order of essentiality: as a picture once painted (nature) is freed from the easel, or from the order of factibility, when it is framed (subsistence) in order to be hung on the wall (existence). Imagery inevitably limping, for it has inevitably to do with things of sensible experience, which are all already existing.

5. Whether it is a question of pure spirits or of men, composed of a spiritual and immortal soul and of a body which subsists with the subsistence of the soul.

Deprived of their body, without which human nature is not complete, the separated souls are not, ontologically, persons. But they keep their moral personality.

6. Ephes. 5, 25-27.

7. *Ibid.*, 29-30.

8. *Adv. Haer.*, Bk. I, c. 10, 2. (Quoted by Father Humbert Clérissac, *Le Mystère de l'Église*, p. 49.)

9. *Sum. theol.*, II-II, q. 83, a. 16, ad 3.

10. The personality of each is elevated in it in dignity by grace. Cf. the encyclical *Mystici Corporis*, p. 33; and Jean-Hervé Nicolas, *Les profondeurs de la grâce*, Paris, Beauchesne, 1969, p. 310.

11. I Cor. 12, 28.–Cf. Rom. 12, 4-7.

12. Ephes. 4, 15-16.

13. II Cor. 5, 17.

14. Col. 3, 10.

15. I Cor. 15, 47-49.

16. Rom. 8, 29.

17. II Cor. 3, 18.

18. Humbert Clérissac, *Le Mystère de l'Église*, 5th ed., Paris, Le Cerf, 1918, p. 43.

19. Apoc. 12, 1-6; 21, 9.

NOTES TO CHAPTER IV

1. Cf. further on, Ch. XI.

2. Cf. my article "Faisons-lui une aide semblable à lui," *Nova et Vetera*, Oct.-Dec. 1967.

3. "Concerning the Fall itself, the Council is content with recalling that it consisted in the transgression of a precept given by God. Nothing is said about the nature of this precept, except that it was accompanied by the threat of being subject to death. One refers clearly to the story of Genesis, as the incidental clause "in Paradise" also shows, but nothing more is specified. Exegetes and theologians retain all liberty to scrutinize the sacred text and to interpret it according to their lights, while safeguarding always 'the analogy of faith.' " M. M. Labourdette, *Le Péché originel et les origines de l'homme*, Paris, Alsatia, 1953, p. 36.

4. There is a multitude of assertions which are, in themselves, reform-

able: not only the hypothetical or probable assertions, but also the assertions themselves with which explanatory theory (I do not speak of that which is mere verification of a fact) constructs itself in the sciences of phenomena, which are a knowledge *of the observable as such,* and refrain from piercing the crust of the observable. However far indeed one may extend it the observation remains inevitably limited, it is impossible to extend it infinitely far: so that, in itself, every system of rational interpretation of phenomena on the plane itself of phenomena can have to give way to a different system, occasioned by new observations and more fully comprehensive. No scientific theory is irreformable or *absolutely true;* it is true only relatively to the state of science at the different stages of its progress. In the rationalization of the observable effected by the sciences of phenomena, truth is the adequation of the intelligence with that which falls under an observation as complete as possible at a given time of human history.

It is altogether different with knowledges such as philosophy and theology. Philosophy (metaphysics, epistemology, philosophy of nature, moral philosophy . . .) is capable of emitting irreformable assertions, in other words absolute truths, because it bears on *intelligible being itself,* or the real attained purely and simply (and not only as to the observable as such). When it says the true, and to the extent that it says the true, that which it says is *absolutely true,* and true for always. This is that to which the primary and most deep-seated élan of the intelligence tends, and that for which it is most fundamentally thirsty.

When we say that truth is the adequation of the intelligence and of *that which is,* this is understood therefore primarily and above all of the adequation of the intelligence with "that which is" *purely and simply,* as it is the case for philosophy and theology. And it is understood secondarily (by extension to a type of knowledge enclosed completely in that which appears to the senses) of the adequation of the intelligence with "that which is" *under a certain relation only* (under the relation of observability), as it is the case for the sciences of phenomena.

Philosophy, which bears on the intimate intelligible structure of that which is, absolutely speaking, and theology, which bears on the intimate superintelligible mystery of Him Who is, absolutely speaking, are types of knowledge exceptionally lofty and universal, and exceptionally difficult in themselves. This is why man has so often erred in them.

In science, knowledge less elevated and more narrow, which is a late fruit of human thought (it began only in the sixteenth century to disengage itself in its proper nature), and which bears on the rational interpretation and the rational organization (above all, there where it is possible, mathematization) of that only which appears to the senses, man errs also but does not cease to correct his errors with an inviolable regularity, because the retracing of the work of the intelligence imposed by such a type of knowledge requires particularly rigorous methods and specializations; but the truth with which we have then to do is truth only *secundum quid,* approximate truth.

The Scientists know this; the noninitiated do not know it. Let us turn, in a last remark, to the side of the human community. If the idea that no higher knowledge, neither philosophy, nor theology, is capable of absolute truth became generally accepted, the result would be that the world of culture would find itself,—not through the fault of science,—mystified by science.

For it is the assertions of science, haloed with its dazzling applications, which a multitude of people who are not scientists would take then for "the truth" (absolute) of which by virtue of the very nature of the intelligence they experience unconsciously the need; whereas the scientists would continue to know, and better and better, that, however precious the progresses of science may be, irreformable assertions and absolute truths are not of the domain of the latter.

5. John 16, 29.

6. John 8, 32.

7. Ephes. 5, 29.

8. Ephes. 5, 27.—Cf. Apoc. 19, 7; 21, 2 and 9; 22, 17. She is "the Bride of the Lamb."

9. Ephes. 1, 23.

10. Col. 1, 18; Ephes. 1, 23; 4, 15-16.

11. Ephes. 5, 25; 5, 29-30.

12. I Tim. 3, 15.

13. John 16, 13. *Cum autem venerit ille Spiritus Veritatis, docebit vos omnem veritatem*, ὁδηγήσει ὑμᾶς εἰς τὴν ἀλήθειαν πᾶσαν, he will guide you to all truth. Cf. 14, 26.

14. Cf. I Cor. 3, 16; 6, 19; and Vatican II, *Dogmatic Constitution on the Church*, Ch. I, n. 4.

15. Matt. 28, 20.

16. M. M. Labourdette, *Le Péché originel et les origines de l'homme*, Paris, Alsatia, 1953, p. 57.

17. John 8, 40: *"Nunc autem quaeritis me interficere, hominem, qui veritatem vobis locutus sum, quam audivi a Deo. Me, a man who has told you the truth which I have heard from God, τὴν ἀλήθειαν ἥν ἤχουσα παρὰ τοῦ θεοῦ."*

18. A prudential judgment is *more or less* prudent. A doctrinal proposition is *true or false*. One can speak of perfect or sovereign prudence (it was surely the case of that of Christ). The expression "prudential infallibility," employed by theologians who are dear to me, is for me devoid of sense.

It is fitting therefore, in my opinion, to distinguish between the truths which constitute the *doctrina de moribus* (cf. further on, Ch. VII, pp. 53-54),—they correspond analogically, it seems to me, to what moral philosophy is in the natural order, and the Church teaches them to us *infallibly,*— and the particular applications by which she directs us, at a given epoch and in given cases, *with a prudence of a higher order.*

I shall say, for example, that the indissolubility of marriage is a truth which relates to the doctrinal infallibility of the Church, whereas the prohibition of the crossbow in tournaments, of which I speak in the present section, relates to her prudence, and that in the Conciliar decrees concerning usury, of which I speak also in this section, prudence (as to the diverse means prescribed in order to struggle against usury) mingles with doctrinal infallibility (as to the true role of money,—to use the latter as if it was made in order to engender more money *by itself* is contrary to the natural law; it brings a legitimate gain only by means of the value of a *thing* which it has aided one to obtain or to produce).

It is curious, let us add, to note that as regards prudential decisions, even if made by the supreme authority, grave failures in prudence have been able to occur in very important matters (cf. Chapter XIII, concerning the institution of the Inquisition); whereas the higher prudence of the person of the Church passed in very secondary matters (like the use of the crossbow in tournaments). Everything depends there on the liberty which the high personnel of the Church leaves in its mind to the instrumental motion issuing from the person of the latter, or on the obstacles which it opposes to it under the pressure of very heavy human solicitudes (caused most often, in former times, by the Christian leaders of State).

19. As early as the Council of Nicaea and Pope St. Leo, but above all in the Middle Ages, from Alexander III to Gregory IX.

20. Cf. Beatrice Sabran, *L'Église et la sexualité*, Paris, Ed. du Club de la Culture Française, 1969. Mme Sabran, who is a psychologist, was the pupil of Roland Dalbiez and worked with him. I hope that this remarkable book will have a second edition in which the too numerous typographical mistakes of the first will be corrected.

NOTES TO CHAPTER V

1. Ephes. I, 23.—" . . . the fullness of him who fills the universe in all its parts." Cf. Ch. I, p. 3 and note 3.

2. *Ibid.*—"Et ipsum dedit caput supra omnem Ecclesiam, quae est Corpus ejus, et Plenitudo ejus."

3. Ephes. 4, 11-13.

4. *Ibid.*, 3, 19.

5. Cf. my book *On the Grace and Humanity of Jesus*, New York, Herder and Herder, 1969, pp. 47-87.

6. Apoc. 21, 1 sq. —Cf. *Dogmatic Constitution on the Church*, I, 6. This image of the Apocalypse applies already to the Church in pilgrimage, according as her personality is of the supernatural order.

7. Ephes. I, 23.—Let us follow here the Vulgate; it is St. Jerome who has most faithfully translated this passage.

8. Cf. *Dogmatic Constitution on the Church*, Ch. II, Sect. 12.

9. The Council of Tyre, which in 335 condemned and deposed St. Athanasius, and the Council of Rimini (359), which under imperial pressure finally accepted an unacceptable formula of compromise and of conciliation with the Arians, were assemblies without ecumenical value or authentic authority, which drowned the voice of the Church instead of causing it to be heard. It is to a Council expressing the thought of the whole episcopate and endowed with an authentic authority, to an *ecumenical* Council (in the sense in which the notion has been lived and practiced from the very beginning and defined later) that the wholly gratuitous hypothesis advanced here alludes.

NOTES TO CHAPTER VI

1. Song of Songs 2, 10.

2. Ephes. 5, 27.

3. *The Peasant of the Garonne*, p. 185.
4. II Cor. 5, 21.
5. "La Couronne d'épines," in *Poèmes de Raïssa*.
6. *Dogmatic Constitution on the Church*, Ch. I, Sect. 8.
7. Charles Journet, *Théologie de l'Église*, p. 239.
8. *Dogmatic Constitution on the Church*, Ch. V, Sect. 39.
9. Cf. *Dogmatic Constitution on the Church*, Ch. I, Sect. 8: "at the same time holy and always in need of being purified."
10. Cf. Luke 15, 24.

NOTES TO CHAPTER VII

1. Cf. Ch. Journet, *op. cit.*, t. II, p. 1174; and t. III, pp. 187-200: "It is the doctrine of St. Augustine and of St. Thomas Aquinas, of St. Bernard and of St. John of the Cross."

2. If it is a question of the glorified body of the Lord and of that of Mary, they must, being bodies, exist, since the Ascension and the Assumption, in some physical place. Since the scientists tell me that the universe is expanding, therefore limited, I think quite simply that these two glorified bodies exist *outside of the universe.* One can conceive, it seems to me, that they themselves delimit in mathematical space (in itself, purely ideal) a place which their own existence renders real and which is coextensive with them.

However it may be concerning this last point, if, as I think, they are outside of and beyond our whole universe (does not St. Thomas, III, 57, 4, teach, after St. Paul, *Ephes.* 4, 10, that Christ ascended "high above the heavens," *super omnes coelos?*), it is still in the symbolical sense indicated above that we say that they are "in Heaven." Wherever they are corporally (and it is certainly not the heaven of the astronomers), Christ and His Mother are spiritually nearer to God than any other being, and share in the glory of God to a supreme degree.

3. In this repentance I believe with St. Irenaeus (cf. Ch. Journet, *L'Église du Verbe Incarné*, t. III, p. 549).—On graces by anticipation, cf. *ibid.*, p. 350.

4. Cf. Benedict XII, Const. *Benedictus Deus*, Denz.-Schön., 1000.—The souls of the just before the time of Christ, and who awaited His coming, found themselves—since they were in grace, participation in the divine life,—in a profound happiness, but,—since they had not yet the Beatific Vision,—in desire still: happiness and desire much greater, certainly, than those of children who die without Baptism or without a rite capable of taking the place of it, and before having been able to make their first moral option, and who will never see the divine essence. (They experience however no affliction either internal or external,—cf. St. Thomas, *De Malo*, q. 5, a. 3,—and enjoy all the felicity which nature alone can give,—cf. Journet, *op. cit.*, II, pp. 773-779.—The case of children who die without Baptism has a quite special interest for the philosopher, for it testifies to the fact that all the degrees of being will be finally fulfilled, including that of the purely natural expansion of the animal endowed with reason, who bears in himself, but, in the case considered, without suffering from the aberrations into which wounded

reason throws us in seeking substitutes in order to satisfy it, the natural desire to see the Cause of being.)

Why this long wait of the just who died before the coming of Christ? Apropos of Abraham (verses 8 to 19) and of Moses (verses 23 to 29), and of many others "of whom the world was not worthy," St. Paul tells us, in Chapter 11 of the Epistle to the Hebrews (39-40): "Yet despite the fact that all of these were approved because of their faith, they did not obtain what had been promised. God had made a better plan, a plan which included us. Without us, they were not to be made perfect." (Cf. SPICQ, in *Études bibliques, L'Épître aux Hébreux*, t. II, p. 368.)

The descent of Christ into Hades is an article of faith. The holy Doctors are in disagreement concerning secondary points relating to what He did there (cf. Journet, *op. cit.*, III, pp. 551-552). But on the point that the just retained in waiting saw God only after Jesus had liberated them from it by appearing to them, the apostolic tradition has unanimously transmitted itself from age to age, and I think therefore (a little regretfully, I confess) that the point in question is not a mere conjecture of the Fathers apropos of the descent into Hades, but must be considered as engaging also the faith. There is here a particularly significant example of the fact that theological faith does not bear only on that which has been the object of a Conciliar definition or of a definition *ex cathedra;* not only has the deposit of faith been entrusted also to the teaching of the ordinary magisterium, but further it is immanent in that which I have called (Ch. V, p. 38) the *universality of grace* of the Church (cf. p. 53, apropos of the *sensus fidei* of the universal Church).

In order to return to the descent into Hades, but this time with regard to that which on its subject is only matter of opinion, St. Thomas, with many others, thinks (*Sum. theol.*, III, q. 52) that Christ not only visited there the just in order to infuse into them the light of eternal glory, but that He also spoke to the damned (in what terms, no one knows, not even St. Thomas). In opposition to the opinion of the latter (52, 8), I like to think that, by an act of royal amnesty, Christ also delivered from Purgatory *those whom He wished,* even if they had not yet completed in suffering their time of purification.

5. This is what Cardinal Journet calls the third age of the Church. See further on, Ch. VIII, n. 3 and Ch. IX, n. 7.

6. Here on earth Christ, Whose person was divine, found Himself in His human nature *at once* under the state of glory in the higher part of His soul, because He had there the Beatific Vision, and under the state of way in the lower part of His soul, because He progressed there in grace and charity. (Cf. my book *On the Grace and Humanity of Jesus.*)

The person of the Church, who is a person wholly human (collective person supernaturally one and individuated by virtue of the perfect unity of the image of Christ imprinted in her), finds herself *at once* under the state of glory and under the state of way *by the members* who compose her, and who are different in the two cases,—blessed souls (and holy angels) in one case, men en route toward their final end in the other case.

7. It is the Church thus considered in her integrality that St. Augustine invites us to consider. "The correct order of the Creed demanded that to the Trinity should be subjoined the Church, as one might say, to the Inhabitant His own house, to God His own temple, to the Founder His own city. And

the Church must here be understood in its fullness—not only of that part which is in exile on earth, from the rising of the sun unto its going down praising the Name of the Lord (cf. Ps. 113, 3), and after the end of its ancient captivity singing a new song (cf. Ps. 33, 3), but also of that part which always since its foundation has in heaven adhered to God nor has experienced any fall to do it injury." *Enchiridion*, c. 15, n. 56 [English translation from *Saint Augustine's Enchiridion or Manual to Laurentius Concerning Faith, Hope, and Charity*. Translated from the Benedictine Text with an Introduction and Notes by Ernest Evans. London: S.P.C.K., 1953, pp. 49-50—Tr.].

8. Luke 18, 8.

9. Cf. I Thess. 4, 14-17.

10. Concerning this wholly immaterial communication of thought (the "locution" of the angels), as also concerning the angelic illumination, and the manner in which it descends, in sheets of intelligible light, from the highest angels and the nearest to God to the less high angels, the first dividing their more universal conceptions in order to adapt them to the capacity of the second ones, and to make handsome presents to them of all that which they know, see my article "Le tenant-lieu de théologie chez les simples," *Nova et Vetera*, April-June, 1969, pp. 90-93.

11. The Greco-Slavonic Orthodox Church (to which I shall return in Chapter X) has stopped, in dogmatic matters, at that which it professed and taught at the time of the separation from Rome. Not advancing in the explicitation of the apostolic faith, I shall say that it is *immobile* rather than *infallible*.

12. Denz.-Schön., 3074.

13. Cf. first Council of the Vatican, Denz.-Schön., 3074: "Definimus: Romanum Pontificem, cum ex cathedra loquitur, id est, cum omnium Christanorum pastoris et doctoris munere fungens pro suprema sua Apostolica auctoritate doctrinam de fide vel moribus ab universa Ecclesia tenendam definit, per assistentiam divinam ipsi in beato Petro promissam, ea infallibilitate pollere, qua divinus Redemptor Ecclesiam suam in definienda doctrina de fide vel moribus instructam esse voluit; ideoque ejusmodi Romani Pontificis definitiones ex sese, non autem ex consensu Ecclesiae, irreformabiles esse."

I do not claim at all that the views which I present are contained in this text, but I think that they accord fully with it.

14. "Together with its head, the Roman Pontiff, and never without this head, the episcopal order is the subject of supreme and full power over the universal Church." *Dogmatic Constitution on the Church*, Ch. III, Sect. 22. Cf. further on, Ch. IX, pp. 77-78.

15. "Divine faith is not to be restricted to matters expressly defined by ecumenical Councils, or the Roman Pontiffs, or the Apostolic See: but extends also to matters set forth as divinely revealed by the ordinary magisterium of the whole Church dispersed throughout the world." Pius IX, Ep. *"Tuas libenter"* (Denz.-Schön., 2879). Cf. Charles Journet, *The Church of the Incarnate Word*, Vol. I, London and New York, Sheed and Ward, 1955, pp. 414-415.

It is a question here of the ordinary magisterium in the *entirely strict* sense, or according as, proposing to us as object of faith "that which, as St. Vincent of Lerins says, has been believed everywhere, always and by all" (cf.

Journet, *op. cit.*, p. 416), it implies *complete universality*, not only with regard to the extension over the surface of the earth (all the bishops of the world), but also with regard to the duration in time (all the bishops who have succeeded each other since the apostolic age). I shall say that then the instrumental causality (by reason of which it is the person of the Church who speaks through the episcopate) has an absolute primacy over the proper causality, which, moreover, in the case of the ordinary magisterium as in that even of the extraordinary magisterium, intervenes always in some manner (at least as to the connotations, variable from one epoch to the other, of the words which one employs), but without ever for all that, when it is a question, as here, of the magisterium strictly understood, altering in any way the infallible and irreformable character of that which is formally taught.

Considered in a *broad* sense, the ordinary magisterium can include at one and the same time infallibility in certain respects and fallibility in others, in other words a *mixture* of instrumental causality (in which it is the person of the Church who speaks through it) and of proper causality (as such liable to error, however wise it may be,—I think for example of the Papal encyclicals, cf. further on, pp. 148-149).

(On the other hand, and in order not to omit the worst, it can happen that a bishop, or a few bishops, as at the time of Luther, or a great many, as at the time of Arianism, betray by a grave error the magisterium entrusted to the episcopate and fall into heresy.)

Finally the ordinary magisterium, when, considered in a *still broader* sense, it does not bear on the universal doctrine of faith and of morals, but on a particular and contingent matter, can, without falling into the slightest error against the faith, be itself fallible (just as then this can be also the case even of Conciliar prescriptions entirely regular,—I think for example of the medieval legislation concerning the Jews, which, in the perspective of the mentality of the epoch and in relation to the empirical adjustment to the situations created by history, presented itself to the hierarchy of that time as prudentially required, but which, in itself, was simply iniquitous).

NOTES TO CHAPTER VIII

1. Cf. Ch. Journet, *L'Église du Verbe Incarné*, t. II, p. 163, note 1, apropos of Karl Barth. At the end of this particularly important note, Cardinal Journet writes: "The distinction which Scripture makes between that which we call the 'Christian spiritual' and the 'Christian temporal,' and which Barth notes, without being able to interpret fully the bearing of it, results from the distinction between, on the one hand, natural reason, which exists more or less impaired in the conscience of peoples, and, on the other hand, the order of the evangelical revelation, of which one of the tasks is to specify, to correct, to ratify, to purify the data of the natural order. As it sanctions the primary data of reason concerning the existence of God, because they are normally *praeambula fidei christianae*, Christianity sanctions likewise the data of reason concerning the order of cultural life, because they are normally *praeambula vitae christianae*."

2. Cf. the beautiful book of Père Irénée Vallery-Radot, *Le Prophète de l'Occident*, Paris, Desclée, 1969.

3. I mean by this the Church of Christ come, founded and built by Him. She was preceded by thousands of centuries of human history. The Adamic state, which theologians call "the age of the Father," and which lasted from the creation of man to the Fall, was an age *anterior* to the Church. The latter began to sketch herself (as Church of *Christ to come*) only after the Fall; from that moment, indeed, and to begin by our first parents, man had to be redeemed by the grace of Christ, received at first, and during what an immense duration, by anticipation. From the point of view of the history of salvation, there have therefore been "the age of the awaited Son," with "the economy of the law of nature," followed by "the economy of the Mosaic Law," then "the age (very short in duration, but of an unparalleled importance) of the temporal presence of Christ," and finally "the age of the Holy Spirit," with the Church in her definitive status, or that which I call the Church *of Christ come*, which alone occupies me here. (Cf. Charles Journet, *L'Église du Verbe Incarné*, t. III.)

4. Paul VI, Address to the General Audience of July 9, 1969 (*Docum. Cath.*, August 1, 1969, p. 707).

5. Matt. 16, 15-19. Heaven will declare bound or loosed that which Peter will have bound or loosed on earth. Cf. the Jerusalem Bible, note to this verse.

6. Like every living organism. Cf. Ephes. 4, 15-16: "Through him the whole body grows, and with the proper functioning of the members joined firmly together by each supporting ligament, builds itself up in love."

7. Cyprian, *Epist.* 73, c. 11 (quoted by H. de Lubac, *La Foi chrétienne*, 2nd ed., Paris, Aubier-Montaigne, 1970, p. 223).

8. It is indeed clear that in this text of Matthew, as in the "feed my sheep" of John 21, 15-17, the words of Jesus aim not only at Peter but also at his successors, since it is a question of *the Church of Christ* whom the latter *will build* in the course of time, and in whom all along the course of the centuries that which will be bound or loosed on earth will be bound or loosed in Heaven, just as all along the course of the centuries Peter, in his successors, will feed in her the lambs and the sheep of the Lord.

9. "Ego autem rogavi pro te ut non deficiat fides tua: et tu aliquando conversus confirma fratres tuos." Luke 22, 32.

10. Let us quote here a text of St. Augustine to which Father de Lubac (*op. cit.*, p. 224) refers apropos of the confession of Peter. It is taken from *De Civitate Dei*, 1. 8, c, 54, n. 1: "We therefore, who are Christians and whom one designates by this name, we do not believe in Peter, but in Him in whom Peter believed, and we are thus 'constructed' by the words of Peter announcing Christ." [*Bibliothèque augustinienne*, t. 36, pp. 686-688.—Tr.]

11. Others translate: "you are an obstacle to me."

12. Matt. 16, 21-23.

13. Letter 185.

14. One reads in the Vulgate: "... *et filii Zebedaei, et alii* ex discipulis ejus." Cf. M. J. Lagrange, *L'Evangile de Jésus-Christ*, Paris, J. Gabalda et Cie, 1948, p. 597, n. 1: "We think that 'the two other disciples,' at first unnamed, according to the discreet manner of John, were rightly explained as the sons of Zebedee in a gloss which afterwards passed into the text."

15. John 21, 15-17.
16. *Op. cit.*, p. 600.
17. John 21, 20.
18. Cf. the *Tractatus in Joannem.*
19. To Peter he had said: "I tell you solemnly: as a young man you fastened your belt and went about as you pleased; but when you are older you will stretch out your hands, and another will tie you fast and carry you off against your will" (John 21, 18). Of John he had said: "Suppose I want him to stay until I come, how does that concern you?" (John 21, 22. Which it is necessary to understand: until I come to take his soul with Me, when he will die in My love.).
20. During the first course, which preceded the Pascal meal properly so called. Cf. Jerusalem Bible, Matt. 26, 21, note c.
21. John 13, 4-7; 13, 12-15.
22. Matt. 11, 11-15.
23. Luke 17, 21.
24. *Journal de Raïssa,* pp. 365-366; 367-368; 369; 370: "Le Vrai Visage de Dieu ou l'Amour et la Loi." This text is reproduced *in extenso* at the end of *The Peasant of the Garonne.*

NOTES TO CHAPTER IX

1. Cf. André Feuillet, "La personnalité de Jésus entrevue à partir de sa soumission au rite de repentance du Précurseur," *Revue Biblique,* LXXVII, 1970.
2. "It is entirely fitting, therefore, that one of those who was of our company while the Lord Jesus moved among us, from the baptism of John until the day he was taken up from us, should be named as witness with us to his resurrection.

"At that they nominated two, Joseph (called Barsabbas, also known as Justus) and Matthias. Then they prayed: 'O Lord, you read the hearts of men. Make known to us which of these two you choose for this apostolic ministry, replacing Judas, who deserted the cause and went the way he was destined to go.' They then drew lots between the two men. The choice fell to Matthias, who was added to the eleven Apostles." Acts 1, 21-26.
3. Cf. pp. 84-86.
4. Cf. Matt. 28, 19.
5. Cf. Ephes. 4, 15-16.
6. Cf. Luke 10, 1-20.
7. Or rather, in a universal sense encompassing the whole sequence of time during which the Church will continue to develop,—since the completion of the sacred trajectory Passion-Resurrection-Ascension-Pentecost.

The graces received by men since the Incarnation were graces *of Christ come* in this sense that He was there, and that they passed through His humanity, through "a word, a glance, a touch of Him" (Journet, *op. cit.*, t. III, p. 576). But it is since Pentecost that they have been graces *of Christ come* in this sense that His passage among us had fully ended, and that after having accomplished on the Cross His redemptive mission, and after His

Resurrection and His Ascension, He had sent the Holy Spirit upon the Apostles in order to build His Church.

It is in this second sense that in the preceding chapters I have employed the expression "of Christ come."

8. In other words, by someone, priest or layman, and even if he not be a member of the Church, who desires "to do that which the Church wishes" in giving this Sacrament. It is however a wise custom to rebaptize conditionally,—*si non es baptizatus,*—those who have been baptized by someone of whom one is not sure that he has desired "to do that which the Church wishes."

In order for an adult to enter into participation in the life of God and to be a living member of the *Una, Sancta, Catholica,* he must receive validly and *fruitfully* Baptism (or be fruitfully regenerated by its substitute, "Baptism of desire"). When a child receives validly (even in a dissident religious family) Baptism, which is always the Baptism of the Church of Jesus, he is *ipso facto* incorporated *sacramentaliter et mentaliter* in the *Una, Sancta, Catholica,* in the Church of whom Peter is the leader here on earth.

9. I Peter 2, 9-10.—It is a question here, the Council says, of "that new and perfect covenant which was to be ratified in Christ, and of that more luminous revelation which was to be given through God's very Word made flesh." "Christ instituted this new covenant, that is to say, the new testament, in His blood (cf. I Cor. 11:25), by calling together a people made of Jew and Gentile, making them one, not according to the flesh but **in the Spirit.**"

"The heritage of this people are the dignity and freedom of the sons of God, in whose hearts the Holy Spirit dwells as in His temple. Its law is the new commandment to love as Christ loved us (cf. John 13:34). Its goal is the kingdom of God, which has been begun by God Himself on earth, and which is to be further extended until it is brought to perfection by Him at the end of time. Then Christ our life (cf. Col. 3:4), will appear. . . ."

"The baptized," the Council says further, "by regeneration and the anointing of the Holy Spirit, are consecrated into a spiritual house and a holy priesthood. Thus through all those works befitting Christian men they can offer spiritual sacrifices and proclaim the power of Him who has called them out of darkness into His marvellous light (cf. I Peter, 2:4-10)." *Dogmatic Constitution on the Church,* Ch. 2, Sections 9 and 10.

10. *Dogmatic Constitution on the Church,* Ch. 2, Sect. 10.

11. *Ibid.*

12. Michel Labourdette, *Le sacerdoce et la Mission Ouvrière,* Paris, éd. Bonne Presse, 1959, p. 54.

13. Acts 6, 1-6.

14. I speak of the primacy of Peter and of his successors, which remains immutably. As to the *mode* according to which it is exercised, who will be astonished that it varies with the ages, and that one sees for it forms altogether different at the time of Peter himself, at the time of Gregory VII, and at the present time?

15. "La Collégialité," *Nova et Vetera,* July-September, 1969.

16. An interview concerning the present difficulties of the episcopate which Cardinal Suenens granted to Henri Fesquet (cf. *Le Monde,* May 12, 1970), and which is not lacking in a certain ambiguity, permits me to state once more that consultative organs are often itched by the temptation to

become organs of government, or to take themselves to be such. It is important to remark on this subject that the bishops, as I have said in the text, are free to decide, in the episcopal conferences, that which they desire on the plane of the local churches, (I add that private meetings, between themselves—and with their priests—aiding each to form a personal opinion on the points which preoccupy them, are also very advantageous); but that, as soon as it is a question of the universal Church, the Pope is always free not to submit, if he judges that this would be inopportune, such or such question either to an ecumenical Council (the words "in union with the leader of the Church" imply that he possesses this liberty), or, with greater reason, to an episcopal Synod.

Nothing requires in any case, as Henri Fesquet supposes, "an extension of the notion of collegiality and a deepening of the theology of the local Churches." And let us hope that the new theology of which one is thinking is not a theology for which a dialogue is "free" only if the higher authority to which one is speaking *is not free* to refuse it on any point; a theology which would hold that the episcopal synods are *organs of government*, and that it belongs *to the local Churches* to exercise by their delegates the supreme power in the Church with the Pope, so that the latter (this is the grand idea) is only a mere *primus inter pares:* all theses which, if they were, not furtively insinuated into public opinion, but expressly submitted to an ecumenical Council, would not fail to incur a condemnation.

17. It is a duty of the magisterium to point out to the faithful that which in such or such a doctrine is in itself absolutely incompatible with the faith. In doing this, it limits doubtless in a measure (feeble measure if it does not take any sanctions against the authors) the liberty of research, but it aids also, and greatly, the liberty and the progress of *theological* research: for to point out some theme incompatible with the faith to persons dedicated to an intellectual discipline whose object is to elucidate the data of faith, is to let them see that it would be absurd to employ this doctrinal theme in their research,—which is so much gained for the latter (the absurd is certainly unhealthy for research, its liberty of invention, and its progress). This remark is valid also, for analogous reasons, with regard to Christian philosophy (insofar precisely as it is Christian).

NOTES TO CHAPTER X

1. The formula "No salvation outside the Church" is an abridgment in current language of a declaration of the Council of Florence (1438-1445), Denz.-Schön., 1351: "Firmiter credit, profitetur et praedicat, nullos intra catholicam Ecclesiam non exsistentes, non solum paganos, sed nec Judaeos aut haereticos atque schismaticos, aeternae vitae fieri posse participes." What matters here is the declaration itself, not the manner in which one understood it in that epoch. That in actual fact the Fathers of the Council of Florence themselves understood it,—according to the mentality of the epoch, and without having been conscious of its ambiguity,—of a *visible* belonging to the Church, this seems evident to me. The fact remains that the declaration itself does not at all say it.

It is with time that the ambiguity in question appeared,—and at the same stroke the true sense in which the declaration must be taken. There has therefore been mutation, not with regard to the declaration itself, but with regard to the manner in which those who formulated it understood it. The declaration itself is infallibly true (provided it is rightly understood). The assistance of the Holy Spirit is a thing from above, it bears on things infallibly true to be caused to be declared, not on the personal mentality of those who declare them.

2. I apologize for these summary statements in the view of scholarly specialists, whose microscopes I have left aside. But did I not warn in my preface that this book was written by an ignorant one for ignorant ones like himself.

3. Mikaël Perrin, *Les Hommes en jaune*, Paris, Calmann-Lévy, 1967, p. 60.

4. "*Brahmanism* is the majority religion of India. It comprises, today, more than three hundred million followers. It begins, for the historian, with those texts written in archaic Sanskrit which bear the name of *Veda*: accordingly the designation *Vedism* is reserved for ancient Brahmanism, whereas one calls *Hinduism* the post-Vedic phases of its evolution." (Olivier Lacombe, "Le Brahmanisme," in the collective work *La Mystique et les Mystiques*, Paris, Desclée De Brouwer, 1965, p. 731.)

This well noted, I shall employ here indifferently the words "Brahmanism" or "Hinduism."

5. Be it adulterated as in Islam by a debatable prophet.

6. Cf. my book *Quatre Essais sur l'Esprit dans sa condition charnelle*, nouvelle édition revue et augmentée, Paris, Alsatia, 1956, p. 134.

7. Cf. my book *Les Degrés du Savoir*, Ch. VI (in which it is shown that a mystical experience of the depths of God can only be supernatural. As to natural mystical experience as experience of the *esse* of the self, the idea came to me only later; the first edition of *Quatre Essais* appeared in 1939, that of *Les Degrés du Savoir* in 1932.).

8. Cf. *Quatre Essais*, pp. 148-149.

9. Cf. *ibid.*, pp. 150-151.

10. "From the very fact that the experience we are discussing is a (negative) purely existential experience, and from the fact that existence is transcendent and polyvalent, and is limited only by the essence which receives it, and of which precisely in this case one knows nothing, it is comprehensible that this negative experience, in attaining the existential *esse* of the soul, should at one and the same time attain this proper existence of the soul, existence in its metaphysical amplitude, and the sources of existence, according as the existence of the soul, taken concretely and to the extent that it is the exercise of effectuation *extra nihil*, is something emanating from and suffused by an influx wherefrom it attains its all. This influx is not experienced in itself, of course, but rather the effect which it produces is experienced in itself, and the influx in and through this effect. This is why the experience in question answers indeed in a certain fashion—and to the extent that this is possible in the natural order—to the desire of every thing to rejoin its sources and the principle of its being. It is the sources of being in his soul that man thus attains, thanks to the techniques through which nature reascends toward the spirit against the grain of nature and in a certain way

disjoints its own proper metaphysical texture. The Hindu experience does appear, therefore, to be a mystical experience in the natural order, a fruitive experience of the absolute, of that absolute which is the substantial *esse* of the soul and, in it and through it, of the divine absolute (as cause of being, not as giving Himself as object of fruition)." (*Quatre Essais*, pp. 153-154.)

11. On the *bhakti*, cf. *Quatre Essais*, pp. 162-163.—For the bhakti, and for Ramanoudja, "the salutary way par excellence is that of the knowledge of love adhering to God as person and correlative of grace." Olivier Lacombe, *L'absolu selon le Védânta*, pp. 5-6.

12. On this metaphysics, see in particular the book of Olivier Lacombe, *L'absolu selon le Védânta, les notions de Brahman et d'Atman dans le système de Çankara et Râmânoudja*, Paris, Guethner, 1937; and René Grousset, *Les philosophies indiennes*, Paris, 1931.

13. "Is Buddhism a religion? In the etymological sense of the word, yes: *res-ligiosa*, 'the thing which binds'; the followers are bound by analogous convictions. But in the present sense of the word Theravada Orthodox Buddhism which denies the soul and God is not a religion. . . ." Mikaël Perrin, *Les Hommes en jaune*, Paris, Calmann-Lévy, 1967, p. 19.

"Buddhism is essentially atheistic, and the multitude of the faithful expects from Buddha all that which one hopes from God (. . .) So much and so completely that one would believe oneself finally obliged to hold together two apparently contradictory propositions: 'Buddhism is not a religion, but it is a philosophy.'—'There is no thought more profoundly religious than the doctrine of Buddha.' " And again: "Atheism. Such is indeed, it seems to me, if one wishes to keep for the word 'God' its strict sense of absolutely transcendent Being, the judgment which it is necessary to bear on the religious literature of the Hinayana. Does the Mahayana contradict this atheism? (. . .) The pure essence of Buddheity, the Tathata, admits the multiplicity of the Buddhas who express it and who identify themselves with it (. . .) Behold therefore the Great Vehicle rejoins the Small Vehicle, in a pluralist conception of Beings who, from mortal, have become imperishable; who have become this by their merits, by their works. . . ." Fr. Taymans d'Eypernon, *Les paradoxes du Bouddhisme*, Paris, Desclée De Brouwer, 1947, pp. 239-240, 245-246, 248.

14. Cf. Mikaël Perrin, *op. cit.*, p. 168.

15. *Op. cit.*, p. 309; cf. pp. 295-324.—"What is Zen?" writes Dr. D. T. Suzuki. "It is one of the questions to which it is most difficult to reply; to reply, I mean, to the satisfaction of the questioners; for Zen resists even an attempt at any sort of definition or of description. The best way to understand it will clearly be to study it and to practice it at least a few years in the Meditation Hall (. . .) It is in the very nature of Zen to escape all definition and explanation; in other words, it can never be converted into ideas or described in logical terms." *Essais sur le Bouddhisme Zen*, Paris, éd. Adrien Maisonneuve, 1944, 4 vol., II, p. 65.

Is a somewhat blasé philosopher surprised that the ineffability of Zen has not prevented Dr. Suzuki from writing a lot of learned volumes on it?

16. "It is a question of discouraging the initiate from all rational research, and by this Zen is in the authentic tradition of Buddhism." Mikaël Perrin, *op. cit.*, p. 295. Cf. Suzuki, *op. cit.*, p. 89: "As long as the masters delight in the negations, the denials, the contradictions or the paradoxes, the

task of intellectual speculation is not completely effaced in them. Of course, Zen is not opposed to speculation, since the latter is one of the functions of the mind. But it has followed a very different path (. . .) Language is therefore, for the masters of Zen, a kind of cry or of exclamation directly sprung from their interior spiritual experience." (p. 99.)

On Zen, see also what Arthur Koestler writes about it in his book *The Lotus and the Robot*, New York, The Macmillan Company, 1961.—It is not surprising that for some centuries (until the end of the seventeenth) there was in Japan an admirable Zen art. A spontaneous explosion of pure irrationality can open the doors to the poetry hidden in the supraconscious of the spirit. But when pure spontaneity becomes itself the object of a discipline which wishes to attain it by automatism, poetry vanishes. (Cf. Koestler, p. 264.)

17. This is what the Council suggests when it says that the Moslems, "professing to hold the faith of Abraham, along with us adore the one and merciful God. . . ." (*Dogmatic Constitution on the Church*, Ch. II, Sect. 16). The faith of Abraham was very certainly a supernatural faith.

Still it is necessary to note that as much as it is permitted to judge of such things, the Moslem faith seems to go (except in the great Sufis) to the testimony concerning God, to the *enuntiabile*, more than to the *res* itself, to the superintelligible depths of the divine Being.

18. Louis Gardet, *L'Islam, Religion et Communauté*, Paris, Desclée De Brouwer, 1967, p. 71 et seq.—On the particular connotations of the words "religion" and "faith" in Islam, cf. *ibid.*, pp. 29-38.

19. Cf. Louis Gardet, *op. cit.*, p. 55. Cf. also pp. 64 and 232.

20. Cf. Louis Massignon, *Al Hallâj, martyr mystique de l'Islam*, Paris, Guethner, 1922; in course of republication.—On Moslem Sufism, cf. Louis Gardet, *op. cit.*, pp. 229-242.

21. Cf. the beautiful book of Henri Hartung, *Ces Princes du Management*, Paris, Fayard, 1970.

22. In treating of atheism in other writings (*Raison et Raisons*, Chs. VI and VII; and *La Signification de l'athéisme contemporain*), I made a distinction which I believe well founded, but which I think now badly formulated, between what I called "pseudoatheism" on the one hand and "absolute atheism" or "true atheism" on the other hand. It would be necessary to say in the first case *atheism by conviction of the mind* (it is not at all *pseudo*-atheism, but authentic atheism); and, in the second case, *atheism by option of the heart*. It is not of this second kind of atheism that it is a question here.

23. See on this point my essay "La dialectique immanente du premier acte de liberté," in *Raison et Raisons*, collection of articles of an earlier date, Preface by Charles Journet, Fribourg, Egloff, and Paris, L. U. F., 1947. [English version of this essay appears in *The Range of Reason*, New York, Charles Scribner's Sons, 1952, pp. 66-85.—Tr.]—When I wrote this essay, I had not yet disengaged the notion of supraconscious, so that the essay requires to be completed and corrected in this respect. It is in two other books (*Creative Intuition in Art and Poetry* and *On the Grace and Humanity of Jesus*) that I have insisted on the essential importance of the *supraconscious* of the spirit, that kind of unconscious which, unlike the Freudian unconscious, is not below but above conscious thought.

24. One will find in *Raison et Raisons* (pp. 146-157) a more complete discussion on this subject.

Does one desire an example in an altogether different domain? "Newman had long given up 'choosing his way' and was content to be led by the divine light"—and in the supraconscious of the spirit had already implicit faith in the Church—"yet still the Church of Rome seemed to him to be allied with Antichrist. There are more things in a man's heart than are dreamt of in his philosophy; or even, often enough, in his theology." (Charles Journet, *The Church of the Incarnate Word*, pp. 39-40.)

25. Cf. further on, pp. 104-106.

26. "Through him [Christ] the whole body grows, and with the proper functioning of the members joined firmly together by each supporting ligament, builds itself up in love." *Ephes.* 4, 15-16.

27. On this whole question of the soul of the Church I employ, in order to simplify things, another language than Cardinal Journet, but while following his thought and, I hope, while summarizing it faithfully. For a complete and detailed theological elucidation, I send the reader to the admirably thorough analyses of Tome II of *L'Église du Verbe Incarné (Chapter VI, Section I)*.

There is however a point on which I would take a somewhat different position. With regard to the non-Christians who, having received the grace of Christ, belong invisibly to the Church, is it necessary to think,—it is not my opinion,—that the grace received does not in any way cause them to participate in the coredemptive mission of the Church? (Cf. *op. cit.*, II, p. 236: text completed and nuanced by the remarks of p. 406 to which I can only give my complete agreement.)

On the other hand, I do not think that there is reason to seek differences in the more or less perfect or imperfect degree of this invisible belonging. All (and it is this which matters for their salvation) have before God, more or less lofty and abundant, the grace of Christ, as also, in the supraconscious of the spirit, the light of faith, at least as to the essential data mentioned by St. Paul. And in all of them likewise the *mode* is imperfect under which the grace of Christ, to however lofty a degree in itself such or such a one may have it, finds itself in them with respect to that which the grace of Christ requires in itself as to belonging to the Church.

I would like to note, after this, that, as Cardinal Journet writes (*op. cit.*, II, p. 662), "there is real identity and distinction of reason between the Church and the Communion of Saints." It is the same reality envisaged from two different points of view. I shall say that the idea of "the Church" connotes the soul of the Church above all as informing the whole complex visible organism which is the body of the latter: so that a baptized person in state of grace, if he has kept the Catholic faith, remains visibly and formally a member of the body of the Church, whereas a Moslem or a Buddhist in state of grace is only invisibly, and virtually or initially, a member of this body. And I shall say that the idea of "the Communion of Saints" connotes the soul of the Church above all as sanctifying the individual persons in whom it resides: so that a Buddhist or a Moslem in state of grace is formally—before God—a member of the communion of saints, whereas a Catholic in state of sin and who has kept the faith is—before God—only virtually and initially a member of the communion of saints.

28. Luke 12, 47-48.—"The slave who knew his master's wishes but did not prepare to fulfill them will get a severe beating, whereas the one who did

not know them and who nonetheless deserved to be flogged will get off with fewer stripes. When much has been given a man, much will be required of him. More will be asked of a man to whom more has been entrusted."

29. *Universale salutis sacramentum (Dogmatic Constitution on the Church*, Ch. VII, Sect. 48). Cf. also *Pastoral Constitution on the Church in the Modern World*, Part I, Ch. IV, Sect. 45.

30. *Chrétiens désunis, Principes d'un "oecuménisme" catholique*, Paris, 1937.

31. Supposing that in a few cases this teaching is the same, then it is not any longer a question of *exchange*.

32. I do not speak of *theological exchanges*, because I do not believe in them. A Catholic theologian has great profit in reading a Protestant theologian, especially if the latter is of high stature, like a Karl Barth; but (let us forget for a moment some charismatic pseudotheologians) he does not read him in order to prepare with condiments received from him a half-Protestant half-Catholic theological sauce; he reads him exactly for the same reason as any other author of value, a Marx or a Freud for example: as awakener of questions which he himself will resolve *in his own light*. It is thus that St. Thomas profited from the Greek philosophers and from the Arabian philosophers, and from all that which fell under his hand,—he who would have been able to say, more truly than Mallarmé, "and I have read all the books." Theology is a science; it is not a *hotchpotch*.

33. Ch. Journet, *The Church of the Incarnate Word*, p. 42.

34. Louis Bouyer, *La spiritualité orthodoxe et la spiritualité protestante et anglicane*, Paris, Aubier, 1965, pp. 14-15.

35. Cf. Louis Bouyer, *op. cit.*, pp. 121-124.

36. Cf. the excellent article of Ernest R. Korn, "Aux origines de la pensée moderne," *Revue Thomiste*, 1971-II and III. I quote here some lines from it:

"This repulsion, at the limit of blasphemy, which the God Who punishes and damns arouses in Luther,—is it not rather the very expression of that war which the Reformer conducts against himself? The expression of a combat begun in order to reach a kind of infinity which Luther thinks he has found in the teaching of Tauler and of the *Theologia Deutsch? . . .*

"The struggle which Luther conducts against the limitations of human nature,—it is at the plane of human activity that it establishes itself: it is by a nonfinite and unlimited action that he intends to surmount the limits of the human being.

"The finitude of which he feels an eternal sadness and an infernal grief (and which he identifies with sin and with fault) is the radical finitude of the human being. The Lutheran manner of understanding the Catholic dogma of Original Sin expresses this limitation in terms of 'total corruption of human nature.' Hence this finitude becomes essentially culpable. And how can one be liberated from this culpability, how can one be saved, except by struggling against the human itself, that is to say, as Luther writes, by conducting 'oneself persecution against oneself.' Combat merciless and to the point of total collapse, for in order for salvation to be able to appear, it is necessary that man 'collapse and be annihilated in all his forces, in all his works, in his whole being.' And why? Because 'the nature of God is such,' explains the Reformer, 'that out of nothingness He makes something. This is why, out of him who is not yet nothingness—out of him God cannot either make any-thing'. . . .

"Are not the *Mass-losigkeit* and the *Form-losigkeit* which characterize Luther related to the experience of a total and measureless fluidity which maintains and blends the extreme oppositions: *simul peccator et justus?*

"Antagonism beyond consciousness? But which fills the soul with bitter-ness, with horror, with fright and with eternal sadness, with intolerable and inconsolable terror: infernal griefs, but which for Luther become the very door of Paradise."

37. *Decree on Ecumenism*, Ch. I, Sect. 3.—"The elements or endow-ments," the Council said. I think that the "interior gifts" (such as "the life of grace, faith, hope and charity") are to be classed especially among the "endowments"; whereas among the "elements" are to be classed especially visible things, such as "the written word of God" (and the Sacraments for example,—Baptism above all,—and the teaching of the truths of faith). It is by the words *visible elements* that the text quoted here ends.

38. *Ibid.*, Ch. I, Sect. 3.

39. *Nova et Vetera*, January-March, 1970, "Intercommunion?", p. 3; cf. *ibid.*, p. 7; and also *Revue Thomiste*, 1965-I, p. 45.

40. *Decree on Ecumenism*, Ch. I, Sect. 3.

41. On the Orthodox Churches and on the Protestant Reformation, from the point of view of the theology of the history of salvation, cf. Charles Journet, *Nova et Vetera*, 1967, n. 4 and n. 3.

42. Cf. above, Ch. III, Sect. 5.

43. Turned in upon themselves, and not without the decorum of superi-ority, even of arrogance, characteristic of large collectivities as such, they accuse Catholics of errors in faith, and rebaptize persons who have been baptized in the Catholic Church, whereas the latter acts toward them in an altogether opposite manner.

Nowhere more than in the tragic history of the Eastern schism have the weaknesses of which the personnel of the Church is capable when it acts as proper cause been laid bare, in the midst of circumstances—palace intrigues, political rivalries between the empire of Rome and that of Byzantium, offenses and calumnies—in which on both sides the human played its sad role. The fact remains that Nicholas I, Hadrian II and John VIII only bore witness to their fidelity to their duty and to their mission, and only acted under the inspiration of the Holy Spirit, in affirming against winds and tides the primacy of universal jurisdiction of the Papacy over the whole Church.

That such a rent was able to occur in the history of the Church herself,—this recalls to us that the latter, with her supernatural personality, is com-posed of poor men, and that many in her personnel are subject in times of crisis to moments of aberration. This shows also that the ways which God has used toward His Son, in delivering Him into the hands of men without ceasing to guard Him by His love are also, in altogether different conditions, the ways which He uses toward His Church (as also, in altogether different conditions, toward His ancient people still loved because of its fathers).

44. One can distinguish from this point of view three currents in the Anglican Church: the Anglo-Catholics, the 'middle-of-the-road' Anglicans, and the "evangelical" current, in which Protestant influences operate.

The history of the rupture between the Church of England and Rome still remains obscure. With the question of the divorce of Henry VIII (Wolsey had, it seems, found a means of obtaining the divorce without breaking with Rome, but had fallen into disgrace and the king did not listen to him; cf. J. J. Scarisbrick, *Henry VIII*, London, 1968) there was mingled the question, very complex also, of the ecclesiastical courts: the fear of the severity—unusual—which they owed it to themselves to show toward the gentlemen when many of the latter began to read Protestant books raised against them Parliament, not without disquieting also, it seems, certain bishops: all of which contributed perhaps to cause them to give in to force when Henry VIII had passed by Parliament the *Act of Supremacy* by which the king became the supreme leader of the Church of England. Mrs. Margaret Bowker, of the University of Cambridge, is pursuing historical researches on the subject. Cf. her article that is to appear in the *Transactions of the Royal Historical Society*, 1970 [Vol. 21 (1971), pp. 61-77.—Tr.].

On the other hand, it is interesting to note that there is today in the Church of England an effort of internal readjustment, implying the desire of a greater independence with regard to the Crown in that which concerns the nomination of bishops.

45. Cf. M. J. Lagrange, *Le Messianisme chez les Juifs*, Paris, 1909.

46. Cf. Stuart E. Rosenberg, "Le renouveau contemporain et l'expérience juive," in *La Théologie du renouveau*, Paris, éd. du Cerf, 1968.—I quote from the recension of J. J. de Santo Tomas (*Revue Thomiste*, January-March, 1970, Bulletin d'Histoire de L'Église, p. 136), which continues thus: "1° In seeking by the *Halaka* the concrete realization of the Torah in Jewish life, the rabbis kept for the Holy Book its character of living Word of God, source of self-renewal of the individual and of the community. 'The Book of the people had changed [the Jews] into people of the Book, and, with this Book, this people could survive all exile.' 2° The destruction of the Temple put an end only to the influence of the priests; there remained the Synagogue, less *place* of prayer than group of *adorers*, congregation *in* Israel and *of* Israel, in which one learns to serve God in the study of the Torah, to pray to Him in turning oneself toward Sion, in the expectation of the time of the 'restauration.' 3° For Sion was less a national concept than the symbol of a confidence in the historical intervention of God, like that of Egypt or of the return from Babylon."

47. "True, authorities of the Jews and those who followed their lead pressed for the death of Christ (cf. Jn. 19:6); still, what happened in His passion cannot be blamed upon all the Jews then living, without distinction, nor upon the Jews of today. Although the Church is the new people of God, the Jews should not be presented as repudiated or cursed by God, as if such views followed from the holy Scriptures." Vatican II, *Declaration on the Relationship of the Church to Non-Christian Religions*, Sect. 4.

48. On Islam from the point of view of the theology of the history of salvation, cf. Charles Journet, *Nova et Vetera*, 1967, No. 2.

49. Cf. Olivier Lacombe, "Le Brahmanisme," in the collective work *La mystique et les mystiques*, Paris, Desclée De Brouwer, 1965, p. 732.

50. *Ibid.*, p. 741.

51. "There is in fact, according to the Buddhist, *no* self. What is felt to be the 'I', the self residing in the body, is nothing of the kind. There is no soul or self which exists as a separate essence or entity, or which experiences

physical and mental happenings. There is only the human complexity, made up of the elements and energy which have flowed together in a particular human form, and which are in a constant state of change. The sense of being a 'self', or of being an individual, is a result of the way in which physical entities and energies have been combined in human form. That is why, instead of talking about a soul or self, which might be supposed to exist (and survive) independently of the body, it is far more realistic to talk of 'not-self', or, in the Buddhist terminology, *anatta*." John Bowker, *Problems of Suffering in Religions of the World*, Cambridge, Cambridge University Press, 1970, p. 241.

52. "Justice as a conception is banished from his system, held up to ridicule; as lived exigency, it is the devouring fire from which his protest springs. . . . It seems to me that this contradiction between an extraordinarily lucid and impatient moral conscience and the negation of its reality at the plane of philosophical reason confers on Marxism its explosive character and its force of seduction. I am speaking, of course, of Marx himself, for Marxism has not ceased to be torn between a humanist tendency and a tendency to rigid intellectual and political systematization, of which the Garaudy-Althusser debate, is only an episode." G. M. M. Cottier, *Horizons de l'athéisme*, Paris, Éd. du Cerf, 1969, p. 113.

Cf. also John Bowker, *op. cit.*, pp. 138-140.

53. From a Hippy hymn, in the musical comedy *Hair*.

54. Cf. the interesting article of Émile Bailleux, "L'universel Adam et le péché originel," in the *Revue Thomiste*, Oct.-Nov., 1969. The exegetico-paleontologic presupposition in the perspective of which this article has been written is far from being established, and I regard it as philosophically debatable. But theologians do well to keep themselves ready for every eventuality.

55. Cf. *Sum. theol.*, I-II, 5, 7.—Cf. also my essay "La dialectique immanente du premier acte de liberté," in *Raison et Raisons* (Paris and Fribourg, Egloff, 1947).

56. This consubstantial desire is a natural desire which goes beyond the limitations of nature (*transnatural desire*) by reason of the Adamic grace in which man was created and which he has lost. "From the moment that grace (grace of Adam or grace of Christ) and faith are given to the human species, there we are infinitized, even if later on we lose grace, and even if we lose the faith. Even in a humanity which has lived in the state of innocence and which has lost Adamic grace, even in a humanity which has been Christian and from which faith departs, and with faith the properly supernatural desires, well, in the two cases, the transnatural desires remain stimulated, sharpened." *Neuf leçons sur les notions premières de la philosophie morale*, Paris, Téqui, 1950, pp. 106-107.

57. "Chronique d'Ecclésiologie," *Revue Thomiste*, 1969, No. 2, pp. 301-302.

58. *L'Église du Verbe Incarné*, II, Paris, 1951, p. 1114.

59. On this subject see the excellent essay of Father Marie-Joseph Nicolas ("La Co-rédemption," *Revue Thomiste*, 1947-I) from which I have given some quotations in *The Peasant of the Garonne* (pp. 248 et seq.).

60. *Sermons*, t. II, p. 247.—Cf. Charles Journet, *L'Église du Verbe Incarné*, t. II, p. 329.

NOTES TO CHAPTER XI

1. Cf. my book *On the Grace and Humanity of Jesus*, pp. 50-87.— According to the interpretation which I have proposed there, it is in the higher part or the supraconscious paradise of His soul that on earth the grace of Christ was limitless (grace of Jesus as *comprehensor*). In the lower part of His soul, or the world of consciousness, this grace was finite (grace of Jesus as *viator*), and it did not cease to grow until the death on the Cross.

2. Cf. the beautiful book of Father M. J. Nicolas on the mystery of Mary, *Théotokos*, Tournai, Desclée, 1965.

3. As the second Council of the Vatican recalled (*Dogmatic Constitution on the Church*, Sect. 60), Christ is the sole Mediator, in the full and rigorous sense of the word. But nothing prevents, says St. Thomas (*Sum. theol.*, III, 26, 1), that others than Christ be termed mediators, in a secondary and "ministerial" sense. And in this sense, the mediation of Mary "is altogether first, altogether unique. If the beings whom God, by His Incarnation, brings closest to Him are also those whom He associates more closely in His action upon others, it is indeed His mother that Christ associates with Himself first and more closely than any other for His work of 'divinization' of the world, of universal extension of the effects of the Incarnation. . . . At each of these three moments: the Incarnation, the Redemption, the glorious Life of Christ, her mediation is the extension to men of her divine maternity." M. J. Nicolas, *Théotokos*, Desclée, 1965, p. 190.

4. *Quadragesimale de evangelio aeterno*, sermo X, cap. 3, Opera omnia, Lyon, 1650, t. II, p. 57. "Nam omnium gratiarum quae humano generi descendunt, sicut quod Deus generalis est dator et Christus generalis mediator, sic per gloriosam Virginem generaliter dispensantur. Nam ipsa est collum Capitis nostri, per quod omnia spiritualia dona Corpori ejus mystico communicantur. Ideo Cant. 7 de ipso dicitur: *Collum tuum sicut turris eburnea.* (Cant. VII, 5; cf. V, 4)."

5. The second Council of the Vatican has insisted on the role of model which Mary had with regard to the Church. Cf. *Dogmatic Constitution on the Church*, Ch. 8, Sections 63, 64, 65.

6. The Church of *Christ to come* was, since Adam and Eve penitent, the Church *in preparation*. The Church here on earth was only formally constituted—with her organic structure in achieved act, and with her personality—as *Church of Christ come*, after the flames of Pentecost on the Apostles and on their queen.

I would be inclined to think that the Church of Heaven was formally constituted as such, with her body unified under her eternally living Leader, and with her personality, from the day of the Ascension,—the Blessed Virgin having thus been here on earth, for a time (as from Pentecost as regards the Church of the earth), the instrument which God used in order to give to the Church her personality in Heaven and on earth.

7. Except that of the Blessed Virgin, through the instrumentality of which, we have just seen, the Church receives her personality, and which is immanent in this personality.

8. If they have lost grace and charity, but not the faith.

9. If they have lost the faith.

10. This is why the questions which the medieval theologians posed to

themselves concerning a Pope who would become heretical seem to me wholly academic. Envisaging the case, by an hypothesis which I consider to be gratuitous, it is necessary to say, with Cardinal Journet and the theologians in question, that the Council would not at all have to *depose* this heretical Pope (as if the Council was superior to the Pope), but only to *state* the fact of heresy, the fact that he himself, having ceased, by his heresy, to be a member of the Church, has divested himself of his primacy in the Church; in short the Council would only have to "take cognizance of an accomplished fact." (Cf. Ch. Journet, "Le Pape et l'Église," in the newspaper *La Croix*, October 3, 1969.)

11. Each of them shows us some aspect of her face, no one of them shows it to us entirely; for no one is as holy as she. In each appears the perfection of charity,—according to his own mode,—but his individual limitations and those of his environment and of his time reveal themselves also.

12. Cf. Vatican II, *Constitution on the Sacred Liturgy*, Sect. 84: "By tradition going back to early Christian times, the divine Office is arranged so that the whole course of the day and night is made holy by the praises of God. Therefore, when this wonderful song of praise is worthily rendered by priests and others who are deputed for this purpose by Church ordinance, or by the faithful praying together with the priest in an approved form, then *it is truly the voice of the bride addressing her bridegroom*; it is the very prayer which Christ Himself, together with His body, addresses to the Father."

Ibid., Sect. 99: " . . . The divine Office is the voice of the Church, that is, of the whole mystical body publicly praising God."

13. I am not forgetting that the fomenters of schism and the great heresiarchs were also, at first, members, and often very noteworthy members, of the personnel of the Church; but they broke with the latter, and find themselves therefore outside the field of my present reflections.

14. Cf. my book *God and the Permission of Evil.*—If this first initiative of nothingness does not take place, the divine motion, received first as shatterable, is then rendered unshatterable.

15. He accomplishes it freely, for he could have, supposing his will had been previously perverted, rendered himself inapt, having already opted for evil, to receive this instrumental divine motion (which is given at once as unshatterable). He can also mingle in that which he is instrumentally moved to do elements of his own invention which can not be righteous.

16. Cf. *Sum. theol.*, III, 64, 1.

17. In the broad sense of the word, according as God uses her in order to move the minister of the Sacrament, as I indicate here, and according as it is Christ Himself Who offers to God the Sacrifice of the Mass through the instrumentality of the Church.—Cf. note 21.

18. *Sum. theol.*, III, 64, 8, c and ad 1, ad 2.

19. III, 64, 1, ad 2.

20. It would be futile to think that the expression has a merely juridical sense and that "to act in the person of the Church" is only to act as representative of the latter: for then, if the intention of the Church is not in the priest, the words pronounced by this "representative" belong to appearances and to fiction. It is necessary that the intention of the Church be *really* there, even if the priest is distracted and inattentive. (If the representative of

a country says to a country at war "my country is sending you a thousand airplanes in order to help you," and if these airplanes are not really sent, the assurances given by this representative are only appearance and fiction.)

21. In order to sum up everything, I shall say that in the sacramental order there are three persons to be considered:

God omnipotent, Who uses the humanity of Christ, conjoined instrument of His divinity, and Who is the principal Agent, supreme and absolutely first;

the holy and indeficient person of the Church, the Offerer here on earth of worship and of sacrifice, and the Effector of the Sacraments, who is at one and the same time second principal agent and, in the broad sense of the word, instrumental agent of God;

the minister of the Sacrament, who is instrumental agent in the strict sense, the instrumentality of whom the person of the Church uses according as he is human subject through whom she acts, and the instrumentality of whom God uses in giving efficacy to the words which he pronounces and to the gestures which he accomplishes when he confers the Sacraments and when he offers the Sacrifice.

22. Canon of the Mass.

23. Pius IX, Denz.-Schön., 2879.—Cf. Charles Journet, *L'Église du Verbe Incarné*, t. II, p. 534.

24. Cf. above, Ch. VII, pp. 55-56.

25. It is in regard to this essential intention that I understand the assertion of Pius XII when he says (encycl. *Humani Generis*) that the teaching of the encyclicals belongs to the ordinary magisterium.

26. Cf. Charles Journet, *L'Église du Verbe Incarné*, t. II, p. 568, note 1. (My language is very different, but what it enables me to say is, I believe, very much in accord with this very illuminating note.)—Cf. also Georges M. M. Cottier, *Régulation des naissances et développement démographique*, Paris, Desclée De Brouwer, 1969, Introd., p. 9.

27. I could give examples, which have come to me from fervent Christians of whom I am honored to be the friend.

28. Cf. Ch. IX, pp. 84-85 and note 15.

29. If it is true that, as we have seen in Ch. III, God gives to the Church her supernatural personality *by reason of the image of Christ which she bears in her,* one must conclude that it was only as Church of *Christ come* that she began to receive this personality. Formerly, at the different stages in which the Church still in sketch gradually took shape, the grace of *Christ to come* undoubtedly caused such a "moral person" to aspire to become person in the primary and ontological sense of the word. But it was once Christ come that such was the case, and that thus the mystery of the Church was brought to its consummation.

Cf. above, note 6 to Chapter XI.

30. With regard to the Pope, it is fitting to add that the choice made of him,—whatever the mode of election may be,—implies a certain acceptance or ratification on the side of the person herself of the Church, in this sense that then, as principal agent using the electoral college as an instrumental cause, she diverts it from designating anyone who would be incapable of guiding the bark and of preserving intact the transmission of the faith. Without such an acceptance or ratification, which makes of the bishop of Rome the leader of

the Church of the earth, the members of the whole hierarchy constituted under his auspices and in communion with him cannot be held to be the "personnel *of the Church*."

The choice in question has moreover nothing to do with the private merits of the man thus designated (so much the better if he is a saint, so much the worse in the contrary case). It is a question of bringing to the Sovereign Pontificate, in given (and sometimes unfortunate) historical circumstances, someone who is sufficiently qualified for the government of the Christian people in all that which concerns the faith and the deposit of the revealed truth. One has remarked that "customs and politics placed aside," the government of a drunk-with-pride and debauched simoniac such as Alexander VI "was generally profitable to the Church. This Pope proved to be always a vigilant guardian of doctrine: he gave several Bulls concerning questions of dogma and of worship. He worked for the propagation of the faith, especially in the New World, which had been discovered at the beginning of his Pontificate" (J. Paquier, *Dictionnaire de théologie catholique*, t. 1, pp. 726-727).

NOTES TO CHAPTER XII

1. Julian Green, *Journal*, II, p. 979.

2. Before him, Gregory VII had dreamed of an expedition into the Holy Land which he wished to lead himself, but the War of the Investitures prevented him from realizing this project. The call to the crusade came from the Papacy of the Middle Ages. It was from the hands of the Pope or from his legates that those who made a vow to participate in the enterprise received the Cross.

3. Which delighted exceedingly Humbert of Romans. Cf. *Gesta Francorum*, p. 202, quoted by Norman Daniel, *Islam and the West*, Edinburgh, 1960, p. 113. This massacre, adds the author, was in fact "the worst medieval profanation of the Holy Land known to us" (*ibid.*, p. 349, n. 12).

4. Cf. his article *Croisades* (*Dictionnaire d'Apologétique*, p. 823), which is a very good summary of his work *L'Église et l'Orient au moyen âge, Les croisades*, Paris, 1907.

5. "Going out, one evening of defeat at Damietta, from the camp of the Crusades, St. Francis came to the Moslem camp to offer himself to the ordeal by fire, for the love of a single Moslem soul, the Ayyubite sultan Mohammad-iba-Abi Bakr al Malik al-Kamil. Driven back far from the glimpsed martyrdom, he knew, by a vision, that on his return to Italy, he would obtain another death of love: it was his stigmatization at Alverno, the day of the Exaltation of the Holy Cross. His compassion for Islam, this true spiritual crusade, the first, the one which Louis IX will imitate at Carthage, had merited for him to become the first compassionate visibly configured with the Crucified, 'who rises from the East, bearing the sign of the living God.' Thus opened, seven centuries ago, the long procession of the vexillaries of the Passion." Louis Massignon, *Les trois prières d'Abraham, Seconde Prière*, Avrault, Tours, hors commerce, p. 56. Cf. p. 25.

6. *Saint François d'Assise*, Paris, Perrin, 1954, p. 307.

7. Norman Daniel, *op. cit.*, p. 113.

8. Luke 9, 54-56.—Cf. John 18, 36.

9. Cf. the beautiful book of Robert Vallery-Radot, *Le Prophète de l'Occident (1130-1153)*, Paris, Desclée, 1969.

10. Allusion to the capture of Edessa by the "atabeks" of Mosul (1144). And it is indeed true that "although the Crusades had at first the appearance of a bold offensive, they were in reality, from the outset, wars of defense." (Louis Bréhier, *loc. cit.*, col. 837.) The first Moslem aggression was that of the Fatimite calif Hakem who, in 1099, had destroyed the Holy Sepulchre, putting an end thus to the free protectorate which the calif Haroun-al-Raschid had conferred on Charlemagne in the year 800. Came then, oppressing the Christians and threatening Byzantium, the invasions of the Seljukian Turks.

11. St. Bernard did not suspect that they echoed the Islamic conception of the shuhadas: those who die "on the way of God" go straight to Heaven. (And the "way of God" included war, even offensive, for the extension of Islam.) It was indeed the idea of the holy war, although the Moslem jihad does not at all evoke in itself an idea of execration and of extermination.

12. Norman Daniel, *op. cit.*, p. 112.

13. Cf. my preface to the book of Alfredo Mendizabel, *Aux Origines d'une Tragédie*, Paris, Desclée De Brouwer, 1937 [Engl. transl.: *The Martyrdom of Spain*, London, Geoffrey Bles, 1938.—Tr.]. The major part of this preface had appeared as an article in the *Nouvelle Revue Francaise*.

14. Bishop Diaz Gomara, bishop of Carthagena.

15. That is to say: object of repulsion for my beloved.

16. As the Jerusalem Bible notes here very rightly (note *a*), "Israel, though unbelieving, 10:21, is still a chosen people, 11:2." That which is clearly confirmed by 11, 16 and 18; and 11, 29.

17. One cannot translate ἀποβολή by the word "rejection," since St. Paul has expressly affirmed (11, 1 and 2) that *God has not rejected his people*. The words "mise à l'écart" ["being set aside"] employed by the Jerusalem Bible render sufficiently well the sense. The Vulgate translates: *amissio*, which one could perhaps render also by the word "defection" in order to signify that as long as they remain in incredulity the Jewish people (still chosen) are deficient in their own predestined "olive-tree," and in the root of the latter, and that they have been amputated from the Body dedicated to the redemptive work, all these members whom the Body has thus lost (*amisit*) until they are again grafted in.

Apropos of 11, 14: Even unbelieving, the chosen people remains a "holy" people, not certainly by their actual conduct with regard to the Gospel (in this respect they have become "enemies," 11, 28), but *by their election*, which is *irrevocable*, 11, 29. This is why the "root" (11, 18) continues to "support" the faithful branches, even those which have been grafted in with Gentiles, and the unbelieving Jews are still *beloved because of the patriarchs* (11, 28).

18. Rom. 9-11.

19. I know well that the "anger" and the "vengeance" of God, and even His "hatred" ("He blessed Jacob and hated Esau") hold a large place in the Bible: manners of speaking proper to Semitic semantics, which puts in the positive (as willed by God) that which He permits only (He "blinds," He "hardens" whom He wishes . . .). Translated into Latin or into our vernacu-

lars, these expressions have not a little contributed to lead astray unreflecting or passionate minds.

20. A furious mob stoned St. Stephen (and the young Saul was in agreement). In 62, another mob threw from the top of the Temple and stoned James the Less, who was then bishop of Jerusalem, while observing so well the Law of Moses that the Jewish common people venerated him (it was the Sanhedrin which had instigated the affair and provoked the riot).

21. It was a question in particular of struggling against the tendency to fast the same days as the Jews and to keep like them the Sabbath Day. In the sixth century St. Gregory the Great will have still to busy himself with the question.

22. "There where the courtesan is, the place [that is to say the Synagogue as assembly of worship] is called a brothel. What am I saying? Not brothel only and theatre, the Synagogue is also cavern of brigands and lair of wild beasts. . . ." The same homily continues: "Living for their stomach, their mouths always open, they do not conduct themselves better than the pigs and the billy goats, in their lewd grossness and the excess of their gluttony. They can do only one thing: stuff themselves with food and get drunk. . . ." *Adversus Judaeos Orationes, Hom. I*, P. G. XLVIII, col. 847-848.

23. "Si expedit odisse homines et gentem aliquam detestari, miro odio aversor circumcisionem, usque hodie enim persequuntur Dominum nostrum Jesum Christum in synagogis Satanae." (Apropos of Psalm 138, 22: *Perfecto odio oderam illos.*)

24. As it will be explicitly codified later by Canon Law. In 1179, the 26th canon of the third ecumenical Lateran Council will declare: *Judaeos subjacere christianis oportet et ab eis pro sola humanitate foveri.* While maintaining the principle of their religious liberty, the fourth Lateran Council (1215) will shackle their life by numerous restrictions destined to protect Christians against their influence.

Let us not forget that if, as I have said, the ecumenical Councils are the voice of the Church, this must clearly be understood of that which concerns the revealed teaching concerning faith and morals. In disciplinary measures in wholly contingent matter like those to which I allude here, or like the prescription of a crusade by the fourth Lateran Council, the Fathers of a Council act as "proper causes" to whom obedience is due, but not as organs causing instrumentally to be heard the voice of the Church of Heaven and of earth, in other words of the person of the Church.

25. When at the same time he did not deem it wrong that one offer material advantages to the Jews in order that they become converted, "he was not at all taken in by the sincerity of the faith thus obtained. 'But,' he said, 'if the men thus gained do not promise to be very good Christians, there is hope that their children will be.' " (*Op. cit.*, p. 115.) Calculation very debatable in itself, but which was not lacking in practical accuracy, if one remembers that one of the grandfathers of St. Theresa of Avila was a Marrano.

26. Cf. Bernhard Blumenkranz, *Juifs et Chrétiens dans le Monde Occidental (430-1096)*, Paris, 1960, p. 380. See also Foreword, p. xix: During the whole Carolingian period no permanent anti-Judaism.

27. In the important work which I have just cited.

28. *Op. cit.*, Foreword, p. xiv.

29. Not without using on both sides the means of pressure or of seduction at one's disposal. (This is why one forbade the Jews to have Christian
slaves.) On the Christian side, one obliged the Jews to assist at sermons which
sometimes were delivered in the synagogues.

30. Neither good temperament nor humor were lacking in that time.
Witness the fine story about Charlemagne and a bishop over fond of expen-
sive curiosities told by the monk of Saint-Gaul. Charlemagne asks a Jewish
shopkeeper to perfume a mouse and to offer it as an Eastern rarity to the
bishop in question, who buys it at a high price; all of which enables the
Emperor to laugh at his expense and to shame him in a synod (*op. cit.*, p. 16).

31. When at the end of the tenth century the Jews will retreat into the
cities, they will group themselves there in districts of their choice. It is at the
end of the following century, in 1084, that the bishop of Spires, Rudiger, has
the Jewish district surrounded by a wall, "in order to avoid," he says, "the
insolent populace's attacking them." Wall which tomorrow will enclose them,
will double itself with an invisible wall of resentment, and will designate them
to the assaults of the persecutors. (Cf. *op. cit.*, p. 39.)

Reserved districts had existed for three centuries in the Moslem countries,
whose theocratic body politic showed itself at first quite benevolent with
regard to its Jewish and Christian guests. As distinctive sign the Jews wore
there a small wheel of yellow color, the Christians a small wheel of blue color.

32. Philip the Fair pursued there no religious aim; he had in view only to
despoil the Jews (as moreover the Lombards or the Templars).

33. Imported from Islam in the twelfth century (1179, third Lateran
Council), absolutely imposed in the sixteenth century (1555, Paul IV),
become out-of-date after the emancipation, officially expunged from Canon
Law by Pius IX.

34. Imported also from Islam in the thirteenth century (1215, fourth
Lateran Council), absolutely imposed at the same time as the ghetto (1555),
fallen into disuse (except for the jurists of the Holy Office) in the eighteenth
century, abolished in the Papal States after the emancipation.

35. One knows that St. Thomas (II-II, 78, 1 ad 2) condemned loan at
interest, which he considered to be usury. In actual fact, the princes appro-
priated the greater part of the interests which the Jews collected from the
poor people, and of which the rate was thereby rendered necessarily excessive.

"The financial role of the Jewish element in the world," writes Louis
Massignon ("L'influence de l'Islam sur la fondation des banques juives," in
Opera minora, t. I, p. 247), "is an accidental role which was imposed on it
only tardily: by the Moslem State. We do not see indeed in antiquity, even in
the Byzantine epoch, that the preponderance, among the bankers, ever
belonged to the Jewish element. At the outset of Islam it was not yet the
case; in the beginning of the ninth century, Jahiz does not consider the Jews
as specialized in banking; this profession is then exercised by Christians. But
one knows that since Islamic canon law forbade Moslems the commerce of
money, and tolerated in Moslem countries no other communities than those
of Christians and those of Jews, the Moslem States had necessarily to
attribute the monopoly of the commerce of money either to Christians or to
Jews; and the Christian financiers were clearly more suspect in their eyes, as
possible spies in the service of the Christian emperors of Byzantium.... It

was therefore the Moslem State which, at the end of the ninth century, specialized the Jewish element in the commerce of money, stigmatizing it thus with a characteristic social stamp, a kind of psychological equivalent of the small wheel."

36. B. Blumenkranz, *op. cit.*, p. 380.

37. The reason invoked by the liturgists was that the Jews had bent the knee before Christ in order to ridicule him (historical error, moreover: it was the Roman soldiers who did this). But in the rubric in question the people saw only a mark of sacred aversion toward them in the very moment that one was praying for them. It seems even, if we believe the sacramentary of Saint-Vast, that the *real* cause of this rubric was to avoid the reactions of hate of the Christian people: *Hic nostrum nullus debet modo flectere corpus, ob populi noxiam ac pariter rabiem.*

38. Toll sheet of Malemort.

39. In his recension (*Revue Thomiste,* January-March, 1970, p. 144) of the book of B. Blumenkranz, *Le Juif médiéval au miroir de l'art chrétien,* Paris, Études Augustiniennes, 1966.

40. *Ibid.*

41. *Ibid.*

42. *Ibid.*

43. B. Blumenkranz, *op. cit.*, p. 135.

44. J. J. De Santo Thomas, article cited, p. 144.

45. Hilary of Poitiers, Ambrose.

46. Cyril of Alexandria: "They have shown themselves deicide," he writes in his Commentary on Isaiah. I do not believe that the expression *deicide people* is found formally in him.

St. Augustine does not use the word, but insists on the collective responsibility of the Jews. Cf. D. Judant, *Judaisme et Christianisme,* Paris, Éd. du Cèdre, 1969, Ch. V.

47. Let us hope that a philosopher worthy of the name will give us some day a good psychoanalysis of history. From the point of view of a concrete psychology, I think that what we call an idea finds itself under two entirely different states according as it is of the merely intellectual order (a concept used by the reason) or according as it affects vitally the whole human subject. In the first case I shall call it "light-idea" when it is true and "word-idea" or "paper-idea" when it is false. In the second case I shall call it "sun-idea" when it is in the service of truth, and radiates ineffably in the supraconscious of the spirit in order to gain from there the intellect and to invade the whole soul; and I shall call it "vampire-idea" when it is in the service of falsehood and rises from the animal unconscious in order to take possession of the human subject.

48. From a letter from one of my Catholic friends, who during his stay in Israel wished to learn Hebrew and had as teacher a "true average Israelian girl, native of central Europe, Esther," I extract the following lines: "With an altogether Israelian frankness and simplicity, she did not scruple to speak out before the whole class (in which I was clearly the only Christian, in the midst of Jewish comrades originally from about fifteen countries of Europe and of Asia, of Africa and of the two Americas) concerning the heavy Judeo-Christian past. And I am profoundly grateful to her for it. All this, it is true, I knew, at least roughly, very roughly, and in the abstract if I may say; but I

had not realized, felt, lived from the interior, from the side of the victims, in their skin, all that which an accumulation of such aberrations throughout twenty centuries could awaken of suffering, of rancor, of scandal. I had before me there, living and sorrowful, the image which a normally constituted Jew or Jewess can form of Christianity, such as they have seen it at work, such as they have experienced it, suffered it, in the quick of their flesh, of their human dignity and of their faith, in the course of history. . . .

"How many times did I hear her evoke the lot of this eternally wandering people, chased from one Christian country, then from another, then again from another. People unceasingly subjected in Christendom to popular scorn and to laws of exception, of segregation, deprived most often of all possibilities of ordinary work, carefully kept in the background, far before they are penned up and packed together in their ghettos; subjected frequently to the infamous wearing of insignia or distinctive hats. People periodically massacred, from the hundreds or so massacres perpetrated in Germany, in the Middle Ages, to the more recent pogroms of Eastern Europe, without forgetting the Crusades, in which the champions of the Cross acquired the knack on the Jewish communities of Europe before going to kill Sarrazin and to burn alive in their synagogues of Jerusalem and other holy places, so many Jews of Palestine. . . .

"Hundreds and hundreds of synagogues burned, bonfires with their holy books (including sometimes the Bible). Incessant and tragic accusations of "ritual murder," or profanation of hosts or of poisoning of the wells at the moment of the epidemics of plague, all this ending clearly in blood baths. In a general manner, antisemitism more or less virulent in the Christian countries and milieus, in the measure ordinarily in which they called themselves and believed themselves Christians, the ordinary teaching of the sermons or of the catechisms (deicide people, accursed people, etc.) having all that which was necessary in order to stir up this antisemitism, which culminated each year at the moment of Holy Week, during which the Jews of the Middle Ages had only to barricade themselves well in their homes if they did not wish to be massacred 'for the love of the crucified Savior.'

"This long history of blood ending in our day in the horrors of the Nazi camps, of their gas chambers and of their crematoriums. . . . Of course Esther and the Israelians distinguish between Nazis and authentic Christians (many of whom risked their life in order to save some of them); but the fact remains that the Nazis were almost all baptized persons, therefore officially Christians, and that their monstrosities were able to surge up only on a terrain already well prepared by the traditional Christian antisemitism.

"I spare you astonished and grieved commentaries on recent Vatican 'politics' and its obstinate refusal to recognize the existence of the State of Israel. . . .

"I shall terminate this sad subject on this phrase of Esther which I shall never forget: 'It is necessary that you understand well that the cross is for us the accursed symbol of all our misfortunes, of all our persecutions, of all our massacres.' And, in actual fact, in Israel, not only has the Red Cross become the Red Star of David, but even the sign '+' of addition in mathematics has been modified also because it evokes the accursed sign. . . . This is frightfully heavy with signification.

"If it is true that a handful of Jews were able to contribute one day, by badly enlightened religious zeal, to the crucifixion of the Savior, 'accomplishing thus the Scriptures,' the Christian people, by a zeal just as unseemly, has persisted in return in crucifying the whole Jewish people, throughout its sorrowful history, resembling strangely a mysterious way of the Cross. And I tell myself sometimes that in the Council Document on Judaism, a small phrase of humble avowal of culpability and of asking for pardon, would perhaps not have been a useless luxury." (September 13, 1969)

49. This edict concerned the Jews of the Papal States.—Prohibition to possess, to write, to translate any impious book, such as a Talmudist or Cabalist one; prohibition to place near their sepulchres any stone bearing an inscription; prohibition to practice their rites outside of their synagogues, for example to sing psalms or to carry torches while transporting to the cemetery the body of their deceased; prohibition to approach nearer the House of Catechumens than the space of thirty canes; prohibition, under pain of the galley and of the confiscation of goods, to dissuade anyone from becoming converted to the holy Catholic faith; obligation to wear the mark of yellow color, which distinguishes them from other people; prohibition to sell or to give to Christians the meat of any animal which they would have killed themselves; prohibition to have shops outside of ghettos; prohibition to have recourse to Christian midwives and Christian nurses, to have Christian menservants or Christian maidservants, etc.

50. The decree of civil emancipation of the Jews was voted two years later by the Constituent Assembly (September 27, 1791).

51. Let us quote here these lines from an author, Mr. Cecil Roth, who is not suspected of sympathy for Christianity: "The Pope, whatever might be his desire to prevent that Christian orthodoxy should be contaminated by contact with them, adhered always to the principle of formal tolerance; in spite of the tendencies of ecclesiastical politics, he never approved the anti-Jewish violences, or atrocities such as the accusation of ritual murder or forced conversion. Each time, he declared himself for reason and moderation in these domains (and even Innocent III, who inspired the most reactionary legislation of the Middle Ages, was no exception). A protecting Bull of Calixtus II, *Sicut Judaeis*, which condemned severely the attacks against the person of Jews and their baptism under constraint, was confirmed at least twenty-two times, from its promulgation in 1120 to the middle of the fifteenth century. From 1130 to 1138, one of the pretenders to the throne of St. Peter was a man of whom the Jewish origins were quite close—Anacletus II (Piero Pierleoni). The Jews of the States of the Pope were almost the only ones in Europe to never experience the massacres and expulsion in all their horror; and small colonies from Rome swarmed into the surrounding territory." (*Histoire du Peuple juif*, Paris, Éditions de la Terre Retrouvée, 1963, pp. 221-222.)—There were nevertheless two attempts at expulsion (edict of Pius V in 1569, broken by Sixtus V in 1586; edict of Clement VIII in 1593, revoked by the same Pope a few months later).

52. *Declaration on the Relationship of the Church to Non-Christian Religions*, Sections 4 and 5.

53. *Le Mystère d'Israël*, Paris, Desclée De Brouwer, 1965.

54. Nor was I denying the rights of the Arabs of Palestine. I shall speak below of these rights; I note immediately that they are by no means, as a certain anti-Israelian political propaganda sometimes seems to suggest, the

unjustly injured rights of a nation which would have been conquered and despoiled by the force of arms.

A bit of history here: Jewish agricultural colonies were founded, at the end of the nineteenth century, and thanks to purchases of lands, by the Zionist pioneers with a view to preparing for the Jews of the Diaspora the creation of a national home on the Promised Land (which, up until the defeat of Turkey in the First World War, and the mandate received by Great Britain, was under Ottoman rule). Following negociations between Chaim Weizmann and the English government, the Balfour Declaration (November 2, 1917) confirmed the right of the Jewish people to this creation. In 1922 Palestine, by virtue of a decision of the United Nations, passed under British mandate. In November, 1947, another decision of the United Nations, prescribing the division of the Holy Land into an Arab State and a Jewish State, and the internationalization of Jerusalem, was rejected by the Arabs,—all of which launched the armed struggle between the Arab League and the Israelians. And on the eve of the expiration (May 15) of the British mandate, Ben Gourion, President of the Executive Committee of the Jews of Palestine, proclaimed (May 14, 1948) the independence of the State of Israel, soon recognized by the principal world powers. The State of Israel was not born of any aggression and invasion of which one knows not what Arab national State in Palestine would have been the victim. It was born of an immigration of rapid growth (not without friction) organizing itself (in conformity with the principle laid down in 1947 by the United Nations Organization) into an independent political unity in a territory under British mandate,—an immigration and an independent political unity both sanctioned by international law.

The rights of the Palestinians are, firstly, those of the human person in each of us, wherever he may be, and which the State of Israel only asks to respect in the Arab population of its territory; and, secondly, their right (whether they have remained in Israel or whether they have gone into Jordan or into other countries) to a compensation which makes up as much as possible for the losses involved for them, not certainly from the fact of an unjust aggression, but from the fact of the legitimate installation of a new national and political unity in a part of a territory which up until then they were the only ones to populate. It was incumbent neither on the Arab countries nor on the State of Israel, but rather on the great powers, to give this compensation. Devoured by national egoism and by their economic and military rivalries, they have failed up till now (I write these lines in April of 1970) in this duty. It is still incumbent on them. It would take energy, intelligence, and *generosity*, —which is to ask much, but is to ask the indispensable.

I do not like to touch on political questions which are situated on an altogether different plane than the one which is proper to the subject of this book. I have nevertheless been obliged to do so in this note in order to explain clearly my thought. Two remarks remain to be made in this order.

In the first place, to desire, as certain ones do (cf. *Témoignage chrétien*, December 11, 1969), "the creation of a secular Palestine, open to all, Arabs and Jews, Moslems, Christians, Israelites and atheists," is, by innuendo, and not without slanderous insinuations with regard to the State of Israel, to desire the disappearance of this State, in other words to desire that which I hold to be an iniquity.

In the second place, to be persuaded, as I am, that the existence of the State of Israel is a just and necessary thing, and to have at heart the love of those who are gathered together in it, as also of the work to which they are called, does not imply at all that one regards without anxiety the nationalist extremism of some among them, nor that one is ready to approve in every circumstance the politics of this State itself. The State of Israel is no more infallible than the others. The fact remains that it is alone in the midst of a hostile world, and is doing what it believes good in order to defend itself; and that with regard to the situation in the Middle East the great powers carry a terribly heavy responsibility. France, alas, has been far from cutting a good figure in the events. It seems that only the American people has kept at the bottom of its soul a sense of human solidarity sufficiently strong that, to the calculations touching national interest which prevail in its politicians as in those of the whole world, there is joined in the anonymous mass a sincere and real friendship for the State of Israel, as for the Jewish people recently persecuted in such a tragic and unforgettable manner.

55. Gen. 13, 5; 15, 18; 17, 8.
56. Gen. 28, 13.
57. Exodus 3, 8; 6, 8.
58. Ez. 37, 12 and 14 and 25.
59. "Anti-Israelism" is the exact word. One prefers to say today "anti-Zionism." It is always easy (the imagination and passion are there for that, it suffices to cease to control them, and also to rely on the idle gossip of some extremists, who are never lacking) to create a myth such as that "Zionism" which one pictures to oneself as an organized movement tending to put the Jews of the whole world in the service of the State of Israel, and which one reproaches (*Témoignage chrétien*, number cited in note 54) "its racial character, its expansionist will, the confusion which it maintains between the sacred and the temporal, its materialist interpretation of the Bible and the utilization of the Holy Books in a political purpose." In this fantastic enumeration, it is the accusation of theocracy ("confusion of the sacred and of the temporal") which appears the most ridiculous, when one knows that in Israel the least well disposed ones toward their State are the more religious Jews, and that on the other hand it is in Islam that the State is conceived as sacral. As to "the materialist interpretation of the Bible," it consists undoubtedly in believing that which is written in it? And when one speaks of "racial character," does one wish to reduce to "race" the moral community and the immense historical heritage which explain that there is a Jewish people? Finally, is it for the State of Israel "expansionist will" to defend its threatened existence and its right to be there?

The Christians who declare themselves anti-Zionists can declare at the same time, in all good faith, that they are not anti-Semites, and that they have moreover given proof of this during the occupation. They do not see that myths like the "Zionism" in question are the ways through which antisemitism penetrates most insidiously into the imagination and the heart of people. The anti-Zionist propaganda at work today, and of which the political origins are easily discernible, is in actual fact a well-orchestrated anti-Semite propaganda.

It is perhaps not profitless to quote here some lines drawn from *Le Mystère d'Israël* (pp. 245-246). "On account of the formation of the Israelian

State," I wrote in 1964, "the condition of Israel in the world has entered into an entirely new phase. Henceforth this condition is, if I may say, bipolar: it implies at one and the same time the diaspora among the Gentiles, which has not ceased and which is required by the very vocation of Israel,—and the political unity of the Israelian people in such and such a given point of the globe, through which we see decidedly ended the vestiges of the regime of the ghetto, and decidedly begun the first foundations of a realization in time of the hope of Israel. Thus it is no longer only the long tragic tension between Israel and the world which the philosopher of history has henceforth to consider. It is also, in the bosom of Israel itself, a fraternal tension between the Jewish State of the Holy Land and the Jewish population of the Dispersion, which relate, so to speak, to two different centers of gravitation, and of which the needs, the purposes and the destinies are distinct, but which in a no less important measure remain nevertheless essentially linked and interdependent, in the material order and in the spiritual order."

60. Rom. 11, 15. It is to this whole chapter that I refer here.—The persons who, like Mme Judant, take as mythical the belief in the conversion of the Jewish people in a distant future, display, I do not contest it, an erudition as vast as it is tendentious, but it seems doubtful that they have read closely the Epistle to the Romans. "If you were cut off from the natural wild olive and, contrary to nature, were grafted into the cultivated olive, so much the more will they who belong to it by nature be grafted into their own olive tree. Brothers, I do not want you to be ignorant of this mystery lest *you be conceited* (Pr. 3, 7): blindness has come upon part of Israel until the full number of Gentiles enter in, and then all Israel will be saved." (11, 24-26.)

61. Rom. 11, 1-2.

62. Rom. 11, 28.

NOTES TO CHAPTER XIII

1. On the sacral regime cf. Charles Journet, *L'Église du Verbe Incarné*, t. 1, pp. 280-425 ("Régime de la Chrétienté sacrale"); and my book *Integral Humanism*, pp. 143-153.

2. *In Cant.*, serm. 64.

"Drive the heretics out of the Church: but do not kill them; for they are made like you in the image of God," wrote St. Hildegarde.

3. Letter to the Archbishop of Rheims, Henri, brother of King Louis VII the Younger.

Let us quote also the letter written in 1043 by the Bishop of Liége, Wazon, to the Bishop of Châlons, Roger, who had consulted him: "God does not wish the death of the sinner but his conversion. Did not Christ give us the example of gentleness toward the heretics, whereas, omnipotent, He endured the opprobriums, the insults, the cruelties of the Jews and finally the torment on the Cross? And when, in His parable, He advised to let the cockle grow with the good grain until the harvest, did He not teach us that the wicked must live with the righteous until the Judgment of God Who alone will separate them? ... Those whom the world considers today as cockle, can be, when the harvest will come, gathered into His barn by God along with the wheat.... Those whom we regard as the enemies of God, can be put by Him above us in Heaven."

However true and noble they may be, these lines, like those of Alexander III quoted in my text, furnish us a testimony of the gentleness of heart and of the elevation of thought of the one who wrote them, more than a clear principle of discernment in order to solve a practical problem. The kings and their counsellors saw in them only a testimony of weakness.

4. These Bulls thus caused rigorously to pass into practice the prescriptions enacted by the third Lateran Council in 1179 and the Council of Verona in 1184, and repeated by Innocent III at the fourth Lateran Council in 1215.

The functions of inquisitors had first been exercised by the Cistercian legates. Gregory IX entrusted the Dominicans with them. The first general Inquisitor of the kingdom of France was Robert le Bougre (himself a converted Catharian,—one said commonly "bulgare" or "bougre" for "cathare"). He acted both in the name of the Pope and in the name of the king.

For a detailed historical account of that which I have summed up in this paragraph, cf. Jean Guiraud, article *Inquisition*, in the *Dictionnaire d'Apologétique*, col. 823 to 853.

The Inquisition prosecuted the Catharians, the Waldenses (cf. Jean Marx, *L'Inquisition en Dauphiné*), the Beguin disciples of Joachim of Flora and of Jean d'Olive; and also, in the fifteenth century, the sorcerers; and even the persons guilty of certain misdemeanors of common law.

5. Cf. Jean Guiraud, *op. cit.*, col. 868 et seq.; and Ch. Journet, *L'Église du Verbe Incarné*, t. 1, p. 378, note 1.

6. Very little: The accused were not confronted with the witnesses who accused them, and they did not know their names; at the time when one granted them lawyers, these had as their role only to advise them in their defense or to urge them to confess, and they never appeared in court; a system of informing which violated natural law forced the father and the mother to accuse their children, the husband to accuse his wife, and reciprocally. Cf. E. Vacandard, *Dict. de théol.*, col. 2038-2041.

The Bull *Cum adversus*, of Innocent IV, 31st October 1243, approved "the constitution *Commissi Nobis* of Frederick II, in which it is said that the sons of heretics shall escape the punishments provided by the law even against them—deprivation of goods, refusal of public offices and honours—if they denounce the secret heresy of their own father." Later a Bull of Pius V (*Bullarium romanum*, Turin, 1862, t. VII, p. 430) forbade "physicians to go on visiting the sick who should not have confessed themselves within three days or were not in a position to present a certificate of confession." Ch. Journet, *The Church of the Incarnate Word*, Vol. I, p. 297, n. 2.

7. What I call here the *teaching* authority of the Church consists above all in her "declaratory power," which makes known that which God has revealed (and which we believe *on the word of God*), but also in her "canonical power," when it makes known to us, in order to assure through the centuries the preservation of the revealed deposit in its integrity, that which is to be believed *on the word of the Church*. Cf. further on, Ch. XIV, pp. 203-206.

8. St. Bernard, in the *De Consideratione*, speaks also of the two swords,

but by the second sword he understands the material sword which is "in the hand of the soldier," and which can be drawn *at the order* of Peter, but not *by his hand, tuo forsitan nutu, etsi non tua manu* (IV, cap. 3, a. 7). St. Thomas takes up again the same views in *in IV Sent.*, dist. 37. On the contrary, the second sword, such as I understand it, that of the coercive authority possessed by the Church, is *normally* drawn *by the hand* of Peter (and, in the case of the sacral regime, drawn also on his order by the hand of the prince).

If the Church possesses thus the sword of the coercive authority, as that of the teaching authority, it is because she is a society complete and master of herself (*societas perfecta*, in the jargon of the philosophers), and composed of human beings who are not pure spirits. The ecclesiastical authority—in its own domain and without having recourse to the civil power—can therefore, by reason of an immediate end of the spiritual order, impose on one of her members, especially on one of the members of her personnel, a penalty intrinsically and in itself temporal, such as "fine, restriction of liberty, privation of an office or of a benefit, etc." (Ch. Journet, *L'Église du Verbe Incarné*, t. I, p. 333, note 1). A priest, in the Confessional, can in certain circumstances prescribe to a penitent the payment of a fine.

With regard to the vocabulary employed by us: the coercive authority implies also legislative authority and judiciary authority (cf. Charles Journet, *The Church of the Incarnate Word*, Vol. I, pp. 184-185), but it is by the coercion that it finally completes itself and that it discharges decidedly the office of sword. It is therefore indeed by the words "*constraining* or *coercive* authority" that I had to designate it here.

A last remark much more general: the two "swords" of which it is a question in these pages, as also the diverse powers possessed by the Church (by the person of the Church), designate the foundation by reason of which, in the diverse domains considered, the *personnel of the Church* has, in the name of God, either authority in order to exercise its activity as *proper cause*, or role of *instrumental cause* when it is the person herself of the Church who through Him speaks and acts.

9. Cf. *Code of Canon Law*, Can. 2213 S 1; cf. Charles Journet, *op. cit.*, pp. 260-263.

10. John 18, 10.

11. Matt. 26, 52.

12. They had perfectly the right to use the sword of coercive authority, since the Church possesses this sword, and even to use it, that which is normal in a sacral regime, by having recourse to the action of the prince and of the secular arm.

That which was, *in itself* and objectively speaking, a singularly grave mistake (without doubt historically almost inevitable, but in itself injurious to God) was to have, in creating the institution of the Inquisition, used the sword in question *otherwise than the Lord permitted,* in a manner which betrayed His spirit and which violated the first prescription of the New Law brought by Him.

13. Cf. Charles Journet, *op. cit.*, p. 232: "Then were held those Councils of Toledo so remarkable for their dogmatic definitions on the Trinity and the Incarnation, but of which it has been said, in respect of their practical

ordinances, that they were 'less Councils than assemblies of the Spanish monarchy, content to do no more, or little more, than register the decrees of their sovereigns.' "

14. I employ this word with reluctance, and at the risk of paining theologians who are dear to me. But *magis amica veritas.* The hypocrisy (or "legal fiction" as E. Vacandard says) was moreover very careful to conceal itself by the words. One did not "deliver"; one *abandoned* the guilty person to the secular arm. And in doing this, one pushed even charity as far as to use a pious formula which I have recalled in the text, entreating the secular arm to spare the guilty person mutilation and death. But if a prince refused to burn the heretics whom the Inquisition thus "abandoned" to him, he was excommunicated and exposed to all the penalties reserved to the supporters of heresy. Cf. Vacandard, *Dict. de théol.*, col. 2051 and 2065.—Likewise one employed torture in order to make the accused confess, but the confessions were assumed free (*ibid.*, col. 2043).

15. I say "Church tribunal" as I say "personnel of the Church." The institution of the Inquisition relates to the *personnel* of the Church. It has nothing to do with an institution essential to the *person* of the Church, like that of the Sacraments for example, and which relates to Christ, *caput super Ecclesiam.*

16. St. Raymond of Penafort, St. Peter of Verona (called also St. Peter Martyr), St. Pius V. . . .

17. Cf. the courageous book of Pierre-Henri Simon, *Contra la torture*, Paris, éd. du Seuil, 1957. "The practice of torture is one of the shames of humanity. . . ." However, "with the exception of the Jewish people, the nations of the Mediterranean world, in the centuries in which their most beautiful cultures flourished, knew, accepted, practiced punitive or inter-rogative torture. . . . Neither Plato, nor Aristotle, nor Cicero, nor Pliny, nor Seneca, protest against the principle, if they happen to deplore the excess of cruelty in the application . . . " (pp. 24-27). In 866 torture was condemned in an absolute manner by Pope Nicholas I. P. H. Simon cites this admirably just text, which did not prevent the Christian Middle Ages, from the moment they rediscovered Roman Law, from returning to the juridical use of torture with a frightful good conscience.

The book of Pierre Henri-Simon is a cry of indignation against the use made of torture by officers and soldiers of the French army during the Algerian War. Let the author be thanked for having borne witness for justice and for having protested for the honor of France.

18. Cf. Arthur London, *L'Aveu*, Paris, Gallimard.

19. With regard to the stake as a means of putting to death, it was more spectacular, but not much more cruel and barbarous than the guillotine or hanging. In my opinion it is only in the case of legitimate defense or of defensive war that the putting to death of a human being is not a sin of homicide, and capital punishment is in itself such a sin committed by society. Cf. the book of Albert Naud, *Tu ne tueras point*, Paris, Éd. de la Table Ronde. Apropos of this book, Julian Green writes: "Of the sufferings of the executed, we know almost nothing. It seems certain that the head separated from the body continues to live. For how long a time? One does not know. It lives and suffers frightfully, since all suffering is in the brain, and as long as the nerve centers are not destroyed, the extraordinary torture machine

continues to function. One knows that hanging is sometimes, by an atrocious accident, a decapitation. The electric chair is doubtless the most ingenious and the *slowest* method. The Spanish garrot is the fruit of sadistic imaginations. Formerly one turned the garrot more or less quickly according to the enormity of the crime. . . . At the origin of capital punishment, there was this doubtlessly prehistoric idea that the blood of the person condemned to death will alleviate the wrath of the victim. It is as primitive and as stupid as that . . . " (*Journal*, t. II, Paris, Plon, 1969, p. 1473).

I am not surprised however that a multitude of persons whom I do not at all suspect of barbarism and of cruelty consider, on the faith of opinions commonly received, capital punishment and the guillotine as things normal and necessary: just as in Middle Ages one considered as things normal and necessary the stake,—and torture.

20. Except the theologians in order to justify them. In explaining (*Sum. theol.*, II-II, 11, 3) why the heretics must be put to death, St. Thomas showed that the great speculatives, when they pronounce on the concrete, run the risk of being led astray by the regime of civilization and the mentality of their time.

At the time, heresy was so considered to be the supreme crime that the remains or the corpses in putrefaction of those whom the Inquisition condemned for *having been* heretics were exhumed, dragged in the streets through the crowd, while a town crier blared out the name of the guilty and solemnly burned persons.

21. "Give me discernment, . . . The way of truth I have chosen . . . " (Ps. 119, 34-30).

22. "Unless your faith is firm you shall not be firm" (Is. 7, 9).

23. Let us note in passing that it is from the Spanish Inquisition, at the time of the struggle against Protestantism, that the institution came, today outmoded, of an *Index* of the books whose reading is prohibited. At the request of Charles the Fifth, a partial list was drawn up by the University of Louvain, in 1546. The first general *Index* was published by the Spanish Holy Office in 1559. "The age of Gutenberg," to speak as Marshall McLuhan, had begun a century before.

24. This is why John Bowker, in his splendid book *Problems of Suffering in Religions of the World* (Cambridge, University Press, 1969), makes room for Marxism among the diverse religions which he studies.

25. That which was new: in the fifteenth century Jean Hus had been burned alive (1415) by condemnation of the Council of Constance; Savonarola was burned alive also in 1498.

26. In him as in the Popes of the Middle Ages there was not the slightest will or the slightest calculation to adapt themselves to the common mentality of a world conscious of sacred values but still tainted with barbarism and to this extent morally impure (world, moreover, in process of historical development). They had no need to adapt themselves to this common mentality; they were immersed in it themselves and participated in it in all candor (that is the excuse): contrary to many priests of today, they also victims of their time, but in another manner: for in general their good will leaves no doubt, but it is the good will of naive strategists anxious to *adapt themselves*, with a view to acting on it, to the rotten mentality of a world in full decadence and in full aversion of the sacred, to speak its language and to think like it. The

internal process of self-destruction of "bourgeois society" is such that one day perhaps it will seek in Communism its last recourse; so that the intelligent Marxists would be wrong to hurry, they have scarcely but to await their hour (then the steamroller will pass over the rot. And life? It will be for a subterranean time). Would a Christianity faithful to itself have been able—as by a miracle—to rectify the course of history and to remedy the decadence in question? It was at least a duty to hope this. A Christianity unfaithful to itself can only contribute to aggravate the decadence of a civilization sprung from the Christian Middle Ages (as distant origin) and from the humanism of the Renaissance (as proximate origin), spoiled afterwards by materialism and by money, and entered now into the antihuman age of technocracy.

27. In the collective volume *Au service de la Parole de Dieu*, Mélanges offerts à Mgr. Charue, évêque de Namur,—Gembloux, 1969. (Cf. *Revue Thomiste*, April-June, 1970, p. 319.)

Is this to say that the diverse reforms to the possibility of which I have just alluded would suffice in order to resolve the present crisis? I do not think so. In my opinion, one will resolve this crisis only if, in a more or less great number of years, or of decades, the Sovereign Pontiff convokes a new Council,—doctrinal, this one,—which, without having need to name or to condemn anyone, would declare solemnly the incompatibility with the Catholic faith of a series (probably long) of philosophical and theological aberrations which merit this qualification.

28. I think for example of the Gospel for the fourth Sunday of Advent, in which Mary is a *young girl* who is no longer full of grace but *favored-by-God*, and is not troubled in her heart but *very upset* by the word of the Angel, and does not ask him "How can this be since I do not know man?" but "How is this going to come about for *I am not married?*" and does not say to him at the end "Be it done to me according to thy word," but "Let it be done to me as you say." It is not permitted to change the sacred letter under the pretext of translating it,—with a carefully sought platitude which betrays the sense and which supposes that the Christian people are stupid people.

29. "For God has ordained as the sheperds of His flock not Bishops only, but also Angels." Matins of Christmas, 8th lesson.

30. Luke 12, 32.

NOTES TO CHAPTER XIV

IV

The Condemnation of Galileo

1. To which Galileo does not fail to reply: "To say that Copernicus expresses himself by way of hypothesis and not with the conviction that his theory is consonant with reality, is not to have read him."

Let us note here that the word 'hypothesis' (mathematical hypothesis) did not have the same sense for the theologians of that time as for the scientists. For the scientists an hypothesis is a view of the mind which it is a question of verifying, and *which one seeks to demonstrate as consonant with reality*. For the theologians it was a view of the mind for the pleasure of the mind and *which one refrained from seeking to demonstrate as consonant with reality*.

It was to believe or not to believe heliocentrism *consonant with reality* which was the grand concern, and it was in this that in 1633 Galileo was held to be "vehemently suspect of heresy." (It is also the reason why I have translated—see pages 203 and 207—by *provable* the word *probabilis* employed in the sentence of condemnation.) On their side the scientists had not yet learned to distinguish between science of phenomena and philosophy of nature. As Santillana remarks (p. 47 of his book), Galileo "repeated always that he had spent more years in the study of philosophy than months in that of mathematics." And when he declared that *"the book of Nature* is written in mathematical symbols" (*ibid.*, p. 93), what he thus maintained signified, in his eyes as in those of his contemporaries, that mathematical symbols disclose to us that which Nature is absolutely speaking, or in its intelligible essence and its first reality: philosophy of nature which, in an altogether different perspective, Descartes, his masked rival, introduced in his manner on the scene, and which was contrary to all that which one taught in the schools. It is not surprising that his most implacable and most cunning enemies were to be found in the universities and among their professors. It was as philosopher of nature that he was condemned.

In order to summarize this whole story, in which obscurities are not lacking, what seemed to me the safest course was to follow the very objective exposition of Vacandard in the *Dictionnaire de théologie,* while modifying and completing it by that which Giorgio de Santillana has furnished us in his *Procès de Galilée* (Paris, Club du meilleur livre, 1955), especially (*op. cit.,* pp. 135-166 and 325-340) with regard to the false official report surreptitiously introduced into the dossier, doubtless as early as 1616 (cf. above, pp. 201-204). Galileo always denied having received in 1616 a formal *injunction,* and an attestation of Bellarmine (dated May 26, 1616) confirms that there was at that time mere notification. (Deliberate infraction of an *injunction* of the Holy Office in matters of faith entailed condemnation for heresy.)

2. It is likewise in something infallibly true that we believe *on the word of the Church* in the case of the canonization of saints.

At the first Council of the Vatican, a canon had been prepared with a view to defining as of faith the doctrine affirming that the infallibility of the Church is not "restricted simply to what is contained in the divine revelation," but "extends also to other truths *necessarily required* to ensure the integrity of the revealed deposit." Cf. Ch. Journet, *op. cit.,* p. 343.

It is the formal motive of my theological faith: the first Truth *in dicendo* (I say of my theological faith *in the infallibility of the Church*) which causes me to believe in the nonrevealed truths taught by a Pope speaking *ex cathedra* (like Alexander VII affirming the heretical tenor of the five propositions of Jansen): not, clearly, that *in themselves* (since they are not revealed) they could invoke this formal motive, but because, *insofar as mere intuitively perceived points of application* of my faith in the infallibility of the Church, they are this faith itself intuitively particularized.

Another example invoked by the theologians in their discussion of "ecclesiastical faith" (Paul VI, like every legitimately elected Pope, is the vicar of

Jesus Christ) belongs to an altogether different category. This is also a truth not directly revealed, which is a mere immediately evident point of application of a revealed truth (and which, by this fact, is therefore also an object of my theological faith); but the revealed truth of which it is a question is not the *Una Sancta* and her infallibility; it is this truth of divine faith that the legitimate successor of Peter on the episcopal see of Rome is the vicar of Jesus Christ.

If it is a question after this of acts of the magisterium through which the infallible voice of the person of the Church does not pass, but which require however interior assent by reason of the authority (more or less high) from which they emanate, this assent is doubtless "governed" by theological faith, insofar as it assures us that—in very diverse degrees—the magisterium is assisted in its office; but the assent this time cannot invoke the formal motive of theological faith, nor therefore be produced by it. And it is itself exactly measured by the degree of authority of the teaching in question.

3. When the Pope speaks *ex cathedra*, or when an ecumenical Council declares a decree concerning the doctrine of faith and of morals, one has to do with an infallible decision.—When, in the same matter, a Roman Congregation expresses itself on its own authority, one has to do with a fallible decision (except if it is approved by the Pope in *forma specifica*).—As regards prudential decisions, cf. above, Ch. IV, note 18.

4. Ch. Journet, *op. cit.*, p. 355.

5. Cf. above, p. 201.

6. Cf. above, p. 203.

7. Charles Journet, *op. cit.*, p. 358.

8. Letter to Bishop Dini, Cf. above, pp. 201-202.

9. Same letter.—That Galileo did not really *demonstrate* the movement of the earth is beside the point here. In actual fact, it is only with Newton that heliocentrism imposed itself on all men of science. The proofs invoked by Newton were not demonstrative and were not worth much. But before demonstrating and without being yet able to demonstrate, there is in the mind of the great scientist an intuitive understanding which suffices to give him a conviction of which (rightly or wrongly, that is another affair, and which concerns the progress of science) he has absolutely no doubt. Such was the case for the intuitive genius of Galileo.

10. Cf. above, pp. 207-208 and note 7.

11. The religious obedience required of Galileo would have then been normal; and it would have required him (as in the case of the promises made in 1616,—and badly kept) to recognize interiorly that this interdiction to propagate heliocentrism,—badly motivated in terms of his conscience of scientist,—was nevertheless prudent in itself, in this sense for example that it obliged him to seek in silence scientifically better proofs, and that it gave time to the theologians to understand the independence, with regard to Holy Scripture, of the science of phenomena which was entering from that time into full development. In fact, however, the judges of Galileo went infinitely further than the interdiction which I am supposing here. They *abused* the religious obedience required of Galileo.

Normally, to the decisions of ecclesiastical authority, even fallible and in revocable matter, religious obedience requires interior assent. But, as Jaugey writes (*Le procès de Galilée et la théologie*, p. 118, quoted by Vacandard,

Dict. de Théol., col. 1085), the *religious assent* in question, "in the case of a provisional doctrinal judgment, is not an absolute adhesion, like that which is required for infallible decisions and which excludes all fear of possible error: it is a provisional adhesion, compatible with the thought that perhaps that which one admits will be one day recognized to be wrong. The required intellectual submission finds itself thus proportionate to the motive on which it rests."

When it acts not as instrument of the person of the Church, but as proper cause,—therefore fallible,—the personnel of the Church has its graces of state, from which it slips away in a grave manner only in case of a failure itself grave, like that of the judges of Galileo.

12. This "absurd in philosophy" seems to us today rather comical. The expression nevertheless merits attention. If the theologians of the Holy Office employed it so ingenuously, it was not only that their reason judged Copernicus absurd in comparison with Ptolemy; it was also and above all, I think, because the idea that the earth turns appeared to them as clearly contrary to the witness of the senses. Do we not see with our eyes the sun rise each morning and set each evening? And I confess that, however unfortunate it was in the case, such a confidence in the testimony of the senses touches me in men who are doctors of the invisible. A confidence itself "absurd" and "senseless" in the testimony of the senses is still better, "in philosophy," than idealism.

13. *Op. cit.*, p. 356.

14. By a mere authorization to print given in 1822 (cf. above, p. 209).

V

The Funeral-Pile of Rouen

1. Olivier Leroy, *Sainte Jeanne d'Arc, Les Voix*, Paris, Alsatia, 1954, p. 23 (Quicherat I, 51).

2. St. Michael did not state his name to her. The angels have no need of names or of identity cards like us; they know each other intuitively. It was also in an intuitive manner that Joan knew that it was he; she was "as certain of it as she was of the existence of God." St. Theresa, "speaking of the visions of saints which she had had, remarks that she understood many things which they had expressed without words, *beginning with their identity*" (*Interior Castle*, Mansion VI, Ch. V, from O. Leroy, *op. cit.*, p. 35). One can think that a certain absolutely singular quality of emotion, of spiritual joy ineffably experienced by her connaturalized her with the very being of the saints whom she saw; and that for Joan the same held true in respect of him whom she knew already, through the teaching of her mother, as the leader of the angels and the supreme victorious one, and at the name of whom she felt, although in an incomparably weaker degree, the same absolutely singular tonality of emotion as that which was going to penetrate her before the apparition. This is why she applied intuitively this name, with an entire certitude, and under a charismatic inspiration, to the being whom she saw and who spoke to her then. She *recognized* him.

In order to return to the name of Mi-kâ-El (*Quis ut Deus*), I note further that it is the most fundamental truth concerning God that it manifests. In order that from a high antiquity it should have been attributed by men,—those of Israel,—to the protecting angel of their people, there was needed that an obscure prophetical instinct designate to them the highest of the pure spirits as the witness *par excellence* of the divine Transcendence. It is this, it seems to me, that Olivier Leroy wished to indicate in pages (pp. 134, 135, 139) which are not the most successful ones of his excellent book.

3. Up to that time she had deliberated with herself, weighing the meaning of the words heard, and the wisdom with which they were full. "How did you know that it was, as you say, language of an angel?—I had this will to believe it."

4. At this point, if one is a little *au courant* of modern works (and if one judges them without due consideration), one will stop me perhaps and ask: How could Joan of Arc have seen St. Catherine of Alexandria and St. Margaret of Antioch, since modern criticism has shown the nonexistence of these latter? It certainly seems indeed that the history of these two saints is legendary. But if one can quite easily show that that which one relates of someone is legendary, it is more difficult to show that this someone has not existed. And supposing that this be the case, one can reasonably think, with Edmond Richer, Sorbonist of the eighteenth century, that it was angels who appeared to Joan under the form and the shape of these two saints, of whom the legend, doubtless familiar to the child, was not without relation with her own destiny. (Virgins and martyrs the two of them, and consigned to the fire after having long discussed, Margaret with the Governor, Catherine with fifty doctors. To the latter St. Michael had said to "speak fearlessly." Cf. Jean Guitton, *Problème et Mystère de Jeanne d'Arc*, Paris, Fayard, 1961, pp. 148-150.) It matters little that formerly they did not exist; by the angels who had taken their shape they existed now before Joan and spoke to her.

St. Thomas teaches that the angels can "assume bodies" (*Sum. theol.*, I, 51, 2) presenting all the appearances (visible, tangible, olfactive, etc.) of a human being. Moreover no saint,—except the Lord Himself and His Mother,—is in Heaven with his body. Supposing that St. Catherine and St. Margaret once existed in Alexandria and in Antioch, and that their souls enjoy now the Beatific Vision, these souls would have had also to assume all the appearances of a human being, as also clothes worn by the latter, in order to appear to Joan "really and corporally."

"Whether her two saints are historical or not," writes Olivier Leroy, "Joan had of their life only a valueless knowledge. However, that which she knew of them, that which she honored, venerated in them, had a permanent truth, a truth outside the grasps of past or of future History. In the person of Catherine or of Margaret, she venerated virginity, the love of God, Christian wisdom and the abnegation of martyrdom, and she honored them by imitating them to the point of dying as they. These are not realities which can vanish like an historical fiction." (*Op. cit.*, p. 138.)

5. Cf. Olivier Leroy, *op. cit.*, pp. 132, 133-134.

6. She disobeyed them only two times. This was the second. The first time was the "leap" from the castle-keep of Beaurevoir. For having signed the memorandum she had great repentance, and her saints reproached her for it as a "betrayal" before giving her their pardon. (They had moreover warned her in advance that she would commit this mistake.)

7. Cf. J. B. J. Ayroles, *La Vraie Jeanne d'Arc, La Pucelle devant l'Église de son temps*, Paris, Gaume, 1890, pp. 176, 597, 689.

8. In the interrogatory of the 14th of March, of which there is mention a little below, she repeated that St. Catherine had promised to help her.—Cf. below, note 11.

9. Cf. the fragment entitled *Information Posthume*, and fabricated by Cauchon after the trial. It is a faked and defamatory document which neither the witnesses nor the clerks signed (one of the clerks, Manchon, specified that he had refused to affix his signature to it). Concerning the visit paid to Joan by Cauchon, and concerning the words which he said to her, one cannot doubt. But the reply attributed to Joan (by Jean Toutmouille and by Thomas de Courcelles—"*it seems to me,*" says the latter, "that Joan added: 'I see indeed that I have been deceived' ") is certainly an invention or a falsification. The 30th of May, when she was on the ambo where she was listening to the sermon of Nicolas Midi before being burnt at the stake, she invoked St. Michael and her saints, as she had invoked them at the churchyard of Saint-Ouen. Cf. the testimony of Brother Ladvenu at the trial of rehabilitation: "Says and deposes that always until the end of her life, she maintained and affirmed that her Voices were from God, and that all that which she had done, she had done it on the commandment of God, and that she did not think that she had been deceived by her Voices; and that the revelations which she had had came from God." (Quoted by Olivier Leroy, *op. cit.*, p. 150.) We absolutely do not know that which in her prison she replied to Cauchon, nor if she replied to him.

10. On the prophecies of Joan, see Olivier Leroy, *op. cit.*, Ch. XII, "Prophétie"; Jean Guitton, *op. cit.*, pp. 163-164; and the article "Jeanne d'Arc" by Ph. Dunand, in the *Dictionnaire d'Apologétique.*

11. Olivier Leroy, *op. cit.*, p. 108. Here is the text in which the reply of Joan is recorded: "Respond que saincte Katherine luy a dit qu'elle aurait secours, et qu'elle sçait se ce sera à estre délivrée de la prison, ou quant elle seroit au jugement, s'il y viendroit aucun trouble, par quel moien elle pourroit estre délivrée. Et pense que ce soit ou l'un ou l'autre. Et de plus luy dient ses voix qu'elle sera délivrée par grande victoire; et après lui dient ses voix: 'Pran tout en gré, ne te chaille pas de ton martire; tu t'en viendras enfin en royaulme de paradis'. Et ce luy dient ses voix simplement et absoluement, c'est assavoir sans faillir; et appele ce, martire, pour la paine et adversité qu'elle souffre en prison, et ne sçait se plus grand souffrera; mais s'en actend à Nostre Seigneur." (Q.I., p. 155; and 254.)

12. Cf. M. J. Belon and F. Balme, *Jean Bréhal et la Réhabilitation de Jeanne d'Arc*, Paris, Lethielleux, 1893, p. 2.

13. Cf. *ibid.*, p. 5 and pp. 66-69.

14. Cf. *ibid.*, pp. 157-162.

15. It is that which appears for example in the case of Blessed Juliana of Mount Cornillon, asking in the name of Jesus and finally obtaining the institution of the Feast of the Blessed Sacrament; in the case of St. Catherine of Sienna or of St. Bridget, sent to the Leader of the Church in order to transmit to him the wishes of the Divine Majesty; in the case of St. Margaret Mary, messenger of the desires and of the promises of the Sacred Heart. This appears also in an eminent manner in the case of Joan of Arc.

16. Cf. Olivier Leroy, *op. cit.*, p. 125 (Q. I, 395-396).

It is to this that she also alluded in another reply: "Interrogée s'elle croit que ses voix soient saincte Marguerite et sainte Katherine: respond que ouil, *et de Dieu.*" (Q. I, 457.)

17. "Interrogée s'elle a commandement de ses voix qu'elle ne se submecte point à l'Église militante, qui est en terre, ne au jugement d'icelle: respond . . . [elles] ne commandent point qu'elle ne obéisse à l'Église, nostre Sire premier servi." (Q. I, 326.)

Citing the gloss (of St. Augustine) on the Epistle to the Romans 13, 2 (cf. *Sum. theol.*, II-II, 104, 5), Bréhal writes in his *Recollectio:* "Et ad hoc recte tendit illud verbum Johannae, ubi dixit quod erat subdita Ecclesiae ac Domino Papae et aliis prelatis, Deo primitus servato."

18. "She says also that she relies upon the Church militant provided that this Church does not command her anything impossible, namely to revoke what she has said and done on behalf of God. She will not revoke it for anything in the world, nor for man who lives. She relies upon Our Lord, Whose commandment she will always follow." Ayroles, *op. cit.*, p. 252.

19. A good theologian could have explained to her why. It is perhaps what the two Dominicans would have done who wished to give her explanations, clear this time, on the Church militant and the Church triumphant, and whom Cauchon violently rejected.

Another witness said that Joan did not distinguish between the Church militant and the Church triumphant. She distinguished them very well, but she knew that they are a single and same Church.

20. Testimony of Isambart de la Pierre.

21. Cf. Ayroles, *op. cit.*, p. 168.

22. *Ibid.*, p. 689.—I retain these words *scientific doctors* (they amuse me and they enlighten me). At that time the *science* in question was the sophisticated traditional theology of the masters of the University of Paris, and it served them to defend the faith against the infection of heresy of which Joan the apostate and the idolatress was the bearer. Today it is *the same intellectual race* which we see at work; it has only passed into the opposite camp; the *science* of our new *scientifici doctores* is the "human sciences" and the philosophies of the day, with which they fabricate a so-called theology (scientific also) entirely turned toward the world, that of the pseudotheologians to whom I alluded in the Preface.

An obscure and powerful instinct persuades them with good reason that theology must proceed to an immense effort of integration and interpretation of the newly acquired knowledges concerning man and concerning the world, but *on condition of remaining itself,* and of making a no less immense effort of discernment: that which they do not see, because they no longer know what theology is. They think that the human sciences, psychoanalysis, the theory of evolution, ethnology, sociology, etc. are "theological places."

And they think that the essential function of theology is "the criticism of the Church,"—because they do not know what the Church is. Are they not moreover above her, since they constitute now the true magisterium, by virtue of the authority of "Science," whereas the concern of the hierarchy, which attributes to itself still magisterium by virtue of the authority of God, of Christ and of the apostles, is in the eyes of *scientifici doctores* only administration?

They think also that it is they *who made* the second Council of the

Vatican. This very remarkable illusion leads one to suppose that the considerable—but purely consultative—role which the theologians (and certain ones of those who were but lately suspected) played in the preparatorily constituted commissions of specialists has gone to the head of our new Reformers, and has caused them to believe that this role played by "the theologians" was the decisive and capital role. Perhaps they have had the gentle impression that the episcopate was composed in general only of incompetents and semiignorants in theology? Well, even if such a proudly arrogant impression had been somewhat well-founded, they did not have enough faith, and enough authentically theological light, in order to understand that in an ecumenical Council, it is by the episcopate gathered together in union with the Pope,—by it, in nowise by the theologians in its service,—that, even in the epochs in which He does not shine in that *human science* which is theology, *divine truth* is expressed and made explicit under the inspiration of the Holy Spirit Who has been promised to the Church, and Who makes then of it the very voice of the Church.

23. Belon and Balme, *op. cit.*, p. 104.

24. Cf. *ibid.*, p. 42, note 7 (Q. I, 392).

25. Cf. *ibid.*, p. 43, note 3 (Q. I, 205).—And again (Ayroles, p. 251): "As regards submission to the Church, she says that she would like to bear honor and reverence to the Church militant with all her power; but to trust for her deeds in this Church, it is necessary that I trust in Our Lord Who caused me to do them."

26. Cf. Julian Green, *Journal*, t. II, p. 1407: "I find quite troubling the declarations of this saint who makes a distinction between the terrestrial Church and the Church of above 'which alone she claims to obey.' " Julian Green, in the eyes of whom this saint "remains the greatest because she is the most abandoned," spoke of the question to a priest friend of his who replied to him with an unpardonable thoughtlessness.

27. As Julian Green notes (*op. cit.*, p. 1409) she was ready also to present herself before the Council, but when a Dominican asked her if she would agree to go to the Council of Basel, and when she said yes, Cauchon shouted at the Dominican: "Be silent, by the devil!"

28. Cf. Belon and Balme, *op. cit.*, p. 41, note 3 (Q. I, 175).

29. In his *Recollectio*, Jean Bréhal writes very justly: "Fideliter et pie sensisse apparet de unitate ecclesiae. Nam catholica veritas nullam difficultatem inducit, quin regnancium seu fruencium in celis ac militantium in terris una sit societas et unica ecclesia. Ut autem dicit sanctus Doctor (III, q. 8, a. 3 and 4), multitudo ordinata in unum secundum distinctos actus et officia unum corpus similitudinarie dicitur. Corpus vero misticum ecclesie non solum consistit ex hominibus, sed etiam ex angelis; quoniam ad unum finem, qui est gloria divine fruicionis, ordinantur et homines et angeli. Unde secundum statum dumtaxat accipitur hujusmodi distinctio. Secundum enim statum vie, congregacio fidelium est in qua comprehenduntur omnes homines a principio mundi usque ad finem ejus, cujuscumque condicionis sint, justi vel injusti, fideles et infideles, qui, quamdiu viatores existunt, ad congregacionem ecclesie sive actu sive potentia pertinent. Secundum autem statum patrie, est congregatio comprehendencium et fruencium, que dignior pars est, eo quod illi Deo actu uniuntur. Unde non est mirum, si Johanna, de hiis que ex inspiracione et revelacione dixit et gessit, Deo in primis et huic summe

congregacioni se potissimum retulit; quoniam ex ea parte procedebant, et ideo illud summum judicatorium maxime exigebant." (Belon and Balme, *op. cit.*, p. 101.)

All this is true, in many words. And Joan in her own manner knew it still better than Bréhal.

30. I find this phrase in the book, in other respects excellent, of Belon and Balme: "Joan of Arc was truly a new Judith, sent to the people of Israel when it was necessary almost to despair of its salvation" (p. 104). Behold France promoted to the rank of chosen people! This book appeared in 1893.

One has been astonished that the Church waited five centuries before canonizing Joan of Arc. But if this canonization had taken place sooner, it is probable that the misinterpretation committed regarding it by national sentiment would have run the risk of implanting itself definitively.

31. Cf. Ayroles, *op. cit.*, pp. 57-58.

32. Cf. Jean Guitton, *op. cit.*, pp. 207-214.—Theresa had "the idea that the task of Joan is not finished." And what is very striking, "it is that Theresa, at several moments of her supreme audacity, in an 'unconscious-supraconscious,' almost identified herself with Joan of Arc, that she at least linked herself with Joan by a mysterious and mystical assimilation. . . . For Merejkovsky, Joan and Theresa were the two most modern and most revolutionary saints—and of a revolution which is scarcely beginning, which carries us into a new age."

33. Cf. *ibid.*, p. 212: "She thinks that at death, one is dubbed a knight in order to begin one's functions as an Angel of God. Just as the coronation of Rheims, which Joan set up and presided over, is an act of knighthood, so also for Theresa the entry into Heaven, place of *eminent* action where she is finally going to be able to work according to *all the dimensions* of her vocation. During her mortal and furtive life, she had in *love* the recapitulation of her divergent vocations, impossible to exercise together on earth, even if she had been a super-Joan.—Henceforth, liberated from this mantle of flesh which limits all action, she is going to spread her wings. One has perhaps not yet sufficiently shown how much this is paradoxical, original, *inspired*."

Jean Guitton quotes then these astonishing lines of Theresa: "The thought of heavenly happiness does not cause me any joy, but still I ask myself sometimes how it will be possible for me to be happy without suffering. Jesus without doubt will change my nature, otherwise I would miss suffering and the vale of tears."

34. The present crisis is a general crisis of civilization which has repercussions upon the Church, and affects in the first place clerics forgetful of the interior reform required above all. The old spirit of clericalism (reversed, but still extant) could persuade these clerics who kneel now before the world that without being directed and brigaded by them Christian laymen cannot accomplish properly that which they have to do for the world. And this would not be good for them or for the world.

I add that in the struggle against the dehumanization of the world by scientific progress, however admirable it may be in itself, and by a civilization enslaved to techocracy, it seems to me that a role of first rank belongs normally to those technicians and technologists who have concern for man and for the spiritual. (Cf. the positions taken by M. Fernand Lapland, Departmental President, in the *Bulletin* de l'Association Française pour le Développement de l'Enseignement technique, Section du Vaucluse.)

NOTES TO CHAPTER XV

1. Ph. Dunand, art. "Jeanne d'Arc," *Dict. d'Apol.*, col. 1251.

2. Charles Journet, *The Church of the Incarnate Word*, Vol. I, p. 350. Cf. above, Ch. XI, pp. 147-148, and note 15 of Ch. VII.

3. One hears it said often that in the time of temporal power certain Popes did not hesitate to employ spiritual means such as excommunication in political conflicts or wars with some adversary. I am anxious to note here that if we consider things closely history does not furnish any example of such an error; one observes on the contrary the extreme attention of the Popes to respect always the distinction between the two domains. The primacy accorded to the means of repression caused a great number of interdicts and of excommunications which one is entitled to judge excessive, but which has nothing to do with a diversion of spiritual arms for the benefit of temporal advantages.

On Popes Nicholas I (858-867) and John VIII, who symbolize the apogee of the Papacy in the High Middle Ages, cf. W. Ullemann, *The Growth of Papal Government in the Middle Ages*, 1962.

4. Supposing that one will have resolved this pernicious ambiguity, the word "Church" will keep still, under other relations, an ambiguity which Jean Bréhal noted a long time ago, and which entails no disadvantage, for it does not run the risk of leading astray the mind. This word designates above all the universal Church in her proper mystery, which is object of our faith and on which so much insistence is placed in the present book. But it designates also such and such a "Church" (Catholic) of a given rite; and such and such a local "Church," "the Church of Lyons" for example; and such and such a dissident "Church," "the Anglican Church" for example.

In speaking in his own way of the ambiguity of the word "Church," Bréhal supposed even that the simplicity of Joan of Arc ran the risk of causing her to confuse "the Church" to which the judges of Rouen asked her to submit and "the Church" to which one goes every Sunday. But Bréhal nevertheless exaggerated a little.

5. *Curs. theol.*, II-II, q. 1, a. 7; disp. 2, a. 2, n° 10 and 40; t. VII, pp. 233 and 248. Cf. Ch. Journet, *op. cit.*, p. 344.

Index

295